Counterfeiting Labor's Voice

THE WORKING CLASS IN AMERICAN HISTORY

For a list of books in the series, please see our website at www.press.uillinois.edu.

Counterfeiting Labor's Voice

William A. A. Carsey and the Shaping of American Reform Politics

MARK A. LAUSE

UNIVERSITY OF ILLINOIS PRESS
Urbana, Chicago, and Springfield

1 2 3 4 5 C P 5 4 3 2 1
∞ This book is printed on acid-free paper.

Library of Congress Cataloging-in-Publication Data
Names: Lause, Mark A., author.
Title: Counterfeiting labor's voice : William A. A. Carsey and the shaping of American reform politics / Mark A. Lause.
Other titles: William A. A. Carsey and the shaping of American reform politics
Description: Urbana : University of Illinois Press, [2024] | Series: The working class in American history | Includes bibliographical references and index.
Identifiers: LCCN 2023036470 (print) | LCCN 2023036471 (ebook) | ISBN 9780252045783 (cloth) | ISBN 9780252087899 (paperback) | ISBN 9780252056666 (ebook)
Subjects: LCSH: Carsey, William A. A. (William Augustus Adolphus), 1841–1914. | Political activists—United States—Biography. | Tammany Hall (Political organization) | Democratic Party (New York, N.Y.)—History—19th century. | Labor movement—New York (State)—New York—History—19th century. | New York (N.Y.)—Politics and government. | United States—Politics and government—1865–1933.
Classification: LCC F128.47 .L38 2024 (print) | LCC F128.47 (ebook) | DDC 322.40973—dc23/eng/20230927
LC record available at https://lccn.loc.gov/2023036470
LC ebook record available at https://lccn.loc.gov/2023036471

Contents

Acknowledgments

This work owes everything to the colleagues and friends who found it interesting and worth pursuing. The staff at the University of Illinois Press—Tad Ringo, Roberta Sparenberg, Alison Syring Bassford, Leigh Ann Cowan, and Geof Garvey—has, as always, been helpful and encouraging, particularly with the often-confusing resolution of images, for which we thank the HaithiTrust Digital Library. Chad Pearson and others saw parts of it and found it encouraging. Janine Hartman at the University of Cincinnati provided the necessary second pair of eyes for the initial draft. Last, but never least, I remain eternally grateful to my wife, Katherine Allen, who has not only tolerated my work interests for forty years but has continued to do so into my retirement.

Responsibility for the research and the interpretation must necessarily be mine.

Introduction

I would like to introduce Mr. William A. A. Carsey, whose full name was William Augustus Adolphus Carsey. . . . I think. Please watch your hat and coat.

I first encountered Mr. Carsey while I lurked in the corner of a newspaper account of a gaslit meeting called by the American adherents of the International Workingmen's Association (IWA)—later known as the First International. That body involved Karl Marx, Friedrich Engels, Mikhail Bakunin, and, later, Mr. Carsey. The local press described him at the time as "a mason," though he variously described himself as a bricklayer and a builder as well, but he tended to talk a great deal and soon began acquiring official positions. Consulting more of the contemporary press permitted me to slip into the back row and observe many such meetings, where I could not have avoided Carsey's presence.

Dig as I might, I failed to locate a picture of Carsey, but we can see him in our mind's eye preparing for his entrance into such a meeting. The self-described worker took some pains to look the part, being well-dressed, but modestly enough for it to merit no special comment. More imaginatively, we might picture him with a derby cocked to one side of his head as he puffed away on a cigar, chatting eagerly out of the side of his mouth to those at his elbow while focused on what was about to transpire in the room. Though not shy about taking the floor in those meetings, the lion's share of his contribution to the deliberations in those smoked-filled rooms came before or after, in the hallway. Throughout, it served him to look and talk like a brawler, but one reporter described his belligerent language "as one of the tools of trade, and not as an evidence of natural belligerence."[1]

Following his activities through the press indicates a unique level of persistence and leadership in labor politics. From the 1870s through the 1890s, few national gatherings of labor organizations or attempts to launch labor reform parties took place without his presence. Very few figures could justly make such a claim, and the course of Carsey's career offers a window into some of the deepest and most profound continuities that underlie working-class and radical history through those years . . . and beyond. Initially, though, I suspected that he was one of those characters who happily spent precious years—if not decades—as the chief public spokesperson of a tiny group of six to eight people which he (almost always) successfully built into a group no larger.

I could not have misjudged him more completely.

The closer the sources take us to Carsey's work, the clearer we see him collaring participants in labor meetings and working to manage the outcome of such meetings. Digging through the press accounts made ever more obvious his regular association with local and state leaders of the Democratic Party, particularly those revolving around Tammany Hall. Indeed, his obituary later claimed Carsey as a member of the society himself. His self-identification as a self-employed contractor in the construction business fit that association with Tammany, which controlled the lucrative business of city contracts for such work. So did his passing through a series of government jobs. The realization of his associations cast a new light on the inconsistent twists and turns in his leadership of the Independent Labor Party or the other movements that he eventually torpedoed.

Regrettably, our subject chose to leave us no memories, no manuscript collections, and no extensive documented discussions with contemporaries about his own view of his activities. The work in hand is the biography of a public man, based exclusively on his impact as a public man, as a partisan consigliere. The book would certainly not have been possible without the technological innovations that translated a massive body of newspapers into a now-searchable digital format, available to us as close as our home computer. Widespread availability not only offered us multiple, often conflicting, accounts for specific incidents but disclosed enough such incidents to form a clear career pattern, sketching a new picture of a career that emerged from Gilded Age politics.

In his own quiet and obscure way, Carsey helped to manage the developing US two-party system through a particularly precarious juncture in its history. If the social tensions and mass politics created the preconditions for class politics in the metropolis, it also created opportunities for a career such as Carsey's. Through the Gilded Age, he served as the most persistent and patient

Democratic field operative, laboring assiduously to mislead, misdirect, and destroy efforts to sustain independent political parties. Doing so sometimes involved structuring them to make them unworkable, while other times it involved guiding them into fusion with the Democrats or shaping them as predetermined dead end of single-shot protests, such as those of Benjamin F. Butler and Henry George. Carsey did so as part of a strategy to reconstruct pre–Civil War Democratic majorities by shattering every possible electoral option into digestible pieces.

While Carsey's career left a clear record of longevity and importance, his story was hardly unique. He had predecessors going back to the origins of the Democratic Party that engaged in specific efforts to defuse the mass impulse to independent political action, which partly still lingered at the edges of Carsey's activities. Contemporaries such as Walter H. Shupe did similar work, though with less subtlety and success. And their successors have been legion.

Certainly, the older participants in those early meetings of the IWA alongside Carsey had begun a long effort to establish socialist and labor parties, which were attaining some success in other western industrial nations around the end of Carsey's career. British radicals and their allies cultivated Liberal-Labour electoral coalitions culminating in the emergence of an Independent Labour Party in 1893 and a Labour Party in 1900. In France, several currents came together as the Socialist Party in 1902. Overshadowing them all in size, the *Sozialdemokratische Partei Deutschland*, the Social Democratic Party (SDP) that emerged in 1890 from its extended period of illegality in Germany to become the largest Marxist party in Europe, though the electoral structure left it grossly underrepresented. In the United States, however, the dominant two caucus parties thwarted a series of efforts, culminating in a massive Populist upsurge, even as small socialist currents converged in a new Social Democratic Party of America in 1898 and the Socialist Party in 1901, the success of which proved to be easily left in the shadows by the rigidly eighteenth-century caucus party model that prevailed.

In terms of political power, the US working class could not have been more conspicuous by its absence. Fantasists may ascribe the phenomenon to the exceptional sensitivity of the ruling elites in the United States to the needs of its workforce, but the search for defensible reasons has persisted for generations. Most directly, Werner Sombart, the German scholar of capitalism, pointedly asks, *Warum gibt es in den Vereinigten Staaten keinen Sozialismus?* Its published translation in 1976 posed the yet relevant query of 1906: "Why Is There No Socialism in the United States?"[2] Sombart's work addressed the issue through distinct parts of his book. The problems, he argued, ran deeper than the failure of the Socialist Party of the United States to grow to a scale comparable to that of the German SPD, resting on fundamental assumptions of "American exceptionalism."

The absence of a socialist movement competitive within the US party system is inseparable from the broader question about the absence of any class politics or, at least, politics held accountable to more than one class. In asking this question, Robin Archer in 2010 suggested that comparisons to Western Europe exaggerated the perception of American exceptionalism, suggesting that another settler state, Australia, offered a better point of comparison.[3] This entirely reasonable response, though, does leave the assumptions in place.

More recently, Kim Moody addressed Sombart's arguments, with a particular emphasis on the Gilded Age. Looking beyond the veneer of electoral politics, he noted that, as British workers built and consolidated a trade union base that provided the core of what became the Labour Party, a disproportionate number of their US counterparts were in no position to do likewise. They faced not only the massive disenfranchisement of African Americans but the marginalization of recent immigrants and the exceptionally more transient working class.[4] Journalists and later scholars have focused on electoral politics in such a way as to obscure that basic reality.

Recent decades have posed the same question in diverse ways. By the 1980s, others could ask "Why Is There No Green Party in the United States?"[5] The question remained no less relevant after the establishment of a Green Party of the United States (GPUS). The GPUS has consistently and dogmatically avoided behaving as anything more than a nominal party, the existence of which has systemically dead-ended efforts to build anything more than an allied outrider of the Democratic Party. Throughout, aspiring insurgents have avoided the most basic steps necessary to turn protest voters into a voting base or a common structure of membership essential to fielding anything close to a complete alternative ticket. Indeed, after three decades, there is no reason to think that the Greens have had any practical function other than getting progressive-minded voters who would otherwise sit out the election to turn up to cast votes for a few Green candidates and, while they're there, dutifully cast votes for lesser-evil candidates of the major parties. Such consistency over decades represents deliberate choices rather than serial oversights. Sombart's question, writ large, asks not only why there is no socialist or labor or environmental party but no genuinely liberal party. I do not, in any sense, mean by this a synonym for "Democrat" or a swear word interchangeable with what well-heeled right-wing dissemblers have called "the Left" or "the Radical Left." So, others could set aside electoral politics to ask, "Why Are There

No Universal Social Programs in the United States?"[6] Plausible explanations tend to echo those of Sombart.

Without addressing Sombart's arguments at this point, let us acknowledge that the question he poses can be writ even larger. The United States has no major party that is ideologically conservative or libertarian. No tories or Christian democrats. We are not talking about advertising labels and jingles to make a sale, but practical policies reflecting shared ideological underpinnings.

Indeed, as another election bears down on us at this writing, the two-party system is showing flexibility to the point of virtual fluidity, as some of those who fund (and own) it are responding to massive disaffection with its limited alternatives by discussing a new "No Labels Party" that simply favors "pushing our leaders together to solve our country's biggest problems." Notwithstanding the name, it represents the ultimate triumph of labels over substantive political content and a reminder that "our leaders" of either or both parties have historically launched such third parties to prevent a serious challenge to the two withstanding.

The case of William A. A. Carsey, with the details of his career, takes us into the grainy texture of US capitalism and permits and provides a focus on the immediate, practical importance of the two-party structure. The US founders constituted a government on solidly seventeenth- and eighteenth-century British assumptions, absent the monarchy and political parties. As British and European societies moved on to membership-based branch parties, the political parties that did develop in the United States did so well within the strictures of the parliamentary caucus party model. Remarkably, they remained so not just by surviving but by pioneering a mass politics that relegated the citizen qualified to wield the ballot something of civic consumer providing a mandate to rule based on family and demographic identities or the appeal of vague rhetoric, the perception of personal trustworthiness, et cetera. While polls regularly reflect an overwhelming dissatisfaction with this arrangement, the political structure provides no clear mechanism for transcending it.

From this perspective, we might well regard Carsey and his obscure kindred as refounding fathers of the United States, figures who remade US civic culture as an entrepreneurial enterprise firmly rooted in a winner-takes-all two-party system. They pioneered in managing the transition to mass politics. New mass circulation newspapers performed the close needlework in knitting all this together. In 1800, printers worked by hand to set, ink, and print about 200 newspapers. By 1860, the increasingly literate and engaged population had recourse to at least 3,000 newspapers and 7,000 by 1880 and, according to *Rowell's Directory*, 20,000 in 1900. Except for highly specialized titles, machines churned out these later publications in numbers that dwarfed those of their predecessors. Readers shared the news of wars, scandals, and celebrity.

All this activity opened new possibilities for molding what we now call "media image," as well as public perceptions and scripting issues to eclipse matters of greater concerns. Then, too, their importance always was to the management of the party system. Carsey's importance rested less on what he was than on what he presented himself to be. His leadership of paper organizations made him a pioneer of modern "astroturfing" and provides an important demonstration of how his practices predate the internet and television.[7]

As with other works of history, this study is a product of the time of its writings. Back in 2008—back around the time I began to realize Carsey's importance—the corporate media went in search of the voice of the forgotten white workingman it so desperately needed to prove their assumptions. In Ohio, they found and celebrated the wit and wisdom of "Joe the Plumber." The media followed the Republican presidential campaign in recasting a right-wing businessman as the voice of white, blue-collar workers, as he complained about the overtaxing of businesses and the influx of foreigners, as well as explaining how gun control caused the Holocaust in Nazi Germany. In fact, though, Samuel Joseph Wurzelbacher was not even a plumber.

He just played one on television.

The serious misrepresentation here was not with Mr. Wurzelbacher but on the other end of the camera. Eight years later, the same sources presented Donald Trump (a creature of the media with no public existence apart from his "brand") as both a successful billionaire entrepreneur and the spokesperson for those same forgotten white workers. At the same time, media on the coasts managed to blame the outcome of the 2016 presidential election between two prominent New York City figures on the voters of the heartland, particularly those who lived and worked the farthest from the cameras and concerns of the commentators.

As this process became normalized further, Trump's 2024 campaign for reelection declared he would go to Michigan to address the striking union workers, and almost the entirety of the commercial media dutifully repeated what they were told. The non-union parts facility that hosted the event reportedly employs only 150, so most of the 400 to 500 supporters who cheered the former president did not work there. Most seem not to have been autoworkers, much less members of the union or strikers. The *Detroit News* bothered to ask questions, but most of the media never entirely rejected their original description of the campaign's public relations event. Such misrepresentations are not random curios about the superficial appearance of politics, but represent a systemic approach to recording events in which great interests are involved.

Such mythmaking has been as important in shaping US civic culture as genuine issue differences. They did not entail random curios about the superficial appearance of politics but represented part of deeply rooted structures, vital to its functioning.

The past got us to a present where professional impostors and con artists overtly practice their craft from their seats in Congress, that books are banned to protect "freedom," and perspectives on the past discomforting to the powerful are prohibited in the interest of "history." Perhaps a critical eye to that past might have been useful to us earlier.

The case of Carsey underscores the fact that the carefully constructed misrepresentations of working people long predate cable television and electronic media. And, of course, it should caution those who want to understand these issues against being overly credulous.

Even by the friendliest email of a Nigerian prince.

So, I remind you, do watch your hat and coat.

Counterfeiting Labor's Voice

PROLOGUE

Carsey's Paternities

The Son of the Streets and the Odysseys of Father Columbia

Mark how my fame rings out from zone to zone:
A thousand critics shouting: "He's unknown!"
—Ambrose Bierce

New York–born William A. A. Carsey returned to his city as a new kind of mass politics began to emerge. In the winter of 1872–73, the press noted his presence among the remnants of the International Workingmen's Association (IWA). There he made an inauspicious and unsuccessful debut as something of an *agent provocateur*, urging a confrontation with the police. After a January gathering discussed solidarity with workers fighting repression abroad, "Citizen Carsie" rose to remind them of "the violence used by the authorities in carrying out their edicts in America." He described the United States as "more oppressed by her Government than any monarchy" and asked "how he was to act if assaulted by the myrmidons of the law when not committing any offense."[1] Carsey soon turned to a different kind of career, thereafter regularly appearing in Gilded Age national gatherings of labor reformers and radicals, where he labored consistently to stifle or misdirect any moves toward mass independent political action in the interests of the Democratic Party. This obscure but ubiquitous figure should cast a new light on this period of the history of the urban working-class, third-party movements, and the complexities of the two-party system itself.

A son of the two-fisted Catholic immigrant culture of New York City, he grew up in the shadow of the Democratic Party. Through his early life, the party had dominated the mass politics rooted in the rough-and-tumble world of the Lower East Side and on the national scene, where elites of the cotton South prevailed within the party. That elite had then opted for secession and civil war, burdening the postwar party with the challenge of overcoming the unenviable record of the overt treason of its formerly dominant faction. One of Carsey's earliest regular collaborators, Walter Henry Shupe, had been exploring ways to get around the challenge through the use of insurgent efforts in 1864, 1868, and 1872 to reduce Republican majorities. As "Father Columbia," the Ohioan Shupe became one of the noisiest advocates for currency reform, which had a particularly strong appeal among the GOP majorities in the rural North. These considerations informed Carsey's course.

Carsey's Apprenticeship

Carsey grew up as a son of the streets of antebellum New York City. His parents, William Carsey and Mary Margaret McCarthy, had been born, respectively, in England and Ireland. They settled in New York City and likely lived in one of the overcrowded, multifamily rentals for which antebellum Gotham had become famous.[2] They resided among their immigrant neighbors on the Lower East Side.

The record leaves no clear indication of exactly how the Carseys made a living, which implies that they may have often found themselves scrounging to make ends meet. It is likely that their work included the salvage business or the construction trades. The Great Fire of 1835 destroyed 530 to 700 buildings in seventeen blocks toward the eastern side of the tip of Manhattan, generating a long demand for new housing.[3]

The press does report that one Charles Shields, a printer of drug labels, filed suit against the Carseys. This slim morsel of documentation hints that they may also have been selling something like the proverbial "snake oil."[4] Of course, this may be reading too much back into the past from what we know of their son's career.

Their community introduced a new term into common usage. In mid-century, a well-dressed, personable, and talkative man appeared among the respectable classes in the city. In the course of a conversation, he would claim to need a timepiece to make an appointment and ask his interlocutor if he had enough "confidence" to loan his gold watch, with a promised to return it promptly the next day. A certain portion would do so and find themselves minus an expensive timepiece the next day. The arrest of the "confidence man" clarified the law, but many of those who lived much harder lives probably had little sympathy for the gullible gentleman and, perhaps, had a certain appreciation for the unscrupulous cleverness of the "con man."[5]

William A. A. Carsey was born into this family on October 16, 1841. Ten days later, his parents baptized him William Augustus Carsey at Old St. Patrick's on Mulberry Street between Prince and Houston. The US Census of 1850 located their household just to the east, across the Bowery in the Seventeenth Ward.[6] This placed the family in one of the more dynamic and interesting corners of the city.

Through the documentary fog, though, the general features of Carsey's early life are discernible. He surely had modest schooling, but he had wits enough to pick up what he needed as he went along. About half a mile down Mulberry from the church sprawled the Five Points neighborhood, later claimed with a perverse kind of pride to be the worst slum on the planet. Outsiders emphasized the intensity of violence there, and the first guidebooks they put into the hands of visitors to the city cautioned against the dangers of the area.[7] Much of the wealth that changed hands there, however, came through fixed gambling and confidence schemes.

A century before, the old Collect Pond had provided city dwellers with a bucolic refuge. The subsequent construction of a large brewery, a slaughterhouse on what would become Mulberry Street, and such workshops as tanneries destroyed the pond. Rejecting a proposal to restore it for use as a recreational area, the city decided to fill in the pond and allow construction on the building sites there. At the same time, Anthony Street reached east to the junction of Cross and Orange Streets, geographically creating the "Five Points," later renaming the streets Worth, Park, and Baxter. The landfill proved so inexpertly done that the ground subsided into a broad depression, unseating the foundations of houses built there. The lower parts of the streets regularly formed as much as a foot of undrained mud and excrement, leaving standing pools of filth as breeding grounds for ever-renewing swarms of mosquitoes and insect life.

In the years of Carsey's youth, those who could afford to leave had long ago done so, abandoning a filthy, crime-infested neighborhood of the poor and immigrants extending west to Centre, east to the Bowery, north to Canal, and south to Park Row. Near the heart of the neighborhood, the city offered the carrot and the stick in the form of the Hall of Justice and House of Detention, "the Tombs" at Centre and Leonard, and a Methodist project to replace the Old Brewery with the Five Points Mission. More generally, though, as long as the neighborhoods centered on the Sixth Ward continued to turn out reliable and large Democratic ballots, the city took a *laissez-faire* approach to the troublesome area, which suited residents. Although orderly by its own standards, neighborhood life followed an order independent of the city authorities and rooted in the crowded street life of the Bowery b'hoys and g'hals. The gangs themselves embraced the actor Frank Chanfrau's portrayed of Mose the fireman in his record-breaking play, *A Glance at New York*, creating a version of a b'hoy, which, in turn, standardized behaviors.

Part of this order involved a balance of power among rival gangs, periodically adjusted with cudgels. The Roach Guards became the most important Irish Catholic gang around Five Points, but it had various rivals, including the Dead Rabbits, while various anti-immigrant Nativist groups operated farther east as the Bowery B'hoys. These two currents had a true knock-down-and-drag-out at the 1849 Astor Place Riot, sparked by the rivalry between an American and an English actor and leaving between 22 and 31 dead with 120 injured.

Such practices grew naturally enough from crowding the working poor into communities defined by market considerations, but outside forces continually strove to manage them. Gangs became an integral component of a new kind of politics coalescing around Carsey. US political parties generally—and the party of "the common man" particularly—originated from the British model of the eighteenth-century parliamentary caucus but developed in such a way as to require a manageably loyal voter base. Decades before, the American states had dropped the old property requirements for voting, albeit with new constitutions explicitly excluding nonwhites and women, as well as children and the insane. While the nature of the parties left white male voters little access to institutional power beyond their votes, it required the careful cultivation of a partisan preference that would be based largely on sectional, religious, and ethnic identities.[8]

Local Democrats, allied to a party sectionally dominated by slaveholders and fostering a system of racial apartheid in the North, found a special strength among Irish voters, a component that only grew stronger with its relative importance as a rapidly expanding constituency. Stoking fears that emancipated workers of color might come north and take their jobs became a vital Democratic strategy to translate the ethnic resentments of disadvantaged whites into something useful for an alliance with the slaveholders, a classic example of what later students of politics would call "identity politics."[9]

Management of this new mass voting base gave rise to a new political profession beyond officeholders and journalists. Electoral success required not only talented officeholders but also saloonkeepers or shopkeepers in the neighborhoods and employers in the workplace, who could make themselves key figures in getting out the vote. The growing importance of governmental power, contracts, and their scale increasingly monetized the value of their work. As a young man, Carsey saw "Honest John" Kelly and his Tammany Hall organization demonstrate how a skilled management of an immigrant constituency could win office as an alderman, and then as a congressman, and still exercise more power out of office than when holding one.[10]

From their origins, Democrats sought assistance managing their voting base from those actually in the voting base. Even before Carsey's birth, Democrats nominated and elected Ely Moore the president of the local printers' union and made him the first "labor congressman." Indifferent to human slavery, when not an active apologist, he touted the praises he won from leading southern Democrats for his denunciations of "wages slavery." Not long after, the English-born Fitzwilliam Byrdsall—though he claimed to be from the South—participated in and chronicled the struggles of an independent Loco-Foco, or Equal Rights Party, which he helped break into digestible pieces for their assimilation into the Democratic Party, earning himself a job at the US Customs House.[11] Mike Walsh, the street leader of the Spartan Band, followed Moore into the US Congress, while his partner, George Wilkes, launched an innovative career in journalism, ultimately editing the *Police Gazette* and presaging a new kind of sensationalist journalism. On the eve of the war, John Cochrane, among others, cultivated a reform-minded rhetoric appealing to Democrats and tended to find themselves tempted by other alternatives.

Such street leaders, whether plebeian or noisily sympathetic to plebeian concerns, bridged the needs of Democratic machines and the gangs of New York. Walsh's Spartan Band was said to have introduced the use of orchestrated street violence into local elections. Captain Isaiah Rynders, a canalboat operator, operating under Tammany auspices, established a reputation as a gang leader while simultaneously asserting the interests of the party, even as slavery and sectionalism threatened its survival. In particular, Rynders beat the drum as a spread-eagle advocate of an explicitly racialist version of Manifest Destiny, while leading his superpatriotic white supremacist cudgel boys against meetings of Black people, abolitionists, and radicals. Nevertheless, expressing this kind of cultural coherence to the people of the street proved insufficient for the maintenance of order among them.

Any aspiring political street leader had to learn the art of maintaining a balance and unity among the distinct, often rival and sometimes irreconcilable, components. Part of the effort for managing the volatile city was the organization of a municipal police force. At the age of twelve, Carsey first saw their distinctive navy-blue uniforms on his street. Earlier, Peter Cooper had proposed replacing the city's time-honored night watch with a militarized force of 1,200 officers, modeled on that in London. From the beginning, people in the neighborhood had a clear understanding that the police provided the city with a fertile field for political patronage.

Democratic mayor Fernando Wood presided over the first years of the force's existence. After rising to power in the party through Tammany, Wood easily shifted to Mozart Hall when it suited him. Critics regularly accused him doing private deals with interests he publicly attacked, and he baited the critics for alleged British or Irish or abolitionist associations. The son of a merchant, he made his own fortune in shipping and land speculation, as he did a stint in Congress and assumed the mayoralty, where he radically expanded the powers of the office. Reputedly "the richest man in New York," he cultivated the image of a man sympathetic to the laboring poor. A series of extensive and expensive construction projects and a large and controversial new police force not only created several thousand new jobs but could also function as his political enforcers.[12]

When the new Republican Party gained control of the state government in 1857, it challenged the legitimacy of the municipals and authorized a metropolitan police force to enforce the law in the city. The metropolitans organized themselves, but Wood refused to dissolve the municipals, creating chaos across the city. On June 16, the metropolitans marched on City Hall to arrest the mayor, sparking the Great Police Riot in front of City Hall, in which the two police forces battled like uniform editions of the ununiformed gangs. The police riot ended only with the arrival of the state militia.

In part, out of revenge for the dissolution of the municipals, the Dead Rabbits led a coalition of Irish Catholic gangs from around Five Points to celebrate the Fourth of July by violating the turf of the Bowery B'hoys, who chased the Dead Rabbits back to Paradise Square before the metropolitan police intervened, despite the ongoing rivalry with the municipals.

The following morning, the Five Points gangs came back, reinforced by the Roach Guards. They stormed into the Green Dragon, a Broome Street watering hole of the Bowery B'hoys, with the apparent intention of demolishing the place. The neighborhood gangs turned out to confront the raiders on Bayard Street. Periodically, the metropolitans made efforts to break up the conflict, but both sides resisted. The fighting resumed, continuing into the afternoon, when a close formation of police waged a determined effort to separate them until the gangs drove them back again.

Finally, the authorities sent in Captain Rynders, who arrived between 5 and 7 p.m. and climbed a barricade to address both sides. After a hail of stones drove him with his escort from the street, he and the city officials decided to call out the militia. At 9 p.m., parts of two regiments of the state militia showed up, advancing alongside the police with fixed bayonets, and the panicked gangs dispersed. Afterward, shorter and smaller clashes erupted during the week.

The outburst cost eight lives with perhaps a hundred injured, and these numbers seem to have been fudged down a bit. Then sixteen, Carsey would have found it hard to resist participation in the troubles. Although his later history hints at a remarkable flexibility, his Catholic and Irish identities may have inclined him to the side of the Dead Rabbits in the riot. That would have left him and his family living among the hostile nativist Bowery B'hoys. He likely adopted the protective coloration of the neighborhood and his later obsession with the threat of foreigners and foreign labor may have echoed the nativist predilections of the gangs where he had grown up. By the time of the 1858 Shields suit and the departure of the Carseys for the West, they had nothing holding them in the city.

The Carseys left for Kansas against a backdrop of political disasters for the Democrats. The dominant southern wing of the Democratic Party became increasingly insistent about permitting western territories to sanction the legality of slavery as new states, but that position blighted support for the party in the North. The northern Democratic strategy aimed to free federal responsibility for the decision by passing it on to the voters settling in the territory. The result had been a mad sectional scramble over Kansas. As the suit pressed in the city, the Carseys seem to have responded by skiving off to the great American West.

Outpacing the lawsuit proved much easier than outrunning the all-consuming national crisis that tore the country apart. In 1860, a Republican electoral victory placed Abraham Lincoln in the White House and the southern wing of the Democratic Party chose to break up the United States in the name of its freedom to own its workers. By that year's census, the Carseys had established themselves on the Fort Leavenworth Military Reserve in the Kansas Territory. They arrived after the struggle to establish slavery there had fundamentally ended in defeat, but they positioned themselves alongside the US Army. The elder William gave his occupation as a laborer, but he likely did a great deal more than that in his younger days, enough to support a household that included two other adult women and a young girl, as well as his wife Mary and their daughter Kate Carsey.[13] Their eldest son, by that point, had likely left the household and would soon go to war.

Young Carsey had barely turned seventeen when he left the city with his parents and had not yet reached twenty before the secessionists fired on Fort Sumter. He enlisted in the First Kansas, which was, as named, the first regiment in the field from the country's newest state. Mustered into Company C on May 29, he served in a regiment that saw hard fighting in the war's first year as Kansans, Iowans, and Illinoisans struggled to deny nearby Missouri to the Confederacy. After May 1862, the First participated in operations in Tennessee, Mississippi, and Louisiana. In June 1864, the army mustered out Carsey and the rest of the regiment.[14] Carsey's later war record remained remarkably muddled, however, because of his later employment by the Pension Office.

Carsey's later claim that he had participated in General William T. Sherman's March to the Sea as a soldier in the Eighth Kansas was another matter. Certainly, the government's Pension Office not only accepted it as part of his application in 1890 but employed him the following year. Nevertheless, that regiment did not join Sherman's movement from Atlanta to the coast at Savannah, but returned to Tennessee instead, where it actually saw more fighting than it would have seen in Georgia. "I am no light-service man," Carsey later insisted, though the details remain sketchy.[15]

More egregiously, a later press account described him as "Colonel" Carsey. This literal self-promotion became endemic in postwar US political life, particularly in the South and among Democrats eager to emphasize their wartime loyalty and service.

How and exactly when Carsey had just made his way back to Manhattan from Kansas remains uncertain. He later hinted that he had been in Arkansas for a while after the war, though he likely had not. By 1868, he gained local notoriety as the catcher for the Frontiers, the Leavenworth baseball team. Local legends even had Wild Bill Hickok umpiring one of their games. The 1870 US census noted the presence of his father boarding with the Wever family in Leavenworth.[16]

Still, by 1869 or 1870, Carsey seemed to have been returning seasonally to New York City. According to what he reported in a later census, he had married sixteen-year-old Adele Zuleima Ostrander, the daughter of a local dentist.[17] His later work suggests the likelihood he earned a living in the building trades, which also provides the most likely basis for his rapid association with figures in Tammany Hall, who had the gift of awarding city contracts and wielded immense weight in the construction business.

Yet Carsey's residence in the city seems to have been initially tentative. The *New York Times* noted his presence as a catcher for the Socials through the 1870 baseball season, but Kansas papers reported in March 1871, that Carsey, "the old catcher of the Frontiers, late of New York," would play in the West that summer.[18] We know no motive for these moves other than his involvement in the sport.

Baseball actually remained important to Carsey throughout his life. While he was still playing ball, he and Adele had their first child, Wilfred, in 1872. It is interesting that they later gave his year of birth as 1870, adding a few years when their son tried to qualify for ball teams in New York. That concern outweighed any embarrassment associated with the change that left Adele pregnant at the time of their wedding. The old man himself played well into his midforties, and, as a catcher, helped to cultivate his son's skills as a pitcher. The training developed an uncanny ability to read the expectations of the batters who faced him and an outstanding slow curve ball to frustrate them.[19] One suspects that "Kid Carsey" owed much of that ability to his father's experience on a wider field with few rules.

In the course of these movements back and forth between Kansas and New York, Carsey likely interested himself in joining one or more fraternal orders, particularly the Freemasons, with which he was later associated. Their lodges provided men on the move with a regular home away from home and could also exercise some power in local politics. He likely also became familiar with the existence of the new IWA, the fame of which inspired an unsuccessful 1871 effort to organize a section in Lawrence. In a day when understanding of the IWA remained vague, it seemed to be just another fraternal order that united people generally interested in reform, a body that could well be seen as playing a role in politics. One participant in the effort, a union printer named Leonard A. Heil, had been gravely wounded in the 1864 fighting around Nashville, after which, he attended what became Washburn University, and, like Carsey, seems to have launched his career as a Freemason.[20]

When Heil returned to Nashville as an agent of the Atchison, Topeka and Santa Fe Railway, he joined a handful of other veterans and more recent immigrants in another unsuccessful effort to form a section of the IWA. The chair, G. G. Proctor—then president of the local typographical union—had most likely been a sergeant in a Georgia regiment guarding Andersonville Prison during the war, and Confederate veterans seem to have had a significant role in imploding the possibilities of forming a section. Since the days of the Spartan Band, figures associated with the party and various fraternal networks had helped broaden the party's appeal among plebeian voters without necessarily requiring any programmatic adjustments. In this case, Proctor not only officiated at organizing meetings of the IWA but played a key role in the local "Order of Pale Faces," a group supported by such publications as the *Caucasian Guard* and allegedly overlapping with the local Ku Klux Klan.[21] Under the postwar demands of self-reconstruction, Democrats did not hesitate to attempt participation in any association from the IWA to the Klan if it could get them what they wanted.

More important, the Democratic effort to claw itself back into viability embraced the deployment of such associations for a wider variety of complex purposes, including electoral activities. In terms of Carsey's career, the particular course of his most important early collaborator, Walter H. Shupe, charted that broad spectrum of these tactical possibilities.

The Mentorship of Father Columbia

A relentless dynamo of self-promotion, Shupe seemed to have regularly experimented with how plausibly one could recast one's identity and record for political purposes. A native of Zoar, Ohio, he may well have been born in the German Separatist community there, and he graduated from Oberlin, that radical hotbed, before studying law under Senator John Sherman, the brother of the general, and establishing other connections with mostly Democratic leaders. He soon left the law, however, for a feisty but financially unsuccessful bid in the newspaper business. Success eluded him as well as his Democratic Party.[22] Shupe—like so many others—proposed to follow the time-honored route from printer to editor to political power broker, blazed by figures from Ben Franklin to Horace Greeley.

Faced with the prospect of continued fragmentation, isolation, and defeat, Shupe and other Democrats made a concerted effort to weaken the Republicans by encouraging a movement of dissenters to nominate a candidate other than Lincoln. That internal tension among Republicans grew from their original desire to exclude slavery from the territories, while leaving its fate where it existed to the states, and initial war goals remained limited to the preservation of the Union. In late 1861, General John C. Frémont—whose soldiers included Carsey—decided that slavery sustained secessionism in Missouri and issued an order effectively banning the institution from his military department. Determined to keep any such decision at the national level, Lincoln removed him.

Roughly a year later, Lincoln announced that he would issue an Emancipation Proclamation. It declared freedom for any slaves beyond Union lines but sought to placate any Unionist slaveholders in the border states or within federal lines. In other words, while the original Republican platform left slavery in the hands of the states, the proclamation placed federal policy and its military in opposition to the efforts of antislavery Unionists in slaveholding states to eliminate the institution.

The antislavery Germans in St. Louis reached out to other organized German across the country and to veteran abolitionists in hopes of mounting a national revolt against Lincoln's renomination. They managed to gather what discontented forces they could for a Cleveland convention in May, intended to press for Frémont's nomination at the upcoming Republican national convention in June. The more skeptical abolitionists suspected that Frémont might be "working underhand for" Benjamin F. Butler, the Democratic politician-turned-general who had redefined runaway slaves as "contraband of war" to avoid returning them to their owners, as federal law required at that time.[23]

Instead, what was intended to be a national convention of antislavery radicals found itself inundated with Democrats such as Shupe, as well as much of the New York delegation. It resolved itself into a nominating convention to run the general on an independent ticket against Lincoln and self-labeled its new party as "Radical Democratic." To further clarify this outcome, it gave the vice-presidential nomination to none other than John Cochrane, a Tammany Democrat who had just become the state attorney general of New York.

The Frémont-Cochrane challenge simply fizzled. In part, the unexpected level of Democratic participation raised fears among the radicals that independent action could weaken their effort to press for a complete and national emancipationist policy. Through the summer, the more serious of them began abandoning the effort, and, in September, Frémont himself announced that he would not run.

The conclusion Shupe drew after this experience was that the route to his prosperity and influence would more likely run through New York than through Cleveland. Gotham offered many opportunities to those with more ambition than scruples. The unprecedented size and anonymity of the great US metropolis certainly provided residents the freedom to make themselves over, even if only in the sense of how others saw them. There, one could not only reinvent one's past but reshape one's present. Drawn by such opportunities, Shupe turned up in Rockland County, launched the *Columbian* newspaper, and recast himself as "Father Columbia" before moving to New Jersey and shifting his entire business operation to the city.[24] Despite the vicissitudes of his own attempts to wield it, Shupe had mastered the power of the press.

Once resettled there, Shupe expanded his association with local Democratic figures through the Masonic Mission, operating out of the Five Points in New York City. Preoccupied with aiding the sick and wounded in army hospitals, it almost immediately raised enough money to send "about thirty nurses" to the Army of the Potomac. The *National Freemason* reported Shupe's presidency over the project, describing him as "a young man but one just fitted for the position." The work brought him to the attention of Generals Butler and Dan Sickles, the latter a Tammany war hero who had lost a leg at

Gettysburg. Shupe also enjoyed the support of Captain Isaiah Rynders, the Tammany Street enforcer.[25]

Shupe, of course, exaggerated such associations for the press. While he knew Frémont, particularly after the general joined a businessmen's club on Broadway, the Ohio newcomer was not likely to have been "one of his most intimate personal friends." Years later, when Frémont fell ill, Shupe confidently assured reporters that the general's sickness was "not dangerous."[26] Shortly after, the family announced Frémont's funeral.

Contemporaries described Shupe at this point as "a gentle but discontented New York lawyer who started a weekly about that time to advocate the unlimited issue of paper money." He claimed to have more than one hundred thousand subscribers, an incredible claim since he lacked available mechanical printing facilities. "A more experienced publisher," wrote a later reporter, "could probably have bridged the dilemma." Shupe had sold advertising space on the basis of such exaggerated circulation claims and escaped the consequences by declaring bankruptcy, indicating a talent for self-promotion that outstripped his ability to deliver.[27] Nevertheless, the editor was well connected and understood the potential of shaping and managing public perceptions.

For all his sterling qualities, though, Shupe never seemed to learn that the power of the new medium to publicize his activities could work against him as well as for him. He seemed to have rarely avoided seriously litigious personal quarrels with his neighbors, accounts of which hardly reflected well on his reputation. For example, after he settled his residence in New Jersey, he drew up codicils to the will of a resident in nearby Ramapo, even as another, better-established local lawyer had executed other, contradictory codicils. The newspapers followed the issue into the court, where it became clear that someone was being less than truthful.[28]

The more far-sighted Democratic officials had begun to grapple with a "new departure" of their own to escape the old issues of the war. The formula involved a refurbished Jacksonian reformism with a plebeian flair and wartime opposition to the unconstitutional concentrations of power. The most reform-minded Democratic spokespeople began to advocate mild regulatory legislation and a flexible approach to paper money, seasoning the rhetoric to local taste with antimonopolist appeals or white supremacism.[29]

All this shaped the course of a new Liberal Republican Party. It initially came from the same sources as had the 1864 attempted rebellion against Lincoln within the Republican Party. As with the earlier case, desperate Democrats quickly entered and managed to make the cornerstone of the coalition a restoration of the civil rights of former Confederates, which would be a decisive aid in overcoming the Republican advantage. With the default of the South, the New York Democratic Party had become the most powerful within the national organization and secured the 1868 nomination for Governor Horatio Seymour, who was sent to a ritualized defeat at the hands of General Ulysses S. Grant.

By 1870, the Liberal Republicans had launched a national party. In short order, it was so thoroughly populated with Democratic figures that the party of Jefferson, Jackson, and Jefferson Davis opted not to field a regular candidate in 1872. Instead, it simply seconded the Liberal Republican nomination of Horace Greeley, the prominent antebellum radical, now repentant to the point of urging the reintegration of the ex-Confederates into national life.[30]

Whatever their shortcomings, Shupe and other aspiring freelance power brokers became increasingly useful to Democratic purposes. Their work provided a greater flexibility that permitted their exploration of alternatives, leaving it to the rest of the party to choose what might prove best for it. They also provided means to test innovative ideas and approaches without necessarily leaving the party responsible for them.

The "Ohio Idea" and Labor Reform

Those reform Democrats eager to chart a new course for the party had diverse options. Few showed much interest in the periodic local revolts of African American voters in parts of the South against their betrayal by the Republican administrations, but the sectional dominance of the Democratic Party there precluded the need to do anything different. In contrast, the agrarian discontent across the Midwest shook the Republican predispositions of voters there, opening real possibilities for Democratic successes.

Also, the concerns of the new labor movement that had grown out of the war raised other possibilities. Episodically, Democrats in New York had been derailing working-class moves to independent action since the 1820s, but these had never become as persistent as after the Civil War. Labor Reform tickets took the field as early as 1863 in Portland, Maine, or Boston in 1865, both places where Republican victory was virtually assured. The trade unions naturally found themselves tending to be at loggerheads with Republican officialdom, and their new National Labor Union (NLU) and its affiliates produced a series of labor reform tickets. By 1871, the NLU became so disillusioned with the party of rail-splitting Abe that it voted to launch a National Labor Reform Party.[31] Realistically, though, labor organizations had little realistic hope of denting the hegemony of the two-party system on their own, and labor politics increasingly tended to submerge itself and its concerns into the movement of rural discontent and its preoccupation with currency reform.

Shupe's preoccupation with greenbacks became central to the introduction of the issue in metropolitan New York. Preoccupied with stabilizing the economy in the face of a massive war debt, the leadership of both parties had moved toward the idea of pulling the old wartime paper currency from circulation in favor of returning to hard specie to maintain confidence in the payment of the national debt. Radical labor understood this proposition in terms of such cooperative schemes as Josiah Warren's Cincinnati "Time Stores," where shoppers could acquire goods with promissory "Labor Notes," guaranteeing the holder a certain amount of labor from the person issuing it. The wider society, however, understood the proposition in terms of a different kind of "Ohio idea," promoted by Democrats in Shupe's home state. The latter sought to establish permanent government control of a paper currency that would be interchangeable with government bonds earning an interest limited to 3.65 percent. The bipartisan national interest in getting rid of the currency alienated much of the Republican electorate in the rural Midwest, suspicious of the power of northeastern elites and finance capital over the money supply.

When the NLU voted to organize its National Labor Reform Party (NLRP), Andrew Carr Cameron, the Chicago editor of the *Workingman's Advocate*, and his allies used the currency issue to lever the effort toward reform Democrats. Cameron nudged the National Labor Reform Party into existence and dominated its February 1872 convention in Columbus, Ohio.[32] That location ensured that most participants would come from the host state, and railroad passes brought the next-largest delegation, from Pennsylvania, but Cameron's large group from Illinois managed to mediate the convention's course.

The NLRP convention did absolutely nothing to address the problem of organizing itself as a party and adopted a remarkably conservative platform. For example, it translated the old NLU demand for a legislated eight-hour workday for all workers into a proposal for its adoption simply for government employees. Delegates also brushed aside—and mocked—a motion to declare "that the true labor reformer of to-day knows no difference between race, color, sex or nationality." In the end, the platform pinned everything on "the Ohio idea" of "a purely national circulating medium, based on the faith and resources of the nation."

Not content with merely composing a weak platform without a constituency, the NLRP steamrolled objections to nominating a presidential ticket without first building local organizations and support. The rush to do so in February 1872 clarifies the party's primary desire to influence the choice of candidates by their party in the major party conventions that summer. It clearly voted only to consider "men who are identified with the Labor Reform movement, who have endorsed the Labor Platform, and have no political connection with either of the other political parties of the day." Immediately after voting for this, each of the delegations from Pennsylvania, Ohio, Illinois, and New Jersey nominated the governors of their own states. The convention considered and rejected Peter Cooper because of his age and rolled over the few who favored nominating Greeley, then on his way to heading the Liberal Republican ticket, which would be seconded by what remained of a national Democratic Party. Ohio, Indiana, Iowa, and Illinois, with the support of half of Pennsylvania, secured the candidacy of Judge David Davis, Lincoln's old friend who had just left the Republicans. Then it then dropped Joel Parker, the Democratic governor of New Jersey into the vice-presidential slot.[33]

Before adjourning, the NLRP authorized a small clique of the participating Democrats to make any necessary adjustments in the ticket. Anyone familiar with the circumstances had every reason to have expected this. Davis had already stated publicly that he had no interest in any nomination. When he declined, the designated executive committee met in March to express a new preference with absolutely no accountability to any organization at all.[34]

In the end, that authorized committee of the NLRP replaced the convention's nomination with that of Charles O'Conor of New York's Tammany organization. He had been involved in the ongoing effort to break the power of the Tweed Ring. Nevertheless, he had noisily supported southern independence during the war, and he enjoyed a modest national fame as the lead lawyer for Jefferson Davis, the former president of the defunct Confederacy. O'Conor even denied the abolition of slavery on the grounds that such an act would have been unconstitutional.[35]

In practical terms, the NLRP deferred to a long-forgotten national convention of the "Straight-Out" Democrats who resented the party's embrace of the Liberal Republican nomination of Horace Greeley. The Democratic and Liberal Republican papers naturally attacked the September convention of the "Straight-Outs" in Louisville, oddly declaring it to be part of a vast Republican conspiracy to divide the opposition to Grant's reelection. Democrats sometimes even blamed the entire thing on Radical Republicans. In fact, it was the work of the old anti-Lincoln Copperhead Democrats such as Marcus M. "Brick" Pomeroy and O'Conor himself.[36] The rationale for action by Blanton Duncan of Louisville and his friends in 1872 centered on their resentment of the regular Democratic acceptance of the nomination of Greeley, an old abolitionist.

In short, party operatives twisted the first effort to launch a national labor party in US history to their own purposes. Duncan masterminded the convention there. An antebellum editor and a Confederate staff officer, he took charge of a major printing operation in Richmond, where his bullying management swagger drove employees in the wartime secessionist capital to organize a union. He responded by winning government help against the union by putting the image of the thuggish head of the local secret police in the capital on the thousand-dollar Confederate bill.[37] In its 1872 nomination, the NLRP opted for a union-busting slavocrat.

The strange course of the NLRP defined the predisposition of nominally independent parties over the next century. None of these repeated efforts to build a party of the working class in this country would or could have ever happened without the direct intervention of Democratic operatives determined to blunt its independent dynamic. This process might have involved all sorts of planning and conspiratorial coordination, but it did not require it. The basic practices came naturally out of the response of individuals operating under a two-party system grounded in mass politics to benefit their party, their group within the party, and themselves.

Efforts of labor reformers in New York City soon attracted Carsey and Shupe, the former making a conspicuous debut in the papers raising the implicit advocacy of violence on behalf of the workers.

* * *

Of more immediate importance to Carsey and Shupe, 1873 saw both deeply immersed in land speculation under the guise of social reform colonies. Even as Carsey claimed to be a leader of the IWA, he appeared as the vice president of "the Workingmen's Land Association." Sounding very much like one of the old radical land-reform groups, it appealed to the aspirations of urban workers for land ownership, particularly the earlier projects that had involved efforts to attain and colonize land cooperatively. Operating out of 109 Fourth Avenue on the southeast corner of Twelfth Street, Carsey's association offered for sale a thousand house lots on the Long Island Railroad for only $5 each, promising that each lot would be on high ground with good soil and a healthy location.[38] Label-making could still trump reality.

At the same time, Shupe pursued similar schemes on the other side of the metropolitan area. He, too, blended the cooperative promise of utopian rhetoric with the razzle-dazzle of real estate. He sought investors for a planned community—or a city, as determined by the interest of the potential investor—between Spring Valley and Monsey in Rockland County. A local chronicler ascribed this plan for "Alturas" to "the brain work of a lawyer, Walter H. Shupe, but like all other of his schemes, it failed of success, and somebody had to lose by it."[39]

Men on the make such as Carsey or Shupe saw themselves as self-employed self-disciplined entrepreneurs. One might dismiss them as monomaniacal grifters, but the kind of relentless hucksterism central to the economic history of the Gilded Age often involved dabbling in political life and had a decisive impact on the civic ecology of the United States.

CHAPTER 1

Paper Party Power Broker

The Entrepreneurial Roots of Labor Reform Insurgency

Laws, like sausages, cease to inspire respect in proportion as we know how they are made.
—John Godfrey Saxe [1867][1]

By the start of November 1875, William A. A. Carsey addressed a meeting called to organize a new political party. Organizers promised to set up precinct clubs to get "a majority of the voters of the State enrolled in our books," but they announced that they had already formed a state central committee and secured "permanent quarters" without such a membership or input. In the absence of the announced speaker, former congressman Samuel F. Cary of Ohio, Carsey took the floor with a prepared speech on the history of money and monetary policy. Newspaper accounts described this new figure as a mason without identifying whether the word referred to his occupation or the fraternal order or both. The *New York Herald* quipped snidely that Carsey described himself as "a workingman, and certainly his appearance and manner of speech fully bore out the assertion."[2] This represented the first thunderclap of news about his launching a party and would not be his last.

The organizers' innovative approach grew less from a broad-based interest in independent politics than from an endemic crisis in Democratic politics, particularly in New York City. Some of Carsey's predecessors had occasionally used sleight of hand to manage insurgent impulses to their party's advantage, but Carsey began to make a career of it. A building contractor and a real estate broker, he began the transition to political "workingman" through the local organization of the International Workingmen's Association (IWA). He went there, it seemed, because of the IWA's interest in electoral politics, which culminated in the launching of the Industrial Workingmen's Party for municipal elections. In short order, Carsey began to harness local developments into a regional ally of the mass sentiment for currency reform, based in the Midwest.

The Postwar Metropolis

The community to which Carsey returned after the war differed much from that in which he had had been born and raised. Shortly before his birth, the census counted 313,000 residents on Manhattan Island with almost another 80,000 in what would become the boroughs of Brooklyn, Queens, Bronx, and Staten Island. The city to which he returned after the Civil War had reached almost 814,000 on Manhattan—1,478,000 with the other four boroughs, which would be consolidated by the end of the century into Greater New York with the five boroughs and nearly 3,440,000 residents. In practical terms, Carsey would close his career on a stage ten times that which had been available at his birth.

New modes of transport and communication not only wove the boroughs together but did the practical job of knitting the country together, an economic corollary of the war's outcome. The United States had less than 2,800 miles of railroad at the time of Carsey's birth but was nearly 50,000 by the time he returned to Manhattan, and it was about four times that by the close of the century. Nobody had ever seen the telegraph when Carsey's parents had him baptized, but the world had roughly 650,000 miles of wire by the time he returned to the city. And New York City became the epicenter of this rapidly coalescing national network.

The war had deprived the Democratic Party of its antebellum dominance over national politics. Much of its popularity represented a reaction to the hostility to immigrants and alcohol expressed by the Nativists and presumably shared by Whigs and later Republicans, peculiarly allied nationally to the interests of the slaveholding South. The course of secession and war left the party stigmatized as the party of "Rum, Romanism, and Rebellion." More important, with the reliably old Democratic states of the South out of the picture, the party that had generally controlled the US government since its founding in the 1820s seemed incapable of winning a national election.

With the South's loss of relevance, New York Democrats played the key role in the national party, as reflected in its presidential nomination. After running General George B. McClellan of neighboring New Jersey in 1864, the party turned to former New York governor Horatio Seymour for the futile 1868 nomination against war hero Ulysses S. Grant. Four years later, a split among the Republicans allowed the Democratic organization to support Horace Greeley, New York City's most famous newspaperman.[3] Then, in 1876, Samuel J. Tilden carried the party's banner.

That postwar dominance of New York in the Democratic Party did not supersede the southern orientation of its old leadership. In addition to figures such as Wood and Governor Horatio Seymour, August Belmont rode heavy investments in the railroads to prominence. He had learned his trade under the Rothschild's operation in Germany but arrived in America as the financial panic of 1837 bottomed, and started a finance company that grew rapidly with the economy's recovery. Even more than Wood, the Jewish-born Episcopalian had strong southern ties and came to national power himself as the chair of the Democratic National Committee. In the wake of the war, he worked with Tilden to get control of the *New York World*.[4]

With so much at stake in the city itself, New York City Democrats required networks of voter management capable of employing a wide variety of means to get out the vote, ranging from persuasion through the use of patronage to less reputable practices such as bullying or bribing voters and buying, stealing, or destroying their ballots. Reflecting the reliability of such practices to those children of an idealized manufacturing age, they called such networks "machines," the use of the plural being key to New York City politics. The most persistent and famous operated out of Tammany Hall, but it never functioned without rivals, such as Mozart Hall or Canterbury Hall on 663 Broadway and Irving Hall operating out of Irving Place and East Fifteenth Street near Union Square.[5]

Indeed, the 1871–73 struggle over the Tweed Ring demonstrated how Tammany itself was hardly homogeneous. Tammany adherents such as John Kelly and Gideon J. Tucker, as well as prominent Democrats such as Charles O'Conor and Peter Cooper, joined the efforts of Tilden and the new Citizens' Association to ease the hold of Tammany on the party—and that of William Magear Tweed's hold on Tammany. In the end, the enemies of the Tweed Ring successfully broke it up and put Tweed behind bars, after which members of the city government engaged in corrupt practices with much more discretion, tact, and forbearance.

Most important, though, Carsey established or reestablished associations with the building trades, which brought him into contact with the politics of the industry in the city. At the time, the Tweed Ring controlled Tammany

Hall, which controlled the city government and exercised a tight control over municipal contracts for construction. Tammany exercised such power through the Democratic Party.[6] So it was that Carsey found himself an otherwise nondescript but ambitious partisan on its behalf.

Carsey would have found the very texture of politics in the city had changed almost tangibly since his departure. Irish Catholics had won much more acceptance. Those with the money found it a remarkable means of clearing obstacles in the way of their ambitions. Newspapers had larger circulation in a more literate population, and the consolidation and expansion of the police force strengthened the machine's hold over patronage. The need to force nominations by the cudgel declined, and so it happened less often. More subtle means replaced reliance on gangs that crowded the polling place to encourage desired ballot choices and discourage other ones. Brain superseded brawn in the new persuasion techniques, but implementation was hardly straightforward. Public support turned on its perceptions of the parties and their rivalries, which required a new kind of mastery to engineer those perceptions.

Against this background—at some point—Carsey encountered Peter Cooper. Literally a man of the previous century, Cooper had been nurturing American industry for even longer than Belmont had worked on its financial infrastructure. His works had produced the first locomotive made in the United States, and his reputation always rode the rails and the telegraph system that grew alongside them, although he invested heavily in real estate and insurance as well. A Unitarian with Universalist predispositions, he earned his reputation as a philanthropist and articulated concerns about slavery, native peoples in the West, women, and the working poor. His Cooper Union offered a free education to those who could spare the time, including evening classes by gaslight. He, his son Edward Cooper, and son-in-law Abram S. Hewitt shared not only the interests of other ironmongers but a predisposition to the anti-Tammany Democratic forces, the elder Cooper working through Irving Hall.[7] But the defeat of the Tweed Ring made elements within Tammany just as acceptable.

For all the thunder of partisan strife, key Democratic leaders shared more with their Republican counterparts than either party did with their voters. Local elites had grown wealthy from the same kinds of land speculation, the profitable duplication of a British system of finance without the restrictions of tradition and custom, and the emergence of industrial capitalism, particularly the railroads. Although they meant different things to different people over time, their common projects of civic improvement and civil service reform provided a common language with a broad appeal to the electorate in general.

On a personal level, prominent Democrats worked regularly with their locally less powerful Republican counterparts, as did the Coopers with the collector of the Port of New York, the wealthy Chester A. Arthur, one of the leaders of the Republican patronage machine in the city.[8]

Rhetoric aside, the city's elite agreed that manhood suffrage did not bequeath to citizens the status of "voting kings," but a mechanism of engagement to secure political stability. Within this system, those who actually won an election had done the best job of selling the idea of their legitimacy to the electorate and—for this very reason—would be the least likely to face a proverbial mob with torches and pitchforks converging on City Hall. Yet the postwar rise of new kinds of mass workers' organizations, organized around independent concerns and with lofty expectations in the wake of the victory for "free labor," posed a new set of challenges.

Establishing an Internationalist Reputation

As the prospect of labor radicalism surfaced at most nationally strategic centers for the Democratic Party, Carsey ventured to test the waters, winding up in very unlikely company. In the IWA, he sat alongside William West, an old Fourierist and land reformer from the 1840s, and Hugh McGregor, who would go on to later help lead the American Federation of Labor. Another, C. Osborn Ward, stood on the brink of a radical scholarly career that would last into the twentieth century. The older participants could easily recall the prewar days when John Cochrane would show up on behalf of Tammany Hall, offering alliances and making promises. Among them, Carsey sat not as an open representative of Tammany, as had Cochrane, but as a leader of one of the numerous craft unions in the building trades, even claiming later that he had "led strikes in New York."[9]

The most explicitly radical organization in the United States, the IWA also became known as the First International, and in which Karl Marx and Friedrich Engels participated in England. In the United States, the organization splintered along generally ethnic lines, with the German-, French-, and English-speaking (or "American") sections going their own ways, casualties of Marx's desire to consolidate the German elements to survive the factional threat of Mikhail Bakunin and the continental anarchists. After the break, the American and French sections nominally affiliated with Bakunin's Jura Federation, but members invested in their own areas of work rather than the international.

Nevertheless, remnants of the IWA filled a serious void in the local labor movement. The IWA sought to make an issue of the disastrous fire that broke out on Christmas Eve 1872 in the New York Printing Company bookbindery at 85 Centre Street.[10] Most of the fifty "girls" employed there—so called despite the fact that some were in their thirties—escaped with slight wounds and bruises, but there remained "very little doubt but that seven of the employees of Archer, Anderson & Co., the bookbinders occupying the upper floors of the building, were burned to death, some of them within sight of persons on the sidewalk." The dead included two sets of adult sisters and a twelve-year-old boy.

As with the later and much larger 1911 Triangle Shirtwaist Fire, the negligence of the city and the employer doomed the workers. A year before, the city had pointed out the unreliability of the old fire escape, an iron bridge from a fifth-floor rear window to the roof of a building fronting Elm Street. The owners added iron balconies and ladders leading to a building on Centre and Leonard, but they had stopped work on it when it remained fifteen feet short and failed to test or do maintenance on the work that had been done.

Worse, though, the fire department claimed that extinguishing the job ended its job, and the police had nothing left in the budget to pay them for retrieving the bodies. The police also denied that they had the authority to deputize the work either. A heavy snowfall buried the rubble under several feet of snow. When the police did attempt the retrieval toward the close of the year, a storm forced them to pull back.

In addition to the presiding officer, the federal council that met on December 29 at No. 129 Spring Street fathered only nine delegates and one Laurent Clement, a visiting Chicago member. They conducted business amid a simmering plebeian frustration with the failure of the authorities to recover the bodies from the fire. After conducting business, they read "The Centre Street Fire" from the Democratic *New York Herald*, and the council resolved to bypass the authorities and "call upon the people to come forward and assist in the work of exhumation from the ruins." Some pushed to gather at the ruins at ten o'clock the next morning "for the purpose of assisting the relatives of the victims in recovering the bodies," which would have met a direct confrontation with the police. Because the federal council coopted Carsey and another into its ranks, they were identified among the key instigators.[11] In the end, though, cooler heads persuaded the body to meet first with the authorities, and the mayor assured them that he had already ordered the coroner to organize the recovery.

Two weeks later, the council had a "large" attendance to discuss how the group might assist the revolutionary struggle in Cuba. At that point, "Citizen Carsie" "called the attention of the Council to the violence used by the authorities in carrying out their edicts in America." On a roll, he declared America "more oppressed by her Government than any monarchy" and asked "how he was to act if assaulted by the myrmidons of the law when not committing any offense." The veteran radical West responded, "Until the voice of the people cry out, nothing can be stopped; until revolution is carried on by public opinions, we cannot cause a revolution, and so we will have to wait until things progress."[12] Carsey's second attempt to move the International into a direct confrontation with the police fizzled.

Carsey's career as a labor agitator, then, began as an *agent provocateur* in the context of the times. The term came out of the activities of the convicted criminal Eugène François Vidocq, who built a career out of serving the authorities by operating out of uniform and beyond the restraints of law to intimidate, assault, and frame opponents. Originally, such activities aimed at strikers and their use spread later to working-class radicals. The term appeared in the British press by the 1820s, but American papers seem not to have picked it up until the 1850s. *Agents provocateurs* could serve government at any level or private businesses. Over time, the term came to mean specifically a government agent who would use anonymity to recast public and legal perceptions of radicals by provoking acts of violence that could be used to justify repression by the legitimate organs of power.

In the United States, private companies tended to pioneer such techniques before governments, and more local government bodies than federal ones. The way New York City pioneered mass politics naturally involved the unofficial but affiliated bodies such as Tammany Hall and politically controlled street gangs, which had long involved the use of plainclothes operatives engaged in all sorts of smoke and mirrors to conjure perceptions favorable to one faction or another. Carsey, however, would elevate such practices to a much larger and more impactful sense.

Three months after trying to goad the International to confront the police and two months after his debut as a real estate developer advocating "homes for workingmen," Carsey sought to persuade what was left of the "internationals" to move into more nationalist channels. Never overly shy in such circumstances, Carsey offered a resolution expressing his own version of proletarian internationalism:

> Whereas, the employers of labor have organized for the purpose of flooding the country with pauper labor from Europe and Asia to the injury of the labor movement, without corresponding benefit to the laborers thus Imported; therefore, be it Resolved, That our Secretary be Instructed to notify the several

> European councils, and request them to use their utmost endeavors to frustrate this scheme of capitalistic monopolists.

The veteran radicals who heard him likely exchanged meaningful looks and authorized a committee to help the neophyte Carsey better thrash out his ideas.

Carsey also introduced a strange resolution about the Republicans. It noted that President Ulysses S. Grant, in his inaugural message,

> fully recognized the principle of one government for all peoples speaking the same language, and further recommended the substitution of the State for private individuals in the management of railroads, telegraphs and other means of transportation and communication; therefore, the thanks of the council are due, and are hereby tendered to President Grant for thus lending the influence of his great name and position to further the objects of our Association.

This expression of gratitude to Grant for his support of nationalizing basic industry stirred already murky waters. Its passage and publication would have had no impact on the Republicans but would have provided the Democrats with a further conservative argument about the threat of a residual radicalism within the GOP.

The IWA meeting declined to pass the resolutions but decided to harness Carsey's stated interest in political action. It assigned him to work with others to persuade the city's labor organizations to press the state to enforce its new eight-hour law. It also added him on a committee to call a July 4 convention to discuss concerted action in the coming election.

That fall, the financial panic created all the preconditions for serious independent political action. Jay Cooke and Company, a cornerstone of the postwar banking establishment, had sought a $300 million loan from the government to finance its expanded investments in railroads, just as Washington began contracting the money supply in preparation for abandoning greenbacks. As a result, on September 18, Jay Cooke and Company declared bankruptcy, followed by many similar firms toppling like a row of dominos, followed by a ten-day shutdown of the stock market.[13] The events sent a wave of railroad failures, factory layoffs, and closures rippling across the country.

The crisis inspired the remnants of the old federal council of the IWA to resume meeting, with Carsey as one of the key proponents. They met at their old stomping grounds, 242 Spring Street, though most members had already moved on to more promising projects. Still, the *New York Times* called its September meeting "one of the largest held this year." With Carsey in the chair, they heard the report of a committee sent to the Fifth Avenue Hotel to meet with the prominent English freethinker and member of Parliament Charles Bradlaugh. George Maddox, Hugh McGregor, T. R. Klinget, and Theodore H. Banks stood in for the conspicuously absent old members of the IWA leadership, along with Alexander Frey, a future socialist leader. The interview proved to be a farce of sorts, reflecting the chaotic approach of the rump IWA. The meeting did decide to expel Banks and "also resolved to open correspondence with the colored associations throughout the country and requesting them to form sections of the International order."[14]

The International's General Council in London had written Presidents Lincoln and Johnson earlier, and, in the wake of the panic, a committee of its federal council in New York wrote President Ulysses S. Grant. As one of the three signatories, Carsey, "on behalf of the workers of this country," requested "a special session of the Congress of the United States, for the purpose of providing ways and means to meet the financial and labor crisis now upon us." Grant had proposed an extensive series of internal improvements that could "furnish employment to the thousands of workingmen thrown out of employment by the failure of our swindling contract labor system." Moreover, by paying them with "sufficient legal tenders you can cure our financial troubles caused by a lack of currency, and thus enable our Western crops to be brought to market at profitable rates to the producers." They urged the president to act and "not give occasion for your enemies to say that by your delay and lack of statesmanship you allowed the producing institutions of your country and its people to be destroyed."[15]

Nevertheless, no such intervention mitigated the mass unemployment and declining wages as the country entered a desperate winter. By the end of the year, Peter J. McGuire, a carpenter active in the IWA, headed a committee of public safety—conjuring the specter of the recent Paris Commune—that asked to meet with city officials, who simply ignored them.[16] The lack of response inspired plans for a march on city hall, demanding a Labor Relief Bureau. Another group pushed for a meeting on January 5 with a similar result. On January 8, a thousand showed up at Union Square to march on city hall, but the police barred the way. Some then headed off to Tompkins Square to plan for a larger turnout.

McGuire's committee faced panic mongering by the press, the mobilizations of the city police force, and threats to attack any march on city hall. In response, the committee opted just to hold a meeting at the square. Under pressure from the police, officials in charge of the parks denied them a permit, but too late to notify the seven thousand protesters who showed up on

January 13. Late in the morning, the police waded in with their clubs in what the young Samuel Gompers called "an orgy of brutality." The police arrested nearly four dozen, prosecuting several of those who had dared to fight back against them.

In late January, the Committee of Public Safety reacted by threatening political action. It described the record of the two parties as "such as to forfeit confidence; that all public officials should be elected by direct vote of the people and should receive moderate salaries." It declared for civil service reform, the improvement of lakes and canals under the state and national governments, an end to privileges in taxation and land grants for corporations, the reform of patent laws, the repeal of national banking laws and issuance of legal tender directly from the treasury. It also favored the abolition of contract labor on public works, the reduction of the hours of labor, state supervision of education, and graduated taxes. The kicker came with its call for an independent labor party, which a confused press regularly and variously called different names, such as the "Industrial Political Party of the State of New York." In the midst of all this angry rhetoric and militant plans, Carsey came to a certain prominence as the head of a committee for encouraging workers to emigrate to the West.[17]

In February, the police moved to shatter an already badly divided movement. For reasons never fully explained, three officers without a warrant raided the home of Desire Debouchy and his wife, described as "communists, living at No. 168 Bleeker street." When he complained about the hour and the lack of a warrant, one of them put a loaded pistol to his head. They did find a stash of shells for hand grenades under the kindling. He explained that a man named Murphy had made them during the efforts to provide munitions to a besieged Paris in 1870. The court threw out the attempt to prosecute Debouchy on the grounds that he had broken no law. Even the already conservative *New-York Tribune* suggested that "it is time for the police to be checked."[18]

The portrait of revolution as the work of a violent cabal of conspirators would become an American perennial. In one sense, it represented a continuation of the argument that abolitionists rather than nature of slavery itself generated hostility to the institution. It seemed to surface whenever and wherever class grievance pressed too severely or reactionaries required some justification for repression. Significantly, the man described once as the "boss communist" got his "United Order of Bricklayers of New York," likely another paper organization, to condemn "the Communists and Internationals."[19]

Carsey simultaneously began to resurrect his real estate map for the emancipation of the working class. The panic had brought construction to a complete halt across the city, and land values collapsed. Within hours of the police riot in Tompkins Square and the press publicity accorded the threat of the old International, Carsey took an initiative in the name of the International that might also line his own pockets.[20]

Notwithstanding the fact that the International had largely disappeared, Carsey began to present himself as the "President of the General Council of the Internationals." "This is a question of bread, not class or creed," wrote Carsey, and he proposed to broker a resettlement of needed labor to the South. "I am an Arkansas man myself," he claimed, "and know a little of the needs of settlers." He cited the Canadian project of Joseph Arch to provide English immigrants from England with land, housing, and seed in return for work on roads at good wages "till they get settled." In this light, Carsey asked, "Cannot your state do as much, as well as vote money to railroads, and enrich the state, sure of the return of your loan with interest?" "Send me the authority to act, and at my own expense I will enlist and organize a regiment of workers who will enter into the land and subdue it, in the words of the Lord," he wrote, adding that he wanted funding to get the aspiring Arkansans from New York.[21] Technological considerations aside, it represented an approach worthy of any electronic entrepreneurial grifter.

Carsey wrote other southern state governments with a similar proposal, as the head of the IWA. When he approached the government of Louisiana, he supplemented the citation of Arch's work in Canada with the decision of Maine to launch a project to resettle a thousand Swedes in Aroostook County.[22] Once more he offered himself as the conduit of any available state largesse.

Whether as "president" of the IWA or "secretary of the International Association," Carsey defined "the objects and aims of the Internationals." The International, he explained, included sections of German, Austrian, Prussian, Swedish, and Danish members "organized by Carl Marx," as well as Swiss, French, Spanish, Italians, Portuguese, Mexican, South American, Belgian, Dutch, English, and American members. "The Internationals in France, Germany and other of Europe, except Great Britain," he explained, favored "overturning the government by revolution."

In contrast to these more obviously foreign types, continued Carsey, "the Internationals in England and the United States . . . believed that their objects and aims could be accomplished by means of the ballot." Members in those countries, "with whom he and his associates were connected, certainly had no intention of violently overturning society in the manner ascribed to them." They sought only "educating the people up to their standard of equality for all, and in a few years at the farthest they believe that their principles will be favored by the majority of voters."[23]

A January 1874 meeting of the rump federal council of the IWA reported on a series of letters from public officials in response to their proposals. US Senator Roscoe Conkling of New York offered a courteous reply to their suggestion of establishing savings banks through the post offices for workers. More significant were the responses of Republican governor Cushman K. Davis of Minnesota and Democratic lieutenant governor Robert E. Withers of Virginia to Carsey's proposals, that their states grant land to workers as a means of enticing a more industrially skilled population there.[24] This seems to have been part of a concerted effort to approach each of the states with such a project.

Most met Carsey's overtures with a deafening silence. In addition to the rejection by Minnesota and Virginia, though, the *Little Rock Daily Republican* complained that any subsidy to settlers "is wholly out of the question at present." In any event, the thought of bringing "hundreds of half-starved laboring men" to the state in the wake of the Tompkins Square Riot seemed about as enticing to the Arkansas paper as the prospect of bringing legions of the unwashed absinthe-sipping, Hegel-quoting Europeans to Carsey's doorstep in New York.[25]

The *Nashville Union* remained similarly unimpressed by Carsey's explanation of the IWA's goal. "If Mr. Carsey means community of property by his expression 'equality of all,'" asked the paper, "what difference would it make whether it was achieved by ballots or bullets? It is agrarianism all the same."[26] Carsey found that wrapping his real estate schemes with a radical candy coating satisfied nobody.

All this might have discouraged a lesser figure of international standing, but Carsey proved to be made of sterner stuff.

Building a Labor Party

In the aftermath of the national financial crisis, membership in nonelectoral voluntary associations reflected a widespread interest in social reform. Perhaps two million farmers and small-town folk joined the Order of the Patrons of Husbandry—the "Grange," which actively encouraged lobbying on such questions as government regulation of railroad freight rates. Then, too, the Holy and Noble Order of the Knights of Labor was emerging from the Philadelphia needle trades, eventually to gain more than three quarters of a million members. The Junior Sons of '76 in western Pennsylvania, the Sovereigns of Industry in New England and eastern Pennsylvania, the Brotherhood of

Labor in the Midwest, and the Industrial Brotherhood in Missouri gained significant regional followings.

On a local and state level in the Midwest, such developments began shaking loose enough voters predisposed to be Republican to produce a series of new independent parties. The two most significant of them grew from the battle over Grange laws regulating the railroads in Illinois, and the recognition by pro-Democratic reformers in Indianapolis that such issues had traction among Indiana voters as well. In addition to Missouri's Peoples' Party, National Reformers took the field in Michigan, Independents in Nebraska, Antimonopolists in Iowa and Minnesota, and Independent Reformers in Kansas and Wisconsin.[27]

The prospect of a new, midwestern-based national party was not so far-fetched at the time as it seems in hindsight. Twenty years before, the Kansas-Nebraska Act had galvanized the Republican insurgency, and many proponents of a new party after the Civil War thought the Resumption Act of 1874, which mandated the replacement of wartime greenbacks with metal specie, could do something similar. Many proponents of a new party after the Civil War thought they might have found it in the Resumption Act of 1874, which mandated the replacement of wartime greenbacks with metal specie. Others balked at focusing a national movement on paper money, and the Michigan and Kansas insurgents explicitly condemned inflationary measures, as did a vocal minority in Illinois and other states. Nevertheless, the powerful Illinois and Indiana independents favored the greenback focus and coordinated their state conventions of "farmers, mechanics and other citizens" at Springfield and Indianapolis on June 10, 1874, so as to provide a common call to save paper money.[28]

Although real grievances gave right to these insurgencies, Democratic strategists saw them as an opportunity to reduce GOP majorities enough to encourage their hopes to resume the kind of power their party had enjoyed before the war. Republican observer and future president Rutherford B. Hayes rightly warned that these new parties had drawn four-fifths of their voters from the GOP, which offered the Democrats a real, if slim, opportunity to escape the permanent minority status into which its association with slavery, secession, and war seemed to have consigned it.[29]

None of these preconditions for a mass insurgency existed in New York City. For this reason, Carsey found it very easy to provide the voice for a local movement, establishing a position on paper that would also enhance his status and those of his allies within the local Democratic Party. Acting in the name of his defunct local "industrial" party associated with the old Committee of Public Safety and with Tompkins Square, Carsey went to work rallying Democratic figures, such as Theodore E. Tomlinson and others, to meet and consider the new reform proposals. By August, they had met at the Masonic Hall to seek someone who could carry the new party's banner into the fall elections, even as members of the old Committee of Public Safety pointed out that it was not the "party" they had authorized earlier.[30]

They acted to launch the Industrial Political Party, claiming the authority of a vague call as well by New York's Workingmen's Assembly. On October 7, 1874, Carsey chaired their county convention in the Masonic hall, a gathering that tendered their mayoral nomination on October 12 to Charles A. Dana, the owner and editor of the [New York] *Sun*. They did so with the support of the more old-line Democratic *New York Herald*. Its legendary editor, James Gordon Bennett, the antiunion white supremacist, had just died, passing the torch to his son, James Gordon Bennett Jr.[31]

Dana was a former Fourierist, a veteran of Horace Greeley's Republican *New-York Tribune*, and an assistant secretary of war in the Lincoln administration. After taking over the *Sun*, he transformed it into a Democratic organ. Indeed, physically, as well as ideologically, the *Sun* quite literally occupied the same ground as the old Tammany Hall at Nassau and Frankfort, when the latter organization moved into its new headquarters at 141 East Fourteenth Street between Third and Fourth Avenues. Dana immediately declined what had been presented to him as a labor nomination, but there is no evidence indicating that he knew how inaccurate he was in thanking the committee for nomination that "comes fresh and direct from the people, and not from an old, organized party."[32]

Carsey gaveled together a reassembly of the "party" to make another nomination. A few radicals, such as George Blair, showed up, as did some influential local politicians, such as Tomlinson. In the end, they decided to run Dana's editor, John Swinton, a man who had much better and more recent radical credentials in his own right. An old abolitionist—he had been in Kansas during the struggles there—Swinton had publicly confronted the city government over Tompkins Square. He called for firing the police board in a testimony to the state government later reissued as *The Tompkins Square Outrage*.[33]

Swinton hesitated until representatives of the party assured him that they had "no outside affiliations or entanglements, and that it shall in no way be rendered subservient in any other purpose than that which appears on the surface." On October 27, after getting such assurances, Swinton assured them "that my head, heart and hands are, to the full extent of their powers, in sympathy with the suffering and struggling workers of this great city, and that I am one with them in every rational effort to establish justice and secure the rights of human nature." He added that

> The workingmen of this city can elect its Mayor, if they please; those of the State could elect its Governor if they pleased; those of the country could elect its President, if they pleased. The workingmen of each State could control every legislature, and the workingmen of the Union could fill Congress with their actual and proper representatives. They have it in their power to enact and enforce such laws, local and national, of any kind, on every subject, as may seem to them necessary to secure their rights, succor their interests and promote their welfare.[34]

The absence of a full slate successfully restricted the practical function of this "party" to little more than an incentive to draw to the polls the reform-minded who might otherwise not vote. Once there, most such voters would tend to vote against the Republican candidates. Also, entirely disregarding the assurances they had given Swinton, the new party gave its nomination for the Fourteenth State Assembly District to Luke F. Cozans, a candidacy endorsed by Tammany, Peoples Liberal Democratic Convention, German American Independent Citizens' convention, and the Liberal Republicans.[35]

On November 2, "between 200 and 300 workingmen met in Tompkins Square to ratify the nominations of the industrial Political party."[36] Swinton spoke, as did McGuire and John B. Wolff, another old abolitionist and former internationalist. Rabbi Max Lilienthal, president of freethinkers, spoke, as well as Leander Thompson, a persistent voice for labor political independence, "and others." A circular appeared on behalf of the campaign that named a few other candidates as well as Swinton, with no indication that a public nominating meeting ever took place.

At the meeting in Tompkins Square, Blair proposed a series of ringing resolutions. They asserted "the rights, interests and welfare of that vast body of workers" and denounced "the two rival parties which divide the plunder among them, have not only ignored the working masses, but wronged them in every possible way." They claimed the right of the workers to exercise their freedom of speech and assembly and insisted that "unemployed people, of both sexes, not be left to starvation while the granaries are filled with food." The meeting proposed to elect candidates "prepared to take measures to avert the impending calamities of the coming winter, and we demand our opponents to tell what preparations they propose to make." After passing these resolutions, the group moved as a body to their headquarters, Mr. Kohn's wine shop and eatery at 386 Broome Street.

In fact, the more radical proponents of independent political action had already moved on to form a socialist party. The ethnic self-fragmentation of the German adherents of the IWA had continued to purge sections until it had none left to expel but themselves. In April 1874, three former German sections joined a French one and the recently formed Newark labor party to declare the need for a new party. With eight other groups, a July 4 convention launched the Social Democratic Workingmen's Party of North America (SDWP). The SDWP immediately opened talks with the Chicago-based Workingmen's Party of Illinois, the remnants of the IWA, and the United Workers of America. Although the socialists had not fielded their own candidates, some French groups who balked at the prospect of doing so eventually walked out.[37]

Although Carsey's "Industrial Political Party" enjoyed a clear field for gathering in the stray voters of discontented workers, it officially got votes in numbers lower than the numbers of those who participated in its local meetings. Nevertheless, Carsey and a handful of others continued to act in the name of the "party" for many years, as its nominal head. It provided credentials for him and others to participate in various labor conventions elsewhere (and, he would argue, in bargaining for concessions from the Democrats). Early on, the *Times* shrewdly ascribed various ploys by the major parties to weaken the voting strength of their rival and to "the self-seeking of a few individuals" eager to promote their own prospects within a major party.[38] It could have been deliberately describing Carsey's Industrial Workingmen's Party.

Of course, Carsey's activities reflected a general disposition among Democrats to coopt and defang insurgent impulses. As radical workers in New York and Philadelphia began moving toward the kind of social democratic groups that had appeared in Germany, Democrats in the Thirteenth Ward established a "Social Democratic Association," the primary purpose of which would be to participate in Democratic conventions and "to use every exertion to secure" the election of Democratic candidates.[39]

To be clear, Carsey and his peers had created a labor reform "party" radically disconnected from working people that existed only on paper or, more accurately, in the papers. The course of these nominally or aspirationally insurgent bodies should not distract us from the key point: how the Democratic organization, through Carsey, sought to position and script their activities to its benefit. Nor should the actual scale of these tiny groups in New York City obscure their abilities to channel and influence the impact of that much larger national insurgency centered in the Midwest.

The Greenbackers of Gotham

On November 25, 1874, the two major independent parties anchored a national conference at the Real Estate and Manufacturers Hall in Indianapolis. It adopted a Declaration of Principles in which a national focus on "the money question" provided the cornerstone. It could hardly have been accidental that they avoided taking explicit positions on anything else that might form an insurmountable obstacle between them and a convergence with a reformer-led Democratic Party.[40]

The absence of any meaningful platform contrasted with other independent parties that seemed to have, at least in part, galvanized around other issues, making the new National, Independent, or Greenback Party much more than a convergence of those state insurgencies. Minnesota Republicans blocked the efforts of a handful of antimonopolist legislators to secure a Grange law regulating railroads, while their party in Iowa and Wisconsin actively promoted such legislation and Missouri's GOP merged into that state's new People's Party.

Nevertheless, the greenback issue had a distinctive appeal. Although it represented a practical issue for midwestern farmers, it carried peculiar labor associations for people in the cities and the East. It certainly resurrected the old issue of the NLRP of two years before, raising the same prospect of using the "Ohio idea" to construct a notional alliance with the Democrats. Notwithstanding a later tendency to see the issue as a rather dry regulatory proposal, it ran much deeper than a debate over monetary policy. It inspired what arguably became the largest unsuccessful third party in US history, most closely rivaled by its Populist offspring.

The subtext of Greenbackism ran beneath the printing of paper money to assert the need for social control over the money supply. The antebellum community of Modern Times on Long Island had gestated an assault on monopoly, if not capitalism. Edward N. Kellogg, a failed businessman, had spent much of his life formulating a monetary policy fairer to the smaller-scale entrepreneur, and his neighbor, Josiah Warren, had successfully experimented with "Labor Notes" scripts in his Time Store cooperatives. There, one purchased goods with a promissory note for a certain amount of work. Those so inclined, then, could look beyond an issue of the government management to a radical reconstruction of society.

Those who criticized the excesses of postwar capitalism often ascribed the key problem as "middlemen" who stood between the producer and the consumer. To them, management of the money supply might provide government with a mechanism for adjusting the value of wages and the rate of profit. As a greenback editor from Pekin, Illinois, explained to a meeting in St. Louis, "co-operative money should be secured by the masses to secure co-operative government."[41] Simply put, Greenbackism seemed to promise a transitional measure to the "cooperative commonwealth."

An impressive array of old National Labor Union (NLU) leaders tried to capture the attention of midwestern insurgents with another conference in Cleveland's Industrial Hall. They included prominent labor figures, such as Robert Schilling and Richard Trevellick, as well as J. H. Wright of the Industrial Congress and Alexander Troup, a local officer of the printers' union who also served as a cat's-paw for the Democrats. Other participants were Andrew Warner St. John of Carthage, Missouri, whose Industrial Brotherhood had given the old NLU another lease on life.[42] The greenback focus also permitted the convention to welcome such radicals while avoiding any *de facto* exclusion of those ready to do deals with the Democrats.

This approach had a considerable appeal to more radical labor reformers in the East. Horace H. Day, a veteran of both the IWA and the NLRP fiasco, tried to rally others of the more radical participants to a broader platform. In March 1875, "representatives from all the labor organizations in New-York and Pennsylvania, including the Granges and retail coal dealers" anchored a national gathering in Harrisburg. It claimed the mantle of "the Industrial Congress of the United States," but the independent parties of Indiana, Illinois, and the imploded People's Party of Missouri ignored it.[43] The more orthodox Greenbackers naturally viewed Day, with his record of raising the necessity of solidarity regardless of race and gender, as likely to introduce matters that might prove divisive.

Would-be insurgents also dickered over the new party's name, a dispute that reflected deeper conflicts over goals. Many preferred to call themselves independents, but this created some confusion with the state parties of Illinois and Indiana, as well as with the "independent" factions of Republicans and Democrats. The convention decided on "the National party," an implicit criticism of the two sectionally based major parties. Nevertheless, when hostile papers described the group as the Greenback Party, adherents—particularly those eager to emphasize the focus on currency—happily adopted that label.

Carsey, meanwhile, found other Democrats in New York cognizant of the potential of the currency dispute. He, Walter Shupe, former New York secretary of state Gideon J. Tucker, and others saw the issue as a means of rocketing into the leadership of the state's Democratic Party. They argued that the party's national platform in 1868 had endorsed "soft money" and that of 1872 had never revised it. Therefore, the adoption of "hard money" by leaders of the state party organization placed them out from under the umbrella of the national Democratic Party. This left the city's "Greenback Democrats" claiming to be the legitimate Democratic organization in the state. They organized a rival state delegation to challenge that of the state party at the upcoming national Democratic convention.[44]

This effort to redefine the Democrats as something other than the party of "Rum, Romanism, and Rebellion" included a broad spectrum of Democratic figures who had established remarkably mixed records on such matters. Cochrane, Nelson J. Waterbury, and former lieutenant governor Sanford E. Church had remained loyal to the Union. So had Tomlinson, Kelly, and that venerable octogenarian Peter Cooper, though not to the extent of supporting Lincoln's reelection. Charles O'Conor, the son of an Irish revolutionary who had edited the *Shamrock*, however, had remained a pro-Confederate States' Rights Democrat through the war, a position with which Tucker had regularly tinkered as well. Four years earlier, the Straight-Out-Democrats and the rump organization of the NLRP ran O'Conor for president.

Their immediate interest, however, may have had less to do with monetary policy or the old questions of the war than the documentation would indicate. New York's remained the most important state party in the national Democratic Party, and its leaders tended to favor the presidential nomination of Samuel J. Tilden. Tilden had led the assault on the "ring" around William M. Tweed that operated out of Tammany Hall to make fortunes from their control over the distribution of lucrative contracts issued by the municipal government. In doing so, Tilden had considerable support not only in the rival political machines but among the rivals of Tweed within Tammany Hall itself. Tucker had aided him, as did O'Conor. They expected the breaking up of the Tween Ring would end a monopoly over the distribution of the lucrative contracts from the municipal government. Critics of Tweed, in some cases, merely hoped to take charge themselves of what Tweed had been doing, perhaps aspiring to do so with more discretion, tact, and forbearance.

The results tended to leave Tilden's Tammany allies feeling betrayed. Once the prosecutions had dissolved the Tweed Ring, Tilden did not permit a diffusion of the spoils within that organization. In fact, he took measures to strengthen an Irving Hall organization as a counterbalance to Tammany. Tensions later reached a point at which Tammany's chieftain, Kelly, flatly refused to support Tilden's 1876 nomination for president.[45] From this perspective,

Carsey and those Gotham Greenbackers with Tammany associations seem to have been preoccupied with efforts to outflank Tilden and his supporters within the national convention.

Unburdened by that past, younger figures such as Carsey tried to take the initiative in leading the party in New York City out of the wilderness. He and others declaring themselves a "General State Committee" called for a meeting for November 1, 1875, at Glass Hall on Thirty-Fourth Street, near Third Avenue.[46] They aspired to "what is to be called the 'independent' party in this city." It is not surprising that the press reported the meeting as "very thinly attended" and "for the most part consisting of workingmen who had apparently mistaken the character of the meeting." Organizers had announced that Samuel F. Cary of Ohio would attend, but he became a no-show.

The chair explained to this small gathering in the city that those "who have called you together" had actually already "formed a State Central Committee and have secured in this building permanent quarters." They proposed clubs in every precinct and urged attendees to get "a majority of the voters of the State enrolled in our books." Once they had demonstrated their strength in that way, "legislators must act under the direction of their constituency; then we can have laws that will command the respect of the people."

After these preliminaries, Carsey took his place as "the orator of the evening." He presented "a long and rambling review of the origin of trade and commerce, and the first establishment of money." His remarks were standard Greenback fare easily culled from readily available sources, though Carsey may simply not have understood them enough to offer more lively fare. The "short speeches" followed.

In the wake of the meeting, Carsey helped to officer a Working Men's Trades Assembly that sponsored a series of meetings. The Chicago *Workingmen's Advocate* misdescribed him as a member "of the Executive Committee of the Trades Unions" in New York. By mid-January, he called to order a self-described labor meeting with the ostensible purpose of complaining that the aldermen had not responded to a petition of—who else?—the bricklayers. It assembled at the Cooper Union and Carsey nominated Cooper himself to chair it.[47]

The meeting voted "to organize a new party, to be based upon the principle of justice to labor, and to that end requested labor organizations to send delegates to a meeting in Glass Hall on the evening of the 15th inst." Joining Carsey to sign the proposal was George W. Maddox of the old IWA and Troup, a prominent leader of the printer's union most regularly associated with the city's Democratic Party.

The "Greenback Democrats" sustained their organization into 1876. That winter, the Cooper Institute hosted a mass meeting to hear them hold forth on issues of labor and finance. Carsey advertised copies the meeting's proceedings, from his office at 402 West Fifty-First Street.[48]

On March 15, the group hosted what amounted to their own Democratic state convention at Weiting Hall in Syracuse, marking the occasion by renting "a brass band and 100 guns." Tucker opened the proceedings, which included other city Democrats, such as Carsey and Tomlinson, as well as upstate Greenbackers and the ever-hopeful Maddox of the old International. The convention affirmed the position of the Manhattan organization and denounced then-Governor Tilden, exposing "the Governor's connection with Belmont," and voted to challenge the current leadership of the state's Democratic leadership before adjourning *sine die*.[49]

To the side in these gatherings, "endeavoring to avoid notice," sat Peter Cooper. Born to the family of a local hatmaker in a day when George Washington had presided over the government, Cooper had grown wealthy with the city. From an artisan background, he became an innovative inventor and a brilliant investor, particularly associated with the railroads. Cooper later earned fame as a philanthropist—his Cooper Union remains a monumental contribution to the city—and advocated various worthy causes: opposing slavery, supporting the Union cause, and urging Indian reform,[50]

A closer look into Cooper 's associations reveal his glaring connections to "respectable," rather than insurgent, politics. His son-in-law, Abram S. Hewitt had become prominent in Democratic politics. These "Swallowtails" took their name from the fashionable coat of gentlemen and professionals and relished their identification with the destruction of the Tweed Ring, which they equated with the breaking of Tammany Hall. Hewitt had not only waged that fight alongside Tilden, but, in its aftermath, Tilden would take on Hewitt as the campaign manager of his 1876 campaign.

Among these Greenback Democrats, Carsey continued to describe himself as a leader and representative of the "Independent Labor Party of New York," which seems to have had no purpose other than to provide him credentials. As the chair of the Committee on Parade, he informed a May 5 meeting that their last attempt to hold one had resulted in such tiny numbers because of the police "dispersing the men at the rallying points." The meeting responded by electing him the president of the party, after which President Carsey extolled the virtues of James Gordon Bennett Jr., whom they "unanimously nominated as the workingmen's candidate for Mayor."[51]

Bennett, who had never been that directly interested in the rough-and-tumble world of politics (or journalism), had been roped into supporting Carsey's mayoral shenanigans four years earlier, and declined the nomination. In the aftermath of his decision, the Independent Labor Party nominated Carsey, whom the party had run for an aldermanic position two years earlier. Then described as a "bricklayer and employer," that is, a building contractor, Carsey claimed that he had "not voted either the Democratic or Republican tickets" since 1871.[52]

* * *

Carsey's strange 1876 run for mayor represented a singular departure from his career preference for operating more incognito. Reporters dutifully covered the effort but seemed particularly to enjoy the results when Carsey took up a collection at a May 5 meeting at Masonic Hall on Thirteenth Street. Participants began angrily peppering him with accusations of simply pocketing the contributions. An investigating committee also declared that Tucker, Cooper, and others had already given Carsey $150, "which he had not accounted for." Nevertheless, after a prolonged wrangle, the majority voted to sustain Carsey's nomination.[53] Within a matter of hours, Carsey left town, taking his underwritten dog-and-pony show on the road.

A few days later, Carsey and Church turned up together in the Midwest. They had gone there in search of finding allies among the active Democrats ostensibly to challenge the seating of the regular New York delegation at the upcoming national convention in St. Louis. Their actual goal may have been to effect a compromise in the seating of that state delegation that would simply include some Greenback Democrats to a regular delegation, which already included Hewitt and Edward Cooper, the philanthropist's son.[54]

On their way—just a coincidence, as they later described it—Carsey and Church passed through Indianapolis as the national convention of the Independent Party gathered, which took Carsey's operation to a national level.

CHAPTER 2

Independents and Partisan Pantomimes

The Dilemma of Third Parties under a Two-Party System

> We have in this city quite a number of such "striking organizations" both Democratic and Republican; they pass resolutions to order, or pass them before they receive orders, and then try to sell them. These "organizations" sprout up during a campaign, especially a presidential one, regularly every time.
>
> —Unsigned letter from New York, *Topeka Advocate*, 1892

On May 15, 1876, William A. A. Carsey and Sanford Church of New York entered the Academy of Music in Indianapolis. Their primary mission had been to consult select local midwestern Democratic parties about seating their own rival New York delegations at the upcoming national party convention. Along the way, they stopped in to sit with delegates representing the various insurgent state parties of the region. They found plenty of people there seriously interested in building a new party and others just as ready to derail the entire enterprise. Either way, the delegates hoped desperately to use their presidential nomination to establish some connection with the labor movements in the big cities of the East.[1] Carsey and Church might be forgiven had they exchanged excited looks before offering a solution.

The reemergent postwar two-party system imposed severe problems on the initial third-party efforts. Broad social forces bound by habits of faith and institutional mythologies shaped the predispositions to ultimate failure, but the parties structured systems of rewards to encourage individuals to initiate multiple tactical approaches to derail moves toward political independence. The movement learned, of course, and built an increasingly broad support for independent action, but the more threatening the scale of their efforts, the more people pursued such campaigns and the more persistent they became. The 1880 campaign provided tangible evidence of the immense obstacles insurgents faced in the wake of the Civil War and Reconstruction.

How Democrats Named and Shaped a Usable Insurgency

Some founders of what became the National or Independent Party expected to follow the example of the antebellum Republican Party, which had successfully built itself on the popular backlash against the effort to introduce slavery into the western territories. Greenback founders thought the currency question would provide the kind of focus for midwestern farmers that the Kansas conflict had provided for early Republicans. Much of the meaning of Greenbackism, however, remained in the eye of the beholder. Certainly, the most radical among them saw currency reform as a means of raising questions about class, wealth, and power, while the more conservatives among them saw their work as in aid of reform Democratic efforts to readjust interest rates on bonds.

The gathering in Indianapolis reflected this spectrum. The official account reported credentials for 240 delegates, though the *Chicago Inter-Ocean* noted that this actually counted proxies and doubted that "there are many more than 200 all told who belong legitimately to the convention." Having resolved the programmatic positions at earlier national gatherings, the nomination of a presidential ticket remained the convention's clear focus. This discussion recalled that of the earlier National Labor Reform Party (NLRP). Midwestern and southern participants tended to favor former Ohio Governor William Allen, a Democrat, while the Illinois delegation split between two favorite sons Judge Alexander Campbell and, once more, Judge David Davis. The withdrawal of Allen's name left the body with two serious nominations, the proponents of which acknowledged to be too unpredictable or too unknown to take the head of the national ticket for the new party.[2]

At this point, if not sooner, Carsey and Church realized that they had climbed through a narrow window of opportunity that left them in a position to burglarize the nomination. After building for two years, an independent political movement deferred to two of the most partisan representatives of one the most machine-ridden communities in one of the country's least insurgent states north of the Mason-Dixon line. Church nominated Peter

Cooper for president. The decision of the NLRP four years before that Cooper had been too old did not dissuade the 1876 convention. For vice president, Carsey named Democratic US senator Newton Booth, who had recently bolted from the Republicans in California, another state that, like New York, had no midwestern insurgent base on which to build.

Cooper represented the second or third choice of most of the delegates, but Carsey offered a fanciful strategy to justify the nomination. The new party could not become a national power, he argued, unless they could involve the workers of the great eastern cities, for which he and Church professed to speak, and a Cooper candidacy would appeal to them. Moreover, Cooper had the money to pay for his own campaign. Most important, naming a Cooper ticket would provide Greenbackers with a powerful tool to pressure the Democratic National Convention to nominate Davis, after which Cooper could then withdraw. Eager just to get any sort of independent ticket nominated, the convention adopted the nominations.

One suspects that, as Carsey and Church themselves left Indianapolis, they must have experienced episodic waves of incredulity at their success. They had entered a national convention of rural insurgents who needed to appeal to potential voters in the Midwest, mostly predisposed to support Republicans. Then two transients from Tammany presenting themselves as spokesmen for the working classes persuaded them that the best way to do this would be to nominate a septuagenarian eastern urban Jacksonian.

That summer, the Democrats did not name Davis—and there is no documentation that anyone fainted in surprise at this—but nominated Samuel J. Tilden, contrary to the hopes of his Tammany enemies. Meanwhile, the Republicans selected Rutherford B. Hayes. As to the vice presidency, nobody in the Greenback convention had ever had any reason to think that Senator Booth would accept his nomination, and he did not. As with the old NLRP, though, the convention had appointed a committee to make any necessary changes in the ticket. To fill the vice-presidential slot, it picked General Samuel F. Cary, the popular Cincinnati reform Democrat.

Carsey returned to New York and immediately resurrected his Independent Labor Party. On August 11, it held another of its allegedly quarterly meetings at the Masonic Hall and elected him president for another term, after which he explained the difficulties of establishing a public presence for the party. Toward the close of the meeting, Carsey proposed that they nominate for mayor James Gordon Bennett Jr, a Swallowtail Democrat, so called because most of them wore the pricy expensive coats with impressive tails. Under Carsey's leadership, the body—however much substance there was to it—

accepted Bennett, who was "unanimously nominated as the workingmen's candidate for Mayor."[3]

At the same time, Carsey emerged as a leader of the state's nascent Greenback Party set to hold a convention in September in Albany. Upstate, traditional Greenback issues motivated participants, but what it had of an urban organization simply extended the "Greenback Democrat" hostility to Tilden over his dismantling of the Tweed Ring. It contributed much to the peculiar demographics of the Greenback state contention, described as "mostly young men, energetic in appearance, and . . . largely composed of business men." Cooper himself attended, and Marcus Hanlon, the editor of the *American Protectionist*, called the gathering to order with a declaration that Tilden could not win. Then Carsey, who also favored protective tariffs to foster US industry, took the gavel and gave an opening address giving lip service to the currency issue and protesting the impoverished state of the working class. In October, Carsey chaired the Greenback county convention at No. 162 Broadway, doing so as an official of the Independent Labor Party.[4]

Although the promise of the Cooper campaign reflected the failure of the two parties to respond to the needs of the people, the candidate's own understanding of what his presidential campaign represented still seems to remain debatable. A historian of the Progressive Era described the campaign as "a gallant and long-remembered gesture" by "an honest man with a sensitive social conscience" who would be "loved and laughed at and ignored." If the philanthropist actually was a well-meaning figure disconnected from political realities, he surrounded himself with people who were certainly not. For whatever it might be worth, Carsey's ally Shupe later said that the old man had contributed $100,000 to circulate Shupe's own paper, the *Advocate*, adding that Cooper could have gotten more for his money by buying Democratic votes in Indiana at two dollars a pop.[5]

Ockham's razor slices the national Greenback campaign differently. It seems doubtful that Cooper actually wanted to become the president or even sought to wage a serious campaign. Genuine insurgents did hope that his nomination would do well in the rural Republican districts of upstate New York, but Cooper and his circle had quite distinct reasons for nominating him. In truth, the elderly philanthropist was an old friend of Tilden, the Democratic presidential candidate, and his own son-in-law, Abram S. Hewitt, actually managed Tilden's campaign. The Greenback insurgency appealed most directly to former Republican voters among the midwestern insurgents, and its nomination of a national ticket aimed to minimize those who might fall back to their own partisan allegiance while leaving those inclined to vote Democratic perfectly free to do so. Then, too, there are indications that the Greenback Democrats had made their peace with Tilden. Put more bluntly, 1876 saw a popular New Yorker at the head of the Democratic ticket, while an old friend and the father-in-law of his campaign manager headed an ostensibly independent ticket aimed at drawing off votes in the upstate Republican districts.

Carsey, Church, and their strategy did have some impact, though it proved to be neither decisive nor clear. Tilden carried New York with particularly heavy majorities in the city and in Albany County. Most of Cooper's fewer than 2,000 votes in the state did come from voters in otherwise Republican areas, but the numbers remained far too small to matter even had they all voted for Hayes against Tilden. Nationally, Cooper won only 81,740 votes, indicating that the campaign had failed miserably even in the insurgent Midwest.[6]

On the grand scale, the persistent issues of Reconstruction in the South—largely ignored by the candidates and their campaigns—grabbed the election of 1876 by the throat and turned it into a serious constitutional crisis. Tilden had combined the electoral votes of his own New York with the solidly Democratic vote of the white "redeemer governments" of the old Confederacy, giving Tilden 184 of the 185 electoral votes needed to win, leaving Hayes with only 165. Four states, however—Florida, Louisiana, South Carolina, and Oregon—filed conflicting returns, leaving 20 electoral votes in dispute. There existed no clear mechanism for resolving this, and the Congress remained divided, with a Republican majority in the Senate and a Democrat majority in the House of Representatives. Some on both sides threatened armed violence should they be cheated.

Congress passed—and the president signed—an Electoral Commission Act to break the impasse. The House, Senate, and Supreme Court provided five members each to the commission. Of the fifteen, seven would come from each of the parties, with one having strong credentials for nonpartisan judgment (a role briefly filled by the widely admired Judge Davis). The authorities did not charge the commission to find out who had actually won the election, but to formulate an allocation of the disputed electoral votes that would be acceptable to both parties.

When this *ad hoc* deliberative body awarded all the disputed electoral votes to Hayes, Democrats almost immediately began cultivating a myth about 1876 as the stolen election but accepted the "corrupt bargain." In return for an uncontested road to the White House, the Republicans agreed to withdraw the remaining occupation troops in the South. This abandoned what remained of the project of Reconstruction, allowing the overwhelmingly Democratic white elites of the region to return to power. This obviously had long repercussions for the future of race relations and the structure of political power, nationally as well as regionally.

Then, too, a new challenge to the social peace erupted on another quarter.

Early in the summer of 1877, the major railroads announced another of the annual wage cuts they had promulgated after the onset of the depression several years before. The announcement detonated a planned but undeclared strike by the engineers that quickly became general among the trades on the railroads. Through the last half of July, local revolts spread along the tracks just on the heels of the news about the pay cuts.[7] Local Greenbackers in places such as Toledo assumed leadership of the strike, as did the socialists in St. Louis.

The same government that had balked at using federal troops to protect the rights of freed people across the South against the Bourbon Democratic resurgence had no problem turning the guns of the army against strikers. The rails from the West carried cavalry from their punitive operations against the Plains Indians for the defeat of General George A. Custer into Chicago, where they regularly fired on crowds in the immigrant neighborhoods. In St. Louis, former Union and Confederate officers rode at the head of a united force moving against "the rabble."[8] All this provided considerable evidence to the most radical insurgents that the capitalists rather than the working majority had control of the government and both major parties.

In the aftermath, the press talked about a "labor problem" less in terms of the travails of subjugated social class than as a technical problem of managing outbursts of mass discontent prone to generate violence and disorder. *Scribner's Monthly* warned against spoiling the unemployed, and the *New York World* suggested that since class structure in the United States had become more European, the society needed to train US workers to accept a more downscale Old World standard of living. The *Tribune* applauded Jay Gould's assurance that the capitalists had organized "such power that no act of Congress can overcome or resist their decision." A railroad executive recommended feeding those who demanded bread with "the rifle diet for a few days," while other respectable gentlemen proposed using hand grenades to supplement the use of "canister and grape" against strikers and "communistic tramps."[9] Across the country, companies raised private armies and cities built a new and more militarized police power.

Greenback-Labor Party 1877–80

The bipartisan repression of the July 1877 strike movement transformed the idea of a national Greenback Party into reality. The emergent party challenged the bipartisan hostility to paper currency but went far beyond it. It absorbed new political movements like the Workingmen's Party of California, the Farmers' Alliance of rural upstate New York, and the workingmen's parties in the towns upstate that sprang into existence, as well as various local labor reform parties. The National Liberal League, the freethinkers' association, also voted to launch its own National Liberal Party.[10] Greenbackism, in turn, broadened the scope of its platform.

In August, General James Baird Weaver, a prominent Republican leader in Iowa, broke from the party. "I shall act with the Independents," he wrote. More than twenty years before, he had broken with the Democrats over slavery to join the insurgent Republicans and anticipated that others who had done so felt the same draw to independent action that he did.[11] Indeed, tens of thousands made similar choices, and the hollow threat of 1876 began, in places, to cast the shadow of a new mass party in 1877 and 1878.

The country's largest metropolis, however, saw Greenbackism grow less in the number of its adherents than in the multiplication of rival bodies claiming to be associated with the movement. Some of those drawn to such groups may have hoped to build an insurgent party but had different ideas about what that meant. More of the prominent leaders of the organizations, though, seemed more inclined to influence the perceptions and priorities of the established parties. Still others—perhaps inspired by Carsey's successes—sought to manage votes in a way that would serve one or another faction within the two major parties. Over the next few years, sects, would-be power brokers, and major party operatives vied with each other for dominance.[12]

In the midst of these rivalries, some of the most determined individual insurgents organized the country's first explicitly socialist nationwide party. Even as Carsey appeared among the remnants of the International Workingmen's Association (IWA), other veterans of that organization had launched the Social Democratic Workingmen's Party (SDWP). As he had performed his recent shell game among the Greenbackers in Indianapolis, the SDWP had pursued an aggressive regrouping strategy that resulted in the formation of the Workingmen's Party of the United States (WPUS), which agreed that electoral action remained premature. In the wake of the 1877 strikes and emergence of mass electoral upheavals, the WPUS held another convention between Christmas and New Year's 1877–78, to reorganize as the Socialistic Labor Party (SLP).[13]

Several weeks after the socialists launched the SLP, a hefty sampling of the broader insurgent movement braved the blustery Toledo winter to attend a national convention in a drafty schoolhouse on Washington's birthday in 1878. They pledged themselves to build a genuinely independent course at the polls, and, reflecting their strategy and aspirational composition, became the "Greenback-Labor party."[14] In places, at least, the massive disaffection with the two-party rivalry created an almost irresistible dynamic for genuine independent political action.

This insurgent dynamic left Democratic operatives little hope of repeating their success of 1872 and 1876 in derailing or redirecting such sentiment. They made a serious bid, however, to take the leadership of the insurgent party movements or, at least, to cripple any potential rival leaderships. The most sizable such effort came from the Union Greenback clubs of Marcus M. "Brick" Pomeroy with the old *Chicago Democrat*. A vicious Copperhead, he had briefly moved to New York City, where he had been an ally of William M. Tweed. While exaggerating its electoral strength, Pomeroy had been at it consistently over the years since the war and had extensive ties to the movement across the Midwest, which he used in service of the Democrats. The clubs and allied organizations represented or claimed to represent a large section of the rural insurgents while remaining consistently coy about any independent strategy of the Greenback-Labor Party (GLP).[15]

Carsey and his allies took the initiative in organizing the GLP in New York City. Shupe chaired the June 1878 organization of a city general committee. Under his umbrella, Carsey sat alongside the former IWA spokesman Theodore Allen, former Democratic congressman James E. Kerrigan, and the printer Henry Nichols, a later leader of local antimonopolist organizations.[16] In the press of events, the centrifugal forces in such a diverse association would be difficult to resist.

Shupe's prominence in these efforts caused some controversy. He had just emerged from a court battle to defend his reputation professionally and politically. Years earlier, as the editor of *Rockland Advertiser*, he had described a local minister as a moral leper, for which the pastor sued him. The Court of Common Pleas found Shupe guilty and awarded the good reverend $5,000 in damages, and the courts periodically called him to account over the years for his failure to pay, especially after he launched the *Advocate*. Shupe weaseled out of the judgment with a claim of poverty. The Rockland County farm, he shrugged, belonged to his wife and all he got from the newspaper was a salary of only $20 a week. "He refused to tell who owns the concern, which issues over half a million copies a week for half the cost of the whole paper and postage alone."[17] People assumed that Cooper bankrolled the operation, which may have just reflected Shupe's own questionable stories.

In the end, Shupe wound up fleeing a small army of creditors that had begun "to crowd him down." Even as he assumed the leadership of the Greenback movement—or, rather, a temporary role in a small nominal faction thereof—

he filed for bankruptcy in the US Circuit Court "to erect a statutory barrier against them." He claimed assets worth only $387, including a library with an estimated value of $200, while owing nearly $70,000. "His paper like his financial doctrine," stated one newspaper, "is a cheat and a fraud." By the fall of 1878, as the Toledo convention launched the GLP, the press reported rumors that Shupe still faced arrest for libel.[18]

Meanwhile, Shupe caused more problems by openly boasting to GLP leaders such as James Wright of Elmira of his own personal connections to gentlemen of power. Back in Ohio, Shupe noted, he had studied law under Senator John Sherman and had dinner with him. Shupe said that the senator had privately told him that he favored the insurgents and "that he was sick of the old parties; that he would furnish the laboring men the means to organize a labor league throughout the United States." The project required a secret society, however, to funnel the money to where it would be most useful, and Shupe offered to take on himself the burden of implementing the clandestine will of Sherman and Cooper by "appointing the leaders in the different States." "Although Munchausen himself could not have concocted a more absurd story," quipped the *Indianapolis Journal*, "there is nothing in the past history of Walter H. Shupe to lead anyone who knows him to doubt that he told this tale to Mr. Wright substantially as he reports it."[19]

That June, Carsey turned up in Washington, presenting himself as a member of the governing body of the National Greenback Party. He impressed the *Washington Post*, which found him "in dead earnest" and, "perhaps, the most prominent of the New York communists." Property, he said "just about amounts to" theft. They wanted "an income tax, and no exemption from any other tax; less hours of labor; no land subsidies; no monopolies; no contract labor, and no Chinese; no overgrown fortunes, and no extreme poverty." He had "no doubt" that "there be no other riots this summer." "This is a race between the ballot and the bullet," he said, "and I don't know which will win." Carsey assured them, however, that the new party already controlled ten states, "though we don't pretend we can elect a President ourselves."[20] According to the *Post*, after staking out all these far-reaching radical goals in decidedly militant language, the "Boss Communist" argued for would-be insurgents to cast their lot with one of the big parties.

In general, Carsey, Shupe, and others presented themselves on the national stage as leaders of a mass insurgency in New York City, and, once back in the city, assumed the trappings of leadership by virtue of the status accorded them by the national bodies. What they presided over, though, remained nominal at best, and they often had no end of difficulty managing that. In the summer of 1878, when Carsey presided over the initial organizing meeting of the New York City General Committee of the National Greenback Party, George Blair and others demanded to know whether Shupe was the "tool of John Sherman, the de facto secretary of the treasury" and likely to "sell out the National party in New York to him and the Republican party." Shupe replied that such charges came from upstate Greenbackers whom he had irritated by not giving them enough campaign funds. The committee then voted to vindicate him.[21]

These unelected leaders at the preliminary meetings filled the General Committee by picking "representatives" of nonexistent organizations in various districts. When Allen, the old IWA radical, pointed out the absence of anyone on the committee from the Eighteenth District, Carsey replied that the committee had rejected all those previously nominated, particularly that of "a Fourth avenue liquor dealer." The explanation might have landed with a resounding thud in some quarters, as the group that had been meeting in the rooms of a wine seller on Broome Street. When Allen continued to object, Carsey simply declared the meeting adjourned.

Press coverage remained spotty and often failed to connect even the most obvious dots. The Republican *New-York Tribune* followed these Greenback developments enough to discuss whether Carsey and Shupe would "sell out the national party to Sherman." It also ticked off the participants in Carsey's group already well known to be Democrats, noting particularly that Nichols had been "always a Democrat."[22]

In July, the new party held a state convention in Syracuse.[23] But the most elementary preliminary task of validating credentials dropped its deliberations into a black hole. Albany, Troy, and Buffalo sent two delegations each, Brooklyn three, and New York City no less than four. From its quick survey of the partisan history of members of one of the New York delegations, the *New-York Tribune* concluded that participation at the leadership level drew "double the number of voters here from the Democratic party than it does from the Republican party." The papers also reported that two of the several rival delegations from the city represented the Tammany and Anti-Tammany factions of the Democratic Party.

The convention ended in a preplanned shattering. Eager to thwart the general, if muddled, dynamic toward a full-blown insurgent party, Carsey, Shupe, and Hanlon, heading the faction identified with Pomeroy's pro-Democratic clubs, walked out. They held their own convention on July 23 at the Syracuse House. It reportedly gathered about seventy-five delegates.

If the chickens seemed to have come home to roost for Shupe, it did not phase Carsey, a man who had learned how to shift his roost regularly.

Indeed, that summer, Carsey basked in the prestige of testifying before the congressional committee on "the labor question," then holding its hearings in New York City. Its chair, Congressman Hewitt, Cooper's son-in-law, certainly recognized that Carsey knew the flaws in his stated credentials as an editor and a voice for the working class. Self-described as "once President of the Trade and Labour Union; he is now an officer of the Bricklayers' Union, and he is Secretary to the Greenback Labour Party." As such, Carsey urged "the institution of a comprehensive system of internal improvements, and the inflation of the currency to carry on these improvements." He also criticized the public schools and advised moving the military from duties in the ports "to the plains where they are alone needed," replacing them by reassigning sailors to perform those duties on shore. Most important, he wanted to cut government spending and end practices that tended "to grind down the laboring class and employ Chinese and others, against whom American laborers could not compete, because the latter cannot live as the former do." Returning to a recurring theme of his message, Carsey focused class grievances on the encouragement of "swarms of foreigners to drive out native laborers."[24]

Within days—on August 14—Carsey and Shupe convened a citywide Greenback-Labor meeting at the Science Hall on Eighth Street. Their primary purpose, though, seemed to be to warn the public against all other Greenback organizations, a process that continued through September and October. They drew in S. Myra Hall, the suffragist and spiritualist speaking on behalf of "the Congress of Humanity," along with other radicals. Nevertheless, in covering these efforts, even the Democratic *New York Herald* identified this or that participant as, for example, the brother of an official at Tammany Hall.[25]

The Carsey-Shupe faction participated when the state Greenback organization, such as it was, sent a "harmonizing committee" to unify the groups in New York and Brooklyn. The *New York Times* reported on the meetings to establish common ground, where "nearly every person in the room was a faction and claimed the right to subdivide himself into a committee of five." Carsey "deprecated disputation and personalities, but claimed most decidedly that the Shupe party was the only regular Greenback organization in the City of New York." James Connolly insisted that his faction went back to the April 1876 labor convention in Pittsburgh, and others rooted their claims in similar past events. Much centered on claiming the mantle of Cooper, and Carsey claimed that he had personally paid the entire cost of the campaign in the city (which had amounted to depressingly little). The head of the state body, Dr. E. P. Miller, responded that whoever had charge of six hundred boxes of printed ballots for Cooper in the city had sold them to Tammany Hall on election day. After its visit to the city, Miller's committee concluded that most of the so-called Greenback bodies there simply acted on behalf of the Republicans or Tammany Democrats, or anti-Tammany Democrats.[26]

These overtly partisan efforts to intervene in the insurgency were not isolated, because the contextual realities of the two-party system across the country forced all adherents of Greenback-Labor to define themselves with relation to one or the other of the major parties. Many of the noisiest of the "leaders"—however that might be determined—came to favor a pragmatic fusion ticket with one or the other of the old well-heeled parties. This represented an official cooperation usually with the locally weaker of the two major parties—Democrats in much of the North and West and Republicans in the South. This tactic offered insurgents a temptingly effortless way to get a much-needed boost, but, however temporary they might have intended this tactic to be, nowhere did fusion ever lead to the construction of a genuinely independent new insurgent party.

In New York, leaders of the various factions beyond the Carsey-Shupe Democratic effort scurried for alliances with elements of the dominant parties. In October, Greenback elements redoubled their efforts to make nominations of spokespeople for the major parties, sometimes old reform-types such as Theodore Tomlinson but also Edward Cooper and Richard Schell. The more radically minded did the best they could to find a suitable faction with each moving toward their convention. Carsey and Shupe managed to come to an understanding with a group headed by John W. Crump, an earlier Greenback candidate, to stand together against other currents, which they repudiated as not really as insurgent as they were. "Nearly half the audience were boys," in this body that denounced "bogus Greenback" rivals, denounced Edward Cooper as "a born aristocrat, a cheap employer, who always cut down labor to the lowest point, and paid his workmen with store orders." They voted to make independent nominations, which they offered to men of known political purity but also known to be unwilling to run. Weeks before the election, Carsey's group claimed to have committees scrambling in each district to find candidates.[27]

As these efforts failed, Carsey became increasingly public in advocating fusion with the Democrats. Periodically stepping out of his role as an insurgent leader, he spoke as the head of another paper organization called the New York Labor Union to urge lobbying for municipal improvements among leaders of the dominant parties. These would include street repairs and cleaning, the improvement of docks and piers, a new aqueduct, and the filling of the marshes in Harlem. With his own penchant for eccentricity, he added his rather peculiar protest against pushing the "city's street sweepings in our harbor or river, and demand that it be utilized for the farmers of our vicinity to fertilize the barren soils of New Jersey, Westchester, and Long Island, as such a waste of the life-blood of our soil is both unwise and injurious to our people." They also favored direct action by the municipality rather than the chartering of a private company to use Birdsill Holly's system of heating the city with large boilers capable of serving an entire neighborhood.[28] Carsey advocated nothing that did not fall well within the realm of a municipal reformer within the Democratic Party.

In light of the group's inability to find candidates, Carsey decided to run for office himself in the 1878 fall election. He did so to take the wind out of the sails of any possible genuine independent because there is no evidence that he actually campaigned. In the end, the voters of the Nineteenth State Assembly District gave him so few votes that the only documentary record of his having run was his own protest over the returns. Officially credited with only 18 votes, Carsey complained the city had been "counting of votes cast for me as blank and defective," which had denied him another 57 votes, these out of an official total of 4,364 ballots. "It is a violation of law and an insult and injustice to me as a citizen," Carsey insisted.[29]

These Carseyan droplets easily disappeared in the massive tsunami of electoral discontent with two-party business-as-usual politics, dwarfing everything comparable since the appearance of the Republican Party twenty years before. In their own generally accurate shorthand, the Greenbackers boasted of a million votes in their congressional campaigns. The official count gave between 802,000 and 852,000 to candidates exclusively running as Independent, National, Greenback, or Independent Greenback candidates. Greenback candidates running with apparent Democratic support, however—either by renomination, formal endorsement, or a Democratic decision not to run their own candidate against them—added another 303,400, and another 217,000 went to insurgents with similarly apparent Republican support, these bringing the total to nearly 1.4 million. In addition, Independent Democrats running against regularly nominated Democrats got another 150,000, and Independent Republicans in the same circumstance more than 18,000, with another 25,000 divided between Prohibitionists and Socialists.[30] Insurgents of one sort or another elected twenty-two congressmen, but fusion had clearly blunted the impact of the insurgent achievement.

Things became more muddled as others adopted the tactics that Carsey had used so successfully. The *New York Times* later covered many "small parties or factions outside of the two principal political parties."[31] Greenbackers aside, regular Republicans, independent Republicans, German Republicans, Tammany Hall Democrats, Anti-Tammany Hall Democrats in the county, and taxpayers made their own nominations, as did the Bread-Winners and an anti–Customs House party, as well as two Anti-Tammany Democratic groups, one hoping to end Tammany domination of the Democratic Party and another hoping to replace the Tammany leadership. By 1880, the city had no less than ten "third" parties: A Workingmen's Party, a Bread Winners Party, a Greenback Party, an Independent Greenback Party, and a Greenback Labor Party, as well as Independents, Independent Democrats, Independent Republicans, German Republicans, and so on. Then, too, through these years, the SLP and the freethinkers' National Liberal League also prepared to enter into electoral politics.

All these "parties" claimed to advocate the cause of the discontented (as did the Democrats and Republicans themselves), but most hoped to distill that discontent in something other than a unified mass party with a social agenda. Some did represent no more than deliberate ploys by one or the other of the major parties—or a faction thereof—to weaken the voting strength of their rival. Other "parties" represented the work of "the self-seeking of a few individuals" eager to promote their own standing in the eyes of a major party or part of one. The *New York Times* or the *New York Herald* described "each of the four greenback factions in the market, with an auctioneer clamoring for the highest bidder." Within each, "about fifty rascals in the party were forever trying to sell it out," including some of the best-known leaders.[32] The charges such groups made against each other may well have all been correct.

The *New York Times* correctly labeled many of these local manifestations to be ploys by the major parties to weaken the voting strength of their rival and to "the self-seeking of a few individuals" eager to promote their own prospects within a major party. In a clear attempt to minimize the defection of Democratic voters to the insurgents, *The Irish World*, *Pomeroy's Democrat*, *New Haven Union*, and others described Greenbackers in New York, Chicago, and New Haven as working "by stealth to elect as many Republicans as possible." Pomeroy's local ally, Hanlon, did take his own peculiar course in joining reform-minded Republicans in launching their own "People's Party" in the city. They cited the rumored connections of Shupe with Sherman, adding that Sherman's brother-in-law owned the building that housed the Washington office of Shupe's *Advocate*, while a nephew of Sherman served as "one of the confidential clerks in the *Advocate* office in New York.[33]

Notwithstanding his personal connections to Sherman, Shupe made explicit his general orientation to the Democrats, and particularly to Tammany Hall. The story was that Edward Cooper and Hewitt—the son and son-in-law of old Peter Cooper—had agreed that one of them run for office, while the other would manage Cooper, Hewitt, and company, and some Greenbackers claimed credit for Edward's running for mayor in opposition to Hewitt, his brother-in-law, and a "hard money man." "The march of events," explained Shupe, "indicates that John Kelly will soon make overtures to our party. He and we will clasp hands, but he will no longer lead. We shall enter Tammany Hall and assume control of things ourselves. Kelly's power has departed." Once they had taken over Tammany, it would leave Republicans the hard money party while "Greenbackers and allied Democrats—for the Democratic party is absolutely dead as a party; the members that are left of it will join the Greenbackers—will come to the front with the cry of paper money, the name of their party being, as I told you on a former occasion, the National Democratic party."[34]

Notwithstanding such aspirations, the minnow would find it a strain to swallow the shark.

The August 1879 convention in Utica provided another opportunity to resolve these issues. Almost immediately, though, the "old feud" erupted among the rival New York City organizations. The previous state convention's "harmonizing" committee explicitly recognized how "the intrigue of Tammany Hall" or those of its enemies acting "in the interest of Tilden and Company" had shaped the suicidal course of the insurgency there. The 1879 convention agreed specifically to exclude the most obvious example "and the throwing out of Carsey is generally regarded as a victory for the straight-out Greenbackers."[35] Yet the Carsey-Shupe alliance continued to present itself publicly as whatever might best serve their purposes.

More subtly, Carsey began encouraging advocates of change to look beyond electoral politics. At the crest of the insurgency, he wrote Congressman Wright to discuss how best to promote reform among those outside the Congress.[36] The desire to shift efforts away from the troublesome and daunting task of building an insurgency to practical politics seemed reasonable. Those who strove for reform outside politics, however, nevertheless continued voting, and they would tend naturally to vote for the party or candidates seen as most malleable in their favor, which increasingly tended to mean the Democrats.

Yet whether the movement would enter such channels would not be up to Carsey or Shupe.

The 1880 Campaign

Notwithstanding their wishes, Carsey and his organization limped their little paper party into the 1880 presidential election. Perhaps they still cherished the hope of repeating their earlier hijacking of the national insurgency. Proving that old habits die hard, their initial plans to do so actually centered on promulgating the unimaginative and yet groundless notion of a Democratic nomination of the familiar but aging figure of the sixty-five-year-old Judge David Davis.

On the other hand, the scale of this little cluster made it possible for Carsey, Shupe, and their tiny New York group to continue bobbing to the surface of the insurgent wave. The strength of the midwestern drive for a new party, however, had centered on Iowa congressman Weaver. A Jacksonian Democrat originally, he became a founder of the Republican Party in the state and rose to the rank of a brigadier general in the Union Army. The Republican establishment in that state marginalized him, as his genuine sympathy for the farmers and the laboring classes became increasingly apparent.[37] Within the Greenback movement, Weaver spoke for those who genuinely hoped not just to replace individuals in office but to transform the party structure, the political system, and social and economic order itself. Addressing those goals effectively posed the greatest challenge Carsey and Shupe had yet faced.

As early as October 1878, Shupe found the time—between the lawsuits, rumored arrests, and threatened arrests—to visit the *Evening Post* and speculate about the presidential nomination. He made no bones about his preference that the GLP run for president its most prominent adherent in the northeastern states, Benjamin F. Butler. The sexagenarian New Hampshire native, argued Shupe, had become "immensely rich," and had spent a quarter of a million dollars on his recent gubernatorial campaign in Massachusetts. He guessed that the general could spend "fully a million dollars more" on his own presidential run.[38]

Butler's credentials as a Greenback-Labor leader were clear enough, but hardly straightforward. The grandson of a Continental soldier on one side and an Irish rebel on the other, he had grown with the industrial community of Lowell, Massachusetts, where his widowed mother ran a boardinghouse. After studying for the ministry, he taught school, studied law, and won his first cases on behalf of factory girls working in the local mills. In politics, critics described him as "a member of all parties and false to each." In 1860, he had tried to start a campaign to win the presidential nomination for Jefferson Davis and supported the "Southern Rights" faction in that year's breakup of the Democratic Party. Secession drove him from the most pro-South current among Democrats in the North to the most intransigently radical of the Republicans. Butler donned the uniform, took a general's rank, and formulated the first legal basis for the army to not return runaway slaves to the rebels, the argument that runaways were contraband of war.[39] Yet Butler never quite shook his well-earned reputation as a slippery character.

In the postwar Congress, Butler became a key figure among the Radical Republicans and served as the floor manager of the impeachment effort against

President Andrew Johnson. With the subsequent election of Ulysses S. Grant, he worked to secure farsighted, if ill-fated, civil rights legislation, such as the so-called Ku Klux Klan Act criminalizing an active interference with the exercise by citizens of their lawful rights. Along with Senator Charles Sumner, he secured the passage of another civil rights act in 1875, which banned racial discrimination in public accommodations (until the Supreme Court declared it unconstitutional). He also took up women's suffrage and legislated labor reform. Republican leaders became increasingly wary of Butler and blocked his gubernatorial nomination in 1871 and 1873.

After the Republican Party blocked his renomination for Congress, Butler began eyeing a return to the Democratic Party. In 1878, Massachusetts voters elected him governor as a Democrat with additional Labor Reform and Greenback support. It would reelect him twice with similar support. As governor, he appointed the first Black judges in the state and appointed Clara Barton to run the state's reformatory for women, the first woman to hold executive office in the state. He also exposed years of Republican pilfering at the Tewksbury Almshouse, which made him something of a *cause célèbre* among those who disliked the arrogance with which the Republican parties wielded power. Of all the political officeholders of the age, few proved as adept at Butler in gaining the consistent support of both a major party and insurgent efforts.[40]

By the late 1870s, Butler used his considerable influence to unite the insurgents and the Democrats, behind the election of the latter. In this, he had the assistance of many who occupied leading positions among Greenbackers in the state, such as the forty-year-old Charles H. Litchman, a shoemaker from Marblehead, who had been a leader of the Knights of St. Crispin since the late 1860s. At one point, its international grand lodge had hired Butler to defend members charged with criminal conspiracy—and to publish its "abhorrence of Communism, and our firm adherence to law and order." After the 1879 GLP state convention that nominated Butler and Wendell Phillips for governor and lieutenant governor, Litchman attended another convention, one where rump Democrats nominated a ticket that ran Butler but replaced Phillips.[41]

Lichtman's associate, the forty-year-old New York–born congressional clerk Dyer D. Lum, had moved to Northampton after winning an officer's commission in the federal army during the war. There he joined the Massachusetts Labor Reform Party and ran for lieutenant governor on the state Greenback-Labor ticket in 1877. He then went to Washington as a columnist for the *Irish World* and a lobbyist for the eight-hour day. Subsequently, he clerked for the Select Committee on labor conditions under Congressman Wright.[42] Lum associated with radicals of all sorts—that with the Haymarket martyrs made him an anarchist icon of sorts—but he had a shameful blind spot when it came to white supremacism and saw a Democratic resurgence as the essential prerequisite for any fundamental change.

Another, Horace B. Sargent, presided over the state's influential Grand Army of the Republic and headed the Massachusetts delegation to the Greenback-Labor national convention. Neither a shoemaker nor a clerk, Sargent had been an honors graduate from Harvard and became a prominent Boston lawyer, even before service in the Union Army. Related to congressional and high-ranking military leaders, he was then serving his third term as head of the state's Grand Army of the Republic.[43]

This interest in Butler's presidential candidacy—or Congressman Wright's—also resurrected its own version of the old schemes around David Davis. It argued that the GLP could somehow prevail by putting Butler at the head of their ticket on the assumption that the Democrats would then find it irresistible to second the nomination. This formula involved a guessing game of which Democratic candidate would get that party's nod. Butler himself toyed with the idea right up to the convention or, at least, allowed people to think he had it under consideration. In late May 1880, reporters caught up with him as he passed through Cheyenne, Wyoming, on his way west and asked him about a Greenback nomination. "If they only give us a good platform," Butler was quoted as saying, "the honor would be most worthy."[44] We have no reliable evidence that he ever seriously considered it.

State parties, the organization of which varied widely in character, selected their delegations to the June national convention in Chicago's Exposition Hall very differently. For example, contrary to the prominence of the pro-Democratic supporters of Butler in the Massachusetts party, the pro-Democratic clique of Carsey, Shupe, and their allies had no representation in the New York delegation, which consisted of other delegates not necessarily opposed to a strategy centered on the Democrats. Many of the hundreds of delegates shared the views of newspapers such as Andrew C. Cameron's *Workingmen's Advocate* of Chicago or Alexander Troup's *New Haven Union*. They had flirted with independent political action, and often played important roles in shaping a national independent political strategy, though they always veered off at the last minute to become noisy Democratic partisans.

Butler supporters arriving in Chicago found some support for their perspectives came from the West Coast. Dennis Kearney, the San Francisco entrepreneur and demagogue, had taken up the challenge of speaking for workers after the 1877 general strike. He did so by targeting the racial exclusion of the Chinese and doing regular deals with the railroad interests and their Democratic allies. Kearney's Workingmen's Party of California aided in the successful congressional election of the Democratic former general William S. Rosecrans, who was famous for his record in the war and less so for his 1864 order using the army against strikers in St. Louis. Although the numbers attending Kearney's "sand lot" harangues had fallen off precipitously, he and a small group of followers sustained the Workingmen's Party and used it to bring credentials to national conventions.[45]

Some participants took exactly the opposite tack. The Socialists who entered the convention as a body remained actively hostile to any compromise with the capitalist parties. So did most of the southern insurgents, which had many more Black participants back home than the few playing a role in the convention; where they came from, the Democrats represented an inflexibly conservative caste hierarchy. Where organized, farmers and their allies across the Midwest had just broken from Republican antecedents and had little interest in rejoining another party representing the elite.

Reporters understood something of the tensions on the floor of the national convention. The first meeting of the convention adjourned to the chants of "Butler! Butler!" When the nominations opened, the Indiana delegation proposed Butler as "the one man who could civilize and Christianize Massachusetts." Missouri nominated Stephen Dillaye, who requested that the delegation withdraw his name in favor of Butler, which it did. Thereafter, a Pennsylvanian nominated Congressman Wright.[46]

In the end, though, an informal ballot gave Weaver and Wright 235 and 214 votes, respectively, and, after a smattering to favorite sons, Butler was left with 190. Supporters of Wright and Butler briefly scrambled to make common cause, but it was too late. The first formal ballot went to Weaver with 450 of 716 votes, and the convention made the nomination unanimous by acclamation.

The delegates then turned to selecting a vice-presidential candidate. Sargent, the most ardent proponent of Butler, offered the sixty-two-year-old General Absolom M. West of Mississippi. A rare southern industrialist before the war, he had gained his military rank through the management of the wartime railroads. After the war, he had helped form an affiliate of the old National Labor Union in Yalobusha County, but the Socialist Peter J. McGuire, who sat on the platform committee with West, said that he had scoffed at "every advanced proposition . . . with the wearisome platitudes: 'visionary ideas,' 'dangerous burdens,' 'perilous to success,' etc." He opposed women's suffrage and declared that a legislated eight-hour workday violated the rights of the capitalist.[47] In the end, 413 of 714 delegates voted for General Barzalai J. Chambers of Texas, though the ghost of a Butler-West ticket would continue to haunt the movement later.

On Tuesday, July 6, the National Executive Committee of the GLP met at the St. James Hotel in New York City. Leaders of what had been the local insurgency remained conspicuously absent from any references to its activities. Kearney, who had gone back to California, left his credentials with Lum. New Yorkers had selected Ephenetus Howe to represent them, but he had given his seat to George O. Jones of Albany, a relative of US Senator John P. Jones of Nevada. Lum scorned Jones as "a notorious lobbyist," while Jones thought Lum erratic and unreliable.[48] Time would indicate the correctness of both charges, and much of the national committee did not differ much in quality from that sent by most states.

General Weaver proved to be a vigorous and aggressive campaigner. While trying to confine himself to Greenbackism in his acceptance, he appealed broadly to the disaffected of both parties and explicitly embraced demands for "a full ballot, a fair count, and equal rights for all classes, for the laboring man in the Northern factories, mines, and workshops, and for the struggling poor, both Black and white, in the cotton fields of the South."[49] This meant directly taking on the Democratic disenfranchisement of African Americans on his scheduled August tour through the South.

On this question, Weaver and the serious insurgents waged a campaign that sought to be honest, honorable, and principled. Their campaign, however, would not only suffer defeat at the polls but grotesque misrepresentations in both contemporary press and the subsequent historical record.

* * *

Many of the Greenbackers—certainly, their presidential candidate—hoped to replicate the earlier citizen insurgency of farmers, small town professionals, and city workers that launched the Republican Party in the 1850s. Since those days, however, the country had experienced a proliferation of mass-circulation newspapers that, as the career of Carsey had begun to demonstrate, could misrepresent the news they distributed. Also, Weaver's direct confrontation with the shortcomings of Reconstruction and the white supremacist restoration of Democratic rule in the South predisposed Democratic-inclined reformers involved with the third-party movement to turn to the work of destroying it.

Carsey and Shupe had beaten their counterparts from New England to California to this conclusion. For them, the threat of independent political action—and its periodic practice—provided a key tool for personal and group power, but only if one avoided any direct attack on the structures of class and power. They specifically hoped to restore the antebellum hegemony of the Democratic Party, coupled to such Republican issues as the tariffs and the traditional appeals to racial and national purity.

Women and men throwing brickbats down on the newly organized police. ("Four scenes from the riot in the Sixth Ward, New York City between the 'Bowery Boys' and the 'Dead Rabbits.'" *Frank Leslie's illustrated newspaper*, July 18, 1857, 109, Prints and Photographs Division, Library of Congress, LC-USZ62-121644.)

The popular stage persona of a Bowery fireman and political gang leader. (Mose the Bowery B'hoy, 1848. National Portrait Gallery, Smithsonian Institution, Object number S/NPG.95.188. CC0, Creative Commons, no restrictions.)

The politically connected construction industry had a reputation for cutting corners and shoddy work. ("The Modern Builder," *Puck*, January 7, 1880, 726. Courtesy of HathiTrust.)

Tammany Hall headquarters of the machine that managed much of the Democratic Party's plebeian and ethnic voting base. (Tammany Hall and 14th St. West. Photograph ca. 1914. Prints and Photographs Division, Library of Congress. LC-USZ62-10173.)

An elite warning that the dalliance of some Democrats with the "Rag Baby" of "Greenbacks" might become so popular that it could carry off the party. (The Democratic Frankenstein, *Harper's Weekly*, September 9, 1876, 748. Courtesy of HathiTrust.)

Puck goads Tammany's John Kelly about his negligible impact on the campaigns of 1876 and 1880. ("With Puck's Compliments to the Democratic National Convention at Chicago—1884," *Puck*, July 9, 1884, 289. Courtesy of HathiTrust.)

THE GREAT BOODLE MONOPOLY.

"I do fear they will build up the worst railroad monopoly ever seen in this country."—THURMAN.

Kelly of Tammany Hall and Charles A. Dana's *Sun* initially hoped to use Butler against the Democratic presidential nomination of New York governor Grover Cleveland. (The Great Boodle Monopoly, *Harper's Weekly*, November 1, 1884, 730. Courtesy of HathiTrust.)

Skeptical of Ben Butler's antimonopolism, *Puck* shows him scavenging John Kelley's discarded stogie before the "Tammany Cigar Store," which is peddling "Cleveland Cigars." ("Tammany Throws Away Its 'Butt,' and the Monopoly Bootlack Picks It Up." *Puck*, September 24, 1884, 49. Courtesy of HathiTrust.)

Carsey flitted at the edges of Belva A. Lockwood's Equal Rights Party, but—like Puck—he dismissed independent candidates as attention-seeking irrelevancies. ("Now Let the Show Go On! Arrival of the Political Columbine to Join the Political Clown," *Puck*, September 17, 1884, 33. Courtesy of HathiTrust.)

CHAPTER 3

Counterfeiting Class

The Secret Society Tradition and the Deep Origins of the American Federation of Labor

I can hire one half of the working class to kill the other half.

—Attributed to Jay Gould

Five years after William A. A. Carsey and his fellow Democratic operatives named the Greenback presidential ticket, they called for a national conference of labor organizations in Terre Haute, Indiana. In August 1881, delegates filed into a Presbyterian church that also served as the local Temperance Hall. Most came from various secret societies hopeful of launching a federation of labor organizations that could provide an effective rival to the Knights of Labor. In the process, Carsey and his colleagues Forrest-Gumped themselves into having had a hand in founding the Federation of Organized Trades and Labor Unions—what became the American Federation of Labor.

The fate of the Greenback-Labor presidential campaign in 1880 turned much of the impetus of labor reform away from electoral politics toward self-organization at the workplace. Generally, groups strongly associated with Carsey, such as the Amalgamated Labor Union and the Knights of Industry, attempted an effort to organize workers on a national scale to foster organization that would be less likely than the Knights of Labor to confront the probusiness politics of the two major parties. In this context, he claimed more the role of a labor organizer than the role of a political leader.[1] Throughout, Carsey left no evidence indicating that he became any more honest in the one than in the other.

The Reaction to Independent Electoral Politics, 1880–81

James B. Weaver's 1880 Greenback-Labor presidential campaign exposed just how difficult it would be for the aggrieved to unite even in making a coherent statement of their concerns. As the threat of an ongoing third party became more serious, the generally growing interest in it gave rise to more well-defined radical currents, such as the Socialist Labor Party (SLP), which complicated efforts to unify a broader movement. It also clearly attracted new would-be power brokers interested in bargaining not only for reform but also for personal power and standing, even as it also drove some of the more opportunistic conservative strategists back into the Democratic fold.

In the end, everything in the two-party system centered on winning and, in a system requiring the management of mass politics, the process sanctioned—if not required—campaign tactics that might well be dirty, filthy, dishonest, and thoroughly corrupt. In the postwar United States, defeat proved an especially heavy burden to the institutionally minority party, the Democratic, which had been the dominant party for decades before the secession crisis. The situation naturally inclined its partisans to engage in the most distastefully desperate tactics to scramble back into power. The prospect of a serious independent force promised a more effective way to reduce those Republican majorities. The experiment had to be abandoned, however, when the insurgents took the entire matter seriously and sought to launch a real mass party to rival not only the Republicans but also the Democrats.

The course of well-known successful officeholders and government functionaries in the Greenback-Labor Party (GLP) also ensured the failure of Weaver's campaign. Newspaper accounts of the 1880 effort ticked off the departure of ostensible insurgents to support the Democratic ticket, which included Peter Cooper, Samuel F. Cary, Hendrick B. Wright, and locally prominent figures such as Alexander Troup and Blanton Duncan. Then, too, Marcus M. Pomeroy had a large Democratic-centered series of organizations in his farmer alliances, his Union Greenback clubs, and other local groups.[2]

Perhaps the most prominent of Pomeroy's network, Ben Butler performed in such a way as to deflect the coverage of Weaver's visit to Boston's historic Faneuil Hall, where "every available inch of standing, sitting and lounging room was occupied by an enthusiastic audience."[3] Groups of supporters showed up from neighboring communities, and representatives of the Boston socialists sat among the meeting's vice presidents. Still, the two organizers of the event—Charles H. Litchman and E. Moody Boynton of Newburyport—had been Butler men who made every effort to get him onto the platform with

Weaver for a Greenback-Labor rally, even though Butler had already begun to urge voters to cast Democratic ballots.

At that Boston rally, Weaver addressed the lesser-evil strategy. "Can any man give me a reason why the Democratic party cannot vote the Republican ticket, or vice versa?" he asked. "What is the difference between the two parties?" He regularly repeated an appropriate analogy that made veiled allusions to the old issues of the war. The *Iowa State Tribune*, for example, greeted news of Butler's joining the Democrats "in order to carry out my greenback ideas" by asking, "Why didn't you join the Confederacy in order to save the Union?"[4]

Butler adopted that same platform plank only days after Weaver's meeting. Simply ignoring the very existence of the GLP of which he had been a spokesman, he told citizens that it would be their "solemn duty . . . to determine which of the two candidates represented more nearly his convictions." With Weaver already stumping Maine for independent action, Butler announced that he would follow Weaver into Maine, to stump for Winfield S. Hancock and the Democratic ticket.

Like Litchman and Boynton in Boston, Carsey, Walter H. Shupe, and other Tammany allies had managed to take command over the GLP campaign in New York City, though they had rarely, if ever, even supported the party's candidate. Most of the various groups that had aimed at electoral action continued to press for an insurgent vote, though as the election approached, the local organizers and their organizations peeled off to the Democrats.

Weaver's speech at the Cooper Union on September 13 repeated much of the scale and importance of his Boston rally. A Kings County, New York, delegation, largely Brooklyn socialists, met on the southeast corner of the hall at 7:15 a.m. to march as a group to their reserved seats. Even the scornful *New York Herald* acknowledged that Weaver had drawn "the largest audience ever gathered in that building." As in Boston, Butler managed to pass through New York at the same time, deflecting some of the press coverage of the Greenbackers with an ostentatious meeting he held with Hancock before heading on to Ohio on a Democratic campaign tour. Perhaps realizing that his time in the spotlight was passing, Weaver increasingly began to focus his speeches on the dangers of restoring white rule through the Democratic parties in the South.[5] Thereafter, Democrats became more demanding of aspiring allies among former Greenbackers.

At this point, Dyer D. Lum also turned up in New York. One of Butler's leading men who enjoyed a high rank among Massachusetts Greenbackers—which got him a seat on the National Executive Committee—also turned up in New York. There he met with members of the internal circles of James

A. Garfield's Republican campaign, ostensibly to get information about the Greenback-Labor movement. The Republicans paid Lum to assist his travel expenses, and he subsequently got the Democratic *Cincinnati Enquirer* to publish his exposé of the Weaver campaign. It claimed to demonstrate that the Republicans subsidized the GLP's national campaign and had General Weaver in their pocket.

The *New York Star* on October 25 added another piece, a letter that entirely sustained Lum's charges, purporting it to be by Weaver. The Democratic press circulated it despite the denials and obviously different handwriting. One paper frankly acknowledged the entire thing to be forgery but justified publishing it anyway on the grounds that the document accurately reflected what it called Weaver's "peculiar methods and peculiar management."[6]

Democrats reprinted and circulated these materials widely, more and more often including an explanation of why their further coverage of Weaver's campaign would be superfluous, as they already covered the Republican campaign. Republican papers followed suit.[7] In this, the commercial media established a clear precedent for the cone of silence it dropped over the later campaigns by Weaver, Gene Debs, Robert La Follette Sr., Henry A. Wallace, Ralph Nader, and others.

On October 29, Uri Mulford, at the head of what he claimed to be 474 of Pomeroy's Union Greenback clubs, announced that they would vote Democratic, and the announcement was timed to come only five days before the election. "We have got to take the situation as it is now, though it may be averse to our eager desire," he declared, "and, as becomes independent and patriotic citizens, on election day, strike where our political taskmasters, the authors of the prevailing debt nursing and labor-crushing financial system will feel our blows."[8] From Carsey to Mulford, through Butler to Lum, people who had elbowed into the leadership of the insurgency turned their groups to the Democrats.

Moreover, the mechanisms of the two-party vote count in that period ensured that the gears of both the Republican and the Democratic machine would grind away at the third-party movement of 1880. Notwithstanding the civic mantra of the present, systemic, and plausible complaints of vote fraud that had been common in, for example, parts of the South by Democrats and in company towns of the North by Republicans. In such places, local functionaries had the ability to fudge their numbers at the expense of their rival party, which, nevertheless, had a certain amount of power to minimize the siphoning of their own votes. They did not necessarily represent a concerted attempt to change the outcome of an election, but it certainly enhanced the apparent abilities of local party organizers to bring out the vote. Also, in most such circumstances, they also had a certain amount of power to minimize the siphoning off of their own votes. Still, both parties had less restraint should they shave votes of the Greenbackers, who had no power anywhere to do anything like that.

Where voters had cast well over a million insurgent ballots two years before, the 1880 presidential election radically underperformed the old totals. Weaver's final and most sober preelection estimates of public support had ranged from 600,000 to 1,500,000, but the official returns left him with only 306,867. The totals likely reflected considerable fudging in the South, and both contemporaries and later statisticians explicitly miscounted tens of thousands of fusionist ballots in Maine as simply Democratic.[9] Even taking all this into account, the results proved discouraging enough to implode national aspirations among the Greenbackers.

The crushing defeat certainly drove the efforts of most advocates for labor reform away from third-party politics into other means of promoting their version of labor reform. Those who still sought change through the government turned to lobbying of one sort or another. The change tended to leave reform-minded citizens a choice between the largely unsympathetic professions of Republican politicians and the increasingly positive rhetoric of some Democratic politicians who, nevertheless, rarely did much.

Terre Haute and the Origins of the AFL

However temporarily, the decline of interest in third-party politics after 1880 freed Carsey from his role as a spokesperson for labor politics. For several years after the election, he offered a perspective not "to foster or oppress a special class or special interests, but one that will foster and protect and build up our industries, develop our resources, perpetuate our institutions, and make us a wealthy, prosperous, self-supporting nation, with a happy, contented, enlightened, and industrious people," particularly the "prosperity of our great middle and professional classes."[10]

By this point, Carsey and his small circle of allies had something of a *modus operandi*. One reporter offered important insights into the group: "New men in politics, especially those that are wealthy, are sought out by these adventurers, who try to induce them to believe that they are the representatives of the workingmen of this city, and thus manage to get money on various pretexts."[11] In short, the group not only provided useful service to its political masters but found a way to be financially self-supporting, and likely they managed periodically to turn a profit.

The largest workers' organization of the day, the Knights of Labor, concerned Carsey, and there he served. He later claimed to have been "one of the founders" of the order in that he became a member of "the original assembly" among the gold beaters and bricklayers of this city. As he explained it, though, the Knights originally saw their goals as political and insisted that the order had nothing to do with strikes. The trade assemblies of the Knights did, however, engage in such trade union activities. Carsey insisted that the order's proper place was supposed to be politics, where they should be working to put Democrats in office. Indeed, he publicly denounced the Knights of Labor as "a mob rather than an organization."[12]

Shupe, for his part, turned from Greenbackism to what he called "practical antimonopoly" under the auspices of a new secret society, the Sons of Columbia. He may have borrowed the name from a song widely circulated in *Temperance Hymn Book and Minstrel* in his childhood. He claimed that his new secret society "holds that the theory of the postal system is applicable to the railroad and the telegraph, and that all corporations of this kind should be conducted for the common good." It smudged the hint at nationalizing the railroad and telegraph into the mere advocacy that corporations function "for the common good." Almost immediately, he announced "a membership of 800,000 throughout the United States and 88,000 in the State of New York." Perhaps because no reporters fainted into astonished insensibility at such numbers, Shupe came back the following week saying that it "now numbers over 900,000 persons."[13]

Meanwhile, Carsey's search for an alternative to the Knights of Labor settled on the "Knights of Industry." (As an interesting sidenote, the French used *chevalier de l'industrie* to describe grifters.) Carsey described it as a working-class organization dedicated to the original goals of the Knights of Labor. That is, it opposed strikes, fostered class peace through negotiations and mutual respect, and advocated reform through political action. The details of its founding and Carsey's role remains obscure, but, in 1881, it made its debut.[14]

As with Shupe's Sons of Columbia, membership claims for Carsey's Knights became astronomical, but there are few indications of its size, and, in New York City, it may have involved no more than could fit in a small meeting hall or even around a dining room table.

Earlier, when the Knights of Labor faced the problem of trying to build a secret society into a mass movement, those uninterested in such a movement found the claim of having a massive secret society terribly convenient. It permitted one to speak for thousands without having to worry about even showing any visible sign of those numbers. In this case, Carsey in New York could speak on behalf of an organization he described as largely "confined to Missouri and Illinois" or—if he were anywhere in or closer to those states—to Indiana or Pennsylvania or anywhere else beyond the likelihood of easy refutation. A Washington paper mentioned the organization of the Knights of Industry in Boston. Although said to include W. F. Falls, one of the aging wartime strike leaders, the group remained hostile to strikes but stated that its appearance was "not intended to antagonize the Knights of Labor, but to supplement it."[15]

So, who participated in what may have existed of this Knights of Industry, this workers' voice against strikes?

The *Sun* reported a meeting of "wage workers" at the Mechanics' and Trades' Exchange, 198 Broadway, a site usually associated with the owners of construction companies. That self-described labor meeting highlighted "one of the members who employs many men," most likely Carsey. Citing the weakness of unions within the various crafts, he recommended the Knights of Industry, "in which all trades are interested." Assuring his listeners that the organization had already gotten quite strong in Pennsylvania, he demonstrated the local viability of this approach, basing it on the experience of his own "New York Friendly Society of Operative Masons." It reported "that nearly all of the bosses had agreed to give the men $3.50 a day and the chairman of the meeting was of opinion that all of them would do so."[16]

A closer look inspires skepticism. The Knights of Industry remained so ephemeral that Carsey periodically gained renewed press attention through the 1880s by leaking "a rumor" describing it as a brand-new organization to gullible reporters who took the story at face value. Its ghost—if an organization that had barely lived can have a ghost—seems to have limped into the 1890s, being mentioned regularly as having some representation at Populist conventions alongside the Knights of Labor and other groups.[17]

Still, genuine workers' organizations increasingly began to challenge the alleged credentials of Carsey and the Knights of Industry. The Central Labor Union of New York publicly described him and the Knights of Industry "as a political trickster and his trick." As elections rolled around, "he bobs up serenely again at the first opportunity." Halfway across the country, when a Republican paper in Kansas seized on a statement by the Knights of Industry as proof that "workingmen" agreed with them on the tariff, local advocates of the Farmers Alliance exposed the Knights of Industry as more like one of those paper organizations floated by one political party or another for its own purposes.[18]

As soon as the Knights of Industry appeared in print, Carsey announced that it had established a common front with something called the "Amalgamated Labor Union." Carsey described it as yet another secret society, one that had formed in 1878 among other workers discontented with the course of the Knights of Labor.[19] He implied that this other group had grown from disgust with the episodic new militancy of the organization and its departure from the shadows of fraternal secrecy.

At the time, several organizations existed under something like this name. New York City had an "Amalgamated Trades and Labor Union." At the start of 1880, a body of this name sponsored a meeting at the Cooper Institute, which endorsed bills in the legislature for a bureau of labor statistics, the abolition of prison labor, enforcement of the eight-hour law, the abolition of tobacco factories in tenement houses, and a mechanics' lien law. An 1883 meeting in New York City mentioned the participation of members of the Amalgamated Labor Union alongside those of the Knights of Labor and the Central Labor Union.[20] Its activities suggest that it surely was not allied with Carsey's efforts, though its name may have provided some inspiration for his adoption of the name.

Later sources offer a few more candidates for this organization allied to Carsey. His antistrike organization could not have been the "Amalgam[at]ed labor union" that promised aid to upstate New York strikers, alongside the announcement of an "Amalgamated Association" in Pittsburgh "at which some surprising action is anticipated." An organization calling itself the Amalgamated Labor Union also organized a strike of streetcar workers in St. Louis.[21] In short, evidence for the existence of an antistrike workers' organization called the Amalgamated Labor Union in New York seems elusive.

Still, an "Amalgamated Labor Union" of some sort did function in Terre Haute, Indiana, though much of it seems to have been smoke and mirrors, and its nature as a labor organization seems questionable. Prominent figures in the organization were Edward Pagette, a carpenter, and J. R. Backus, a bricklayer, who earlier had associations with the International Workingmen's Association through its 1872 Equal Rights Party project. The *Terre Haute Evening Mail* said that the organization had started in 1881 or "a short time ago" rather than in 1878, as Carsey later claimed. Although "its professed object was the protection of the laboring man," it seemed preoccupied with using civic projects to win a higher visibility in the town.[22]

Genuine labor reformers did express an interest in matters of civic improvement. Back in the wake of the panic, municipal projects became part of the make-work strategy advocated by labor organizations. Then, too, people in and around radical organizations generally argued in favor of technological development, as part of actively offering engineering proposals for methods.

Such plans certainly raised the profile of reformers in their communities and could even ease the lives of working people. Underscoring the role of political connections in all this, the government of New York tapped Edward J. Kean to serve as the chief clerk in their new Bureau of Labor. Kean had been an editor of the *New York Boycotter* and the president of "the Amalgamated Labor Union of New York."[23] So the Amalgamated Labor Union of Terre Haute (hereafter in this chapter referred to as ALU) operated in territory known to Carsey and others.

As part of its effort "to regulate the business of the town," the ALU took on itself the organization of the local celebration of the Fourth of July. It had raised money despite press warnings that it might wind up going into "a contingent fund of the Union, to benefit it or carry on strikes." The *Terre Haute Evening Mail* also reported that the organization balked at holding the celebration when news reached Terre Haute of the July 2 assassination attempt on President James Garfield and the prognosis of his impending death. The paper further complained when they went ahead with the celebration and then severely criticized how the organization organized the celebration. Afterward, the *Mail* warned that the ALU had "cleared about five hundred dollars" from the event.[24] Later, the ALU of Terre Haute faded from news reports as quickly as it had turned up in them.

Although the identity of an ALU allied with Carsey back east remains uncertain, this rather peculiar ALU in Terre Haute likely allied with his Knights of Industry in calling for an "Amalgamated Trades Congress" in Terre Haute on August 2, 1881. Proponents of secret societies were hardly alone in hoping to lay the foundations for "a new secret order to supplant the Knights of Labor, although, on the face of the call, its object was stated to be to establish a national labor congress." Locally, the ALU recruited Mark W. Moore of the Terre Haute Typographical Union to join the organizing committee as its secretary and affix his signature alongside theirs to the circular calling the congress.[25]

The assembly that materialized at the Temperance Hall on the northeast corner of Fifth and Ohio Streets proved to be disappointingly small. The local press reported that the congress "did not prove the success anticipated, the attendance of delegates from abroad being somewhat limited."[26] Participants at least claimed to have come from Chicago, Detroit, Cleveland, St. Louis, Indianapolis, Dayton, and Springfield; others attended as individuals.

Mark L. Crawford of the Chicago Typographical Union made a quick, if not entirely accurate, nose count of the body. He saw only eleven delegates represented *bona fide* unions, while more than fifty presented credentials from organizations of which Crawford had mostly never heard, such as the Sons of

Vulcan, Followers of Lafayette, Washington Guards, and the Lincoln Leaguers. He added that "by digging a little deeper we discovered that they represented purely greenback clubs," which he suspected had partisan Democratic motives. Crawford may have been correct, though some, such as the Sons of Vulcan, represented a residual midwestern survivor of the older, antebellum union, after most of the local affiliates of which had merged into the Amalgamated Association of Iron and Steel Workers a few years earlier.[27]

Crawford and most of the trade unionists bunked at the National Hotel. There, Peter J. McGuire, the carpenter and socialist from the St. Louis Trades and Labor Assembly, organized them into a viable caucus. When the conference reassembled the next day, he persuaded the body to endorse the call for another national conference to meet in three months at the Turner Hall in Pittsburgh to formulate a comprehensive charter and organizational plan.[28] On Wednesday evening, as the delegates in Terre Haute prepared to go home, they held an open-air meeting in what they called the Court Park, presumably the site of the courthouse.

The unionists returned home and went to work preparing a conference of their own. It assembled as planned in Pittsburgh on November 15–18.[29] Crawford reported that the handful present in Terre Haute had grown to a total of 107 trade unionist delegates. He also recalled meeting Jeremiah G. Grandison, an African American member of the Pittsburgh Knights of Labor, who gave "one of the best speeches made on the floor." Such was the strange conception and birth of the Federation of Organized Trades and Labor Unions—what became the American Federation of Labor only a few years later.

Notwithstanding Carsey's standing as an employer, the standards of his Knights of Industry did not necessarily preclude what later emerged as key features of the AFL's approach to organizing. It emphasized fraternal benefits for the membership and mistrusted appeals to protect a wider class interest, embracing the ideal of class peace. Skeptical of strikes as well, it increasingly came to emphasize nonpartisan political connections in lieu of organizing, adding jingoism as a part of the mix, in doses that fluctuated over time.

It seems that somewhere in the institutional DNA of the kind of modern US labor movement that eventually emerged may lurk surprising ideological genetic material.

State-Selected Hired Mouthpiece for Labor

Carsey used his dubious position in the labor movement as a publicist for various policies and positions, on which he willingly sold his time and reputation, such as it was. Western Union solicited his authority as a labor leader to testify on worker opposition to government ownership of the telegraph through its postal functions. Organized labor, he assured the Senate Committee on Interstate Commerce, opposed anything but a "moderate and discreet regulation" that would not "injure the business." Norvin Green of Western Union added Carsey to the payroll because he had the impression that the self-described labor leader could exercise "considerable influence."[30] Companies who needed such services could certainly procure one through their political operatives at Tammany or Irving Hall, but none with the quality of Carsey's experience and prominence.

Indeed, the willingness of Carsey and his circle to rent their self-invented labor credentials to serve private companies extended to assisting those enterprises against various strikes by genuine labor organizations. Carsey's lieutenant, A. H. Gallahue, appeared at hearings on behalf of "the Associated Trades and the Workman's Reform League." An even more obscure figure, Gallahue had come to the city from Ohio, where he had been indicted for petty larceny.[31] In New York City, Gallahue shamelessly flitted from issue to issue as a well-publicized "labor" spokesman.

Gallahue appeared before the Rapid-Transit Commission when it sought to mediate a dispute between the Manhattan Railway Company and the Real Estate Exchange. "He's a fake," shouted one voice from the back as soon as he came to the front. "He represents the elevated road," continued the heckler, even as Gallahue nevertheless presented resolutions that "protested against Government ownership of railroads and telegraphs" and asserted the right of the elevated roads to build extensions. As he left, a worker in the crowd challenged his credentials, to which Gallahue replied by doubling up his fist and threatening "a personal controversy."[32]

Still acting as the president of the Workingmen's Reform League, Gallahue intervened in a series of labor disputes, agreeing to settle job actions "for a consideration." In a dispute in the lumber industry, employers agreed to pay him $100 to get resolutions of support from sixty to eighty trade unions. He produced a Carseyesque list of nonexistent paper organizations that the bosses recognized as illegitimate, because they flatly refused to pay the "consideration." Gallahue actually filed a lawsuit against them, in the course of which the employers noted that the names he had presented had no credentials indicating that they were actually "delegates of any body." The judge dismissed the suit.[33]

On August 4, 1882, a congressional committee on tariffs gave Carsey another platform to speak on behalf of labor.[34] Although elsewhere identifying himself as a builder and an employer, when it served his purposes, he described himself as a member of the bricklayers' union or even a generically described "laborers' union." "I have been president of the laborer's union, a knight of labor, and a socialist," he claimed at one point, "and I know them all thoroughly. I have come to the conclusion that the best way to settle the matter is to bring the workingmen up to the use of the ballot as a means of redress." In this case, he presented himself as one of the latter and claimed to speak on behalf of his "Independent Labor Party of New York," which he described as having been "organized in the year 1874, pursuant to a resolution adopted by the State Trade Assembly at their annual convention of that year, that political action was necessary to the salvation of the working classes."

There, Carsey offered a fuller view of his labor reform politics. He first offered the congressional commission not only an olive branch of class peace. He advocated "not a special class or special interests, but one that will foster and protect and build up our industries, develop our resources, perpetuate our institutions, and make us a wealthy, prosperous, self-supporting nation, with a happy, contented, enlightened, and industrious people." What he proposed, insisted Carsey, would be "in the interest of all classes."

His vision could be achieved less through government mechanisms to regulate the economy and more through fostering the right kind of labor organizations. From the start of his testimony, Carsey denounced "the non-political striking labor union system." Instead, he urged "the education of the working classes in the use of the ballot as a cure for the evils of our labor system, its power to remove the cause, as well as cure the effect, and to the discussion of all questions, political, social, and economic, that affect their interests." In the absence of independent political action, this meant labor organizations that did not function so much as trade unions but as mechanisms to get workers to vote Democratic.

US workers, insisted Carsey, had the "that great power and privilege" of the ballot, which he stated—entirely erroneously—to have been denied "the workingmen of all other civilized or uncivilized countries." The ballot made possible "a truly representative government of the people, by the people, and for the people." The vision would not come about because of any expansion of the suffrage or mass demonstrations but through legislative hearings, cultivating a "wise and unprecedented statesmanship" and "a great precedent for all future legislation."

Carsey enumerated the kind of "wise and unprecedented" approaches he expected such thinking to take. To preserve this exceptional nation, he proposed "the exclusion of all foreign, hostile, competitive interests." The United

States needed little or no international trade, and what was useful should "be carried on by means of American ships manned by American seamen, so that the profit of such trade would inure to our own people." The scheme would involve "a tariff of at least 100 per cent, to allow us to compete with foreign manufacturers, or cease to manufacture goods for a competitive market, or else reduce the American to the wage and (its result) the condition of Europeans, or import the pauper laborer to take the place of the American laborer."[35] Of course, it is hard to know how much of this represented his real thinking, how much that of the people who had employed him, and how much Carsey simply hoped to appeal to the lowest common denominator of the base he hoped to reach.

Carsey's concern that cheap goods would undervalue US manufactures extended to cheap labor. The influx of immigrants subverted the standard of living as thoroughly as cheap goods. The origins of the plebeian base of the Democratic machine in New York City had been immigrants, but the sources of immigration had begun to shift after the Civil War to Eastern and Southern Europe, what Carsey called "the hordes at Castle Garden." "While you are so close to the city of New York," he told them, "I would suggest that it would be wise for you to pay a visit to Castle Garden and see the character of people brought here with these ideas in their heads, to strike and do nothing but strike."[36]

So declared the son of two immigrants.

Carsey also spoke with the authority of his labor party, which had been silently working to do what he recommended labor organizations should do, striving to educate workers politically, and it had "steadily and persistently labored to that end."[37] He told them that his Independent Labor Party was "composed of the leading trades unions in New York. . . . We have got in our ranks the presidents of fifteen or twenty organizations. Those men have all learned by experience that this is the only way we can settle these questions." In fact, the party he claimed to represent never amounted to much and had expired seven or eight years earlier, and whatever organization Carsey represented had little substance to it, if any.

Perhaps because nobody seated at this congressional committee challenged Carsey's claims, he carried his description even further. Not only did his party include the leadership of fifteen to twenty unions but included "representation all through the State and all through the city of New York, and attempts are making all over the United States to organize." Indeed, that claim in this performance seems to have inspired its rebirth as the "National Labor Party," to which Carsey and his colleagues later referred.

In his approach to the labor question, Carsey had no reluctance in responding to employers, as well as politicians, eager to have a "labor voice" for whatever they wanted. When various prominent and wealthy advocates of higher tariffs launched the New York Association for the Protection of American Industry and sought incorporation, they found Carsey a useful name for implying labor support. The Republican protariff *New-York Tribune* noted the "strong names representing a number of our most important interests, and it starts at the right time." Unusually, it added that it had been "certainly a mistake to include the name of W.A.A. Carsey in the list of managers." The paper noted that he "has never brought strength to any one of the many parties and factions he has figured in. Pretending friendship for the workingman, he has been, in fact, always and everywhere a friend to himself only." Nevertheless, Carsey shared the stage with a range of local luminaries at a mass meeting at the Cooper Institute to demonstrate popular support for high tariffs.[38]

By this point, if not earlier, Carsey's role as an agent of Tammany Hall also brought him into a close alliance with Democratic New York governor David Bennett Hill. A veteran of the state assembly from Elmira, Hill had served as the assembly's speaker in 1872. He managed to maneuver through the shifting terrain of local insurgencies in the wake of the 1877 strike, emerging as the mayor of the city before becoming lieutenant governor under the governorship of Grover Cleveland. When Cleveland later went on to the presidency, Hill made his own successful bid for the governor's mansion.[39]

Much of Carsey's peculiar expression of labor interest reflected the views of Governor Hill. In particular, the governor advocated arbitration, legislation on working conditions, and even a shorter workweek to be attained not through worker activism but a state move to make Saturday half-holidays. Hill also made no bones about his view of insurgents and third-party movements: "There is no place in honorable American politics for the political guerillas who do not attach themselves to either of the great political armies, but who, while swearing allegiance to neither, criticize them both and fight first upon one side and then on the other."[40] Carsey's language generally echoed that of the governor, particularly on arbitration, but he was in a position to carry Hill's views of insurgency even further, having established a decade-long record of affiliating with insurgent movements in order to destroy them.

Events, however, would not permit Carsey to make a simple transition to being an open Democratic functionary. The circumstances of the previous decade had brought many new players into the field, and the snarl of the third-party experience had become an insurmountable reality. Indeed, it remains doubtful whether a contemporary participant could have mapped it all out, much less someone trailing much more than a century behind and burdened with a healthy skepticism.

Nevertheless, it would be well to understand how this Gordian knot became so tangled. Operatives of one or the other major parties—or factions of one of the other major parties—had a hand in most initiatives for political independence. Not only did some of them hope to siphon votes from the opposition, but they also sought to multiply insurgent options in order to dissipate their impact. Even more deviously, perhaps, those active on behalf of factions could also have acted to ensure the defeat of their own party if headed by their organized rivals. Indeed, just within Tammany Hall, John Kelly readily arranged maneuvers outside the Democratic organization to thwart the success of some of his competitors within it. Such tactics included efforts to define a new party by ethnicity, neighborhood, or even unique ways of asserting their defense of the laboring class—tickets of "workingmen," "bread winners," "tax payers," etc. There were many notes to play on a third-party instrument without reference to the demands of harmony.

Indeed, as the 1884 election approached, well-connected gentlemen stood poised to play Carsey's game on a national scale for the highest stakes, and harmonizing would be particularly elusive.

Inventing Antimonopolism

Through these years, government at all levels began taking on a greater role in the economy. The rise of new industries, wider markets, and new business practices required government to function as a common vehicle for creating a general consensus so as to manage the adoption of new standards more smoothly. In short, it represented a managerial response to the changing needs of a capitalist economy.

In an age of mass politics, however, this innovation would best be received if cast as a response to public will, shaped by the input of ordinary citizens or those who spoke for them. If one sought to exercise (or not exercise) government control over a new industry or industrial practice, it would be useful to have selected voices of "labor" or "the public" to articulate support for it. An implication would be that the policy would be, at least in part, motivated by the desire to present justice to the people as a higher priority than profits for the owners. From these very Gilded Age considerations grew a peculiar "antimonopolism."

The political advocacy of antimonopolism did not necessarily require electoral action, but it also seemed to offer a more pliable and an ultimately more transformative goal than Greenbackism. Further, the movement for currency reform had emerged among midwestern farmers or, more accurately, the townsmen socially and economically tied to the rural economy who groped toward a coherent formulation of their grievances. Greenback-Labor sought to combine such goals with worker discontent in the wake of the 1877 strike wave, with very mixed results. In contrast, antimonopolism appeared to tap into a radicalism that ran deeper than currency reform, to offer a broader critique of capitalism. To add to the confusion, the railroads and their financiers responded sharply to the threat of not being able to charge "what the market will bear." When testifying before government bodies, their spokespeople accused advocates of regulation, whether they were other businessmen or workers, of advocating "anticorporate communism." In testimony before the congressional committee on commerce in 1882, they warned that "the cry of down with railway monopolies is much like that of the communist of France to destroy the bones of the dead Napoleon."[41]

Truth be told, though, the antimonopolist movement not only represented something less than "anticorporate communism" but also less than a movement for currency reform. The rapid growth of the cities left them heavily dependent on business and industries from the utilities to the railroads. City folk, including merchants and professionals, demanded the regulation of those businesses. Unregulated and often arbitrary freight rates affected the profit of farmers, manufacturers, and anyone who needed the railroad to get a product to market. For years, political and business leaders had urged the legislature to require standardizing rates to match the actual distance the railroads would carry the product.

An even older tradition of hostility against monopoly went back more than half a century to when the Jacksonian Democrats had swept into office based, in part, on grievances about the state chartering of "monopolies." In that case, Democrats came into office to break up chartered monopolies dominated by National Republican–Whig allies and replace them with new monopolies in which Democrats participated. In short, being antimonopoly could mean opposition to specific monopolies and not to monopoly in general, providing not that broader critique of capitalism but merely another venue for competing cabals of capitalists.

From its Jacksonian origins, Democrats periodically protested the dominance of "chartered monopolies." In short, while antimonopolism could sound like a sweeping assault on monopoly capital, its most important adherents might actually be more strictly concerned with a specific business rival.

Carsey's status as an entrepreneur and his electoral interests drew him increasingly toward Shupe's "practical antimonopolism." Rather than rushing to the ballot, Shupe's Sons of Columbia sought to promulgate its own practical measures against monopoly by launching its own Columbian Line of Hudson River steamers to challenge the existing steamboat monopoly. Their great social experiment amounted to finding "how low fares for water transportation can most safely be made, and whether there is any such thing as monopoly as applied to docks and landings."[42]

Shupe gauged his success in the struggle against monopoly by how readily he could obtain the necessary steamboats and begin operations. One paper quipped that, should he successfully undersell the existing monopoly, his operation would secure a new monopoly for itself and charge as much as or more than the old lines, "and so compensating themselves for their abstemiousness previously." Another quipped that Shupe also had an interest in the Baltimore and Ohio railroad, "so that all the members of the order are to patronize that road."[43]

For his part, Carsey moved effortlessly into the leadership of a new nonelectoral, nonpartisan Antimonopoly League in 1881. He did so alongside individuals who had collaborated with him for years, with a few new figures from Brooklyn. Demas G. Barnes, a former Democratic congressman from Orange County who had been running the *Brooklyn Argus* for more than ten years, while dabbling in real estate and the building of the Brooklyn Bridge. Barnes's long-standing involvement in the wholesale drug business, however, put him into partnership with John Francis Henry, a local Republican figure who had run for mayor a few years before and had been persistently urging the party's reorganization. Henry remained important enough in Republican circles to have hosted former president Ulysses S. Grant at his home at 140 Second Place.[44]

Later, Carsey gave a backhanded acknowledgment that his organization lacked popularity with reform-minded workers. The league, he complained, had been "denounced by labor organizations, which had, however, been quick to reap the advantages of its labors." Among those successes, he claimed the Labor Bureau in 1882 and the Railroad Commission. Obviously, many other groups, including "labor organizations" had pressed for such changes. For that reason, one could easily dismiss his criticism of them as little more than projection.[45] Carsey would surely have justified his dismissal of their work on the grounds that it had been ineffective and unsuccessful, while the antimonopolist strategy had borne fruit.

The officers of the league called a convention for the Fourth of July 1883 in Chicago's McCormick Hall, where it launched a National Antimonopoly Party, the meaning of which remained fuzzy. Carsey's own career provides ample evidence of how the organization of a "party" could simply mean the declaration of a paper organization. On a larger scale, of course, the decision of the National Labor Union a dozen years earlier to start the National Labor Reform Party—or of the National Liberal Leagues to launch a National Liberal Party of freethinkers—aimed at nothing more than a paper party formed to vent helplessly against grievances in hopes of pressuring the existing parties. Indeed, some participants in the Greenback Party had no greater aspiration than those for that organization, though the dynamics after 1877 had carried it into far more serious channels.

Throughout the founding of this new party, Carsey made particularly noisy efforts to keep any new formation on a tentative basis. Someone on the credentials committee noted that the Workingmen's Party of California had disintegrated, and the majority voted to deny Dennis Kearney and Stephen Maybell credentials for a nonexistent organization. Perhaps concerned that his wispy New York organizations might get a similar treatment, Carsey plunged into the conflict and "stigmatized the report of the committee as an untruth." He struggled mightily—but unsuccessfully—to get Kearney and Maybell admitted. Nevertheless, even as the convention rejected his effort, it made John F. Henry—formerly a prominent associate of the Antimonopolists—their presiding officer.[46]

Despite Carsey's best efforts, what looked like a new party took form, requiring him to exercise considerable flexibility in trying to address it. Twelve years earlier, going into the 1872 campaign, Democratic operatives had derailed a budding labor party. They moved into the insurgent ranks in 1876, winning the nomination of a man whose son-in-law was running the presidential campaign of the Democrats. Fueled by the 1877 strike and the unexpected independent victories of 1878, insurgent sentiment in the next presidential election could not be derailed as it had been earlier. This required Carsey and others to challenge the effort directly. As 1884 approached, considerable sentiment remained for actually running an independent ticket, if not building a new party.

It remained to be seen whether the entire operation would amount to anything more than Carsey's Independent Labor Party writ large.

* * *

It would be a mistake to see Carsey as simply a political grifter, because his career obviously emerged less from the needs of a US labor movement than from the need for dominant political institutions to deflect the concerns of that movement into harmless channels. After contributing so much to the failure of Greenbackism, Carsey and his fellow thinkers audaciously proclaimed that failure as proof that independent political action could accomplish nothing. This coincided with the emergence of the Knights of Labor from the cocoon of secrecy and the coalescing of national trade union bodies, which Carsey and his fellows sought to coax into nonpartisan reforms that would allegedly preclude the need for an insurgent challenge, particularly if it encouraged the precarious aspirations of the Democrats north of the Mason-Dixon line.

Nevertheless, through 1883–84, a network of political planners had already begun to plan and raise money for a presidential campaign by Ben Butler. The president of that network was a Massachusetts-born technocrat named John F. Boynton who had converted to the Latter-Day Saints and had earlier helped the War Department develop weapons. Most famously while working as a geologist, he had proclaimed the fraudulent stone "Cardiff Giant" to be the fossil of a human giant. Periodically assisting him was Texas congressman John H. Reagan, a former secessionist, and the postmaster general of the defunct Confederate government, who had gotten his department up and functioning across the South in only six weeks. Eager to establish a national regulatory authority over the railroads, Reagan later became a key organizer of the Interstate Commerce Commission. Carsey's old ally, Shupe, promoted the idea among "my Voting Sons and Sensible Daughters in the United States," urging an effort "free and independent of all existing party organizations," though not an ongoing, mass-based "free and independent" party.[47]

Could the wretched of the earth, the discontented of the United States, manage to move their civilization in a more positive direction without asserting an independent power at the ballot box? More immediately pressing questions, from Carsey's perspective, whirled around what he needed to do in 1884, and that depended on what the friends of Butler were up to. That answer would only come in time, and, perhaps, not even then.

CHAPTER 4

Monopolizing Antimonopolism

Ben Butler and the Preemption of Insurgency

> Politics is as much a regular business as the grocery or the dry-goods or the drug business. You've got to be trained up to it or you're sure to fail.
>
> —George Washington Plunkitt

Carsey, who had warned against a "multiplicity of parties" as self-defeating, had a direct hand in a number such electoral formations.[1] The Democratic Party offered the only way to avoid fragmentation. In April 1884, a reporter sniffing around for inside information about the upcoming presidential election approached that "prominent labor reformer," William A. A. Carsey. Carsey proved to be surprisingly well informed about Ben Butler's recent visit to New York City. While there, Butler met secretly with James B. Weaver, the previous Greenback presidential candidate, Francis B. Thurman of the Antimonopoly League, "and others." Carsey explained that the Antimonopolists would adopt Butler as a presidential candidate. Thus strengthened, explained Carsey, Butler would enter the Democratic National Convention with such momentum that the Democrats would embrace him as its candidate rather than run the risk of having to deal with the losses from his running as an independent. Once the Democrats had nominated Butler, Carsey's own labor party "is expected to fall into line, and the thing will be done."[2] This updated the fantasy he had sold the Greenbackers eight years before, which ended with their supporting a Democrat nomination.

Every election, however, posed distinct problems and required particular solutions. Carsey approached the race hoping to avoid what had happened in 1880, when Democratic operatives in the Greenback-Labor project wound up initially fostering what became a genuine effort at an independent campaign. Carsey realized that, although Butler sought the Democratic presidential nomination, he would "make the race any way that he gets the chance." This required Carsey and his followers to support—or, at least, to appear to support—efforts to secure a Butler nomination as an independent in the forlorn hope that his nomination by the Democrats would render irrelevant whatever aid they might have offered from their independent efforts. Or, if Butler lost and stayed in the race as an independent, Carsey and similar operatives ran the risk of working against themselves. Underscoring the unique complexities of 1884, the New York Democrats once more had their own strong contender for the presidential nomination, Governor Grover Cleveland,whose election would permit Carsey's handler, Lieutenant Governor David B. Hill, to move into Cleveland's old position at the governor's mansion. This meant that, even though Carsey publicly tried to persuade insurgents to support the Democratic nomination of Butler, he had to have been hoping that the party would repudiate the general. The challenge would be to deny the initiative for Butler a monopoly over the issue of antimonopolism.

A Nomination . . . of Sorts

One of Carsey's oldest associates in the city, Walter H. Shupe, had ties to Butler going back to his own wartime Masonic project in Virginia. The successes of the Sons of Columbia—or, more accurately, Shupe's success in generating publicity around its name—led to his launching of *Father Columbia's Paper* in September 1883, starting as a monthly with the intention of moving to a weekly campaign paper for 1884. "Let us have a people's selection—a Columbian Plebiscite," he declared, marking a "deliverance from party thralldom." Early on, Shupe and his rather insubstantial Columbian masses had declared their desire to "elect Ben Butler President—because he has proved himself to be the best law executor on earth, the lifelong real friend to labor—and as times are, he and he only, among American living statesmen, can and will bring symmetry and order out of the political chaos and Babel now prevailing." Shupe proposed organizing support groups of ten at each post office to form the basis for county organizations and building toward establishing a presence in the congressional districts.[3] The sources, however, offer no evidence that his proposal ever represented more than wishful thinking or mere flim-flam.

Truth be told, the intensity of the boom for Butler reflected the stresses and strains within the Democratic Party. In part, they reflected the party's success in recovering its old constituencies and gaining new voters. Midwestern adherence had grown strong enough to challenge the predominance that New York had enjoyed in the national party, particularly as with the southern state parties back in force. With some justice, they saw New York's governor Cleveland as a Democratic version of a more conservative Republican monetary policy.

Moreover, even in New York, Cleveland's administration of the state had made serious enemies. From the onset, his regime reflected a certain upstate reaction to the power of the city—its needs, the turbulence of its politics, and the highly publicized corruption of its machine. True, Abram S. Hewitt and August Belmont had no deep animosity to him, and Lieutenant Governor Hill had well-wishers in Manhattan. Among them were not only the veteran Carsey but the neophyte Alton B. Parker, who organized Hill's campaign to replace Cleveland as governor. Still, the former presidential candidate Samuel J. Tilden Jr. remained lukewarm, at best. Then, again, Tilden's nemesis Boss John Kelly of Tammany Hall cordially disliked Cleveland, and Charles A. Dana and his *Sun* publicly declared that they would not support him.[4] Regardless of how the convention turned out, at least some of these anti-Cleveland forces might consider Butler—if not a new political party—a preferable alternative, and their hostility to monopolies would have little to do with it.

Perhaps reflecting a desire to avoid public commitments to Butler, Carsey briefly shifted away from identifying himself as an antimonopolist leader and resurrected his old identification with the "Independent Labor Party." That identity reappeared in the press coverage of a meeting at Clarendon Hall during the fall of 1883, which proposed "to confer with all the industrial organizations of this city, with a view to ascertaining the strength of the independent Labor Party and to secure the support of the workingmen for the platform adopted in Buffalo last year." Other participants were future Carsey lieutenant John W. Kehoe and Dyer D. Lum, Butler's long-standing ally, who would be remembered to his last days as "the Judas of the Greenback party."[5]

In the end, none of them had any certainty at all about what the impact of Butler's bid for the White House would have on the Democratic nomination or its prospects for victory. With the new year, the newly press-promoted "Colonel" Carsey became "the prime mover" in a national conference he scheduled for Philadelphia on January 12. New York papers reported the planned conference, though the press elsewhere, including Philadelphia, seems to have missed it entirely. The conference established a national committee before adjourning, which the *Chicago Tribune* characterized as "the notions of any set of men who might gather in a New York saloon and pretend to be a National Committee."[6]

As Carsey took a New York delegation on the road, he acknowledged that "the feeling is very strong for a people's party and the leading politicians of the country are anxious to become identified with the movement." None of the movement celebrities whose presence had been announced actually showed up, which did not discourage Carsey from presenting the need for policies "to regulate or abolish oppressive monopolies, purify our political system, and to obtain justice for labor." For all that, the conference produced a fine set of Butleresque resolutions supportive of protective tariffs and opposed to both the US registration of ships built abroad and the ownership of property by aliens.[7]

Beneath the charade of political independence, Carsey's hopes remained obviously tied to the prospects that Governor Cleveland and Lieutenant Governor Hill would succeed in their search for higher offices. Early on, then, Carsey clarified that he had "no faith in Gen. Butler at all." He also warned against a "multiplicity of parties" that would weaken the united effort necessary to beat the Republicans, a ploy he had attempted several times to reduce Republican numbers and promote Democratic success. Over the next few weeks, Carsey did reorganize a state executive committee of the National Antimonopolists.[8] Although short on numbers, it still drew prominent Democratic veterans such as Theodore Tomlinson and former congressman James E. Kerrigan. They defined their antimonopolism when they "adopted unanimously" Carsey's resolutions protesting "the flaunting of the red flag at labor meetings," blaming its presence for luring workers into riots like those at Cincinnati or at Tompkins Square in New York. Red flags and radical slogans "lost them the sympathy of the conservative element, without which they could never expect any material amelioration of their condition." Reversing his older tactics, Carsey suggested that proponents of independent political action should hold off on making any nomination until after the major parties had named their candidates, particularly that of the Democrats.

The committee confirmed Carsey's position that it would be "inexpedient" to act before the Democrats made their choice, but inexpediency did not keep him and his group from taking a direct hand in structuring what would become the Butler campaign. Perhaps because the Butler planners had put Shupe in charge of the operations, he hosted a meeting in his office at No. 252 Broadway to finalize plans for the former's nomination along with John H. Reagan of Texas. An old-line Democratic congressman, Reagan had been in the cabinet of the Confederate government and did a remarkably respectable job establishing its postal service quickly. Participants in Shupe's organizing meeting included John W. Keogh and the ubiquitous participants in local Antimonopolist meetings, Thurman, Henry Nichols, and John F. Henry.

The more financially strapped Shupe was inexorably drawn into Butler's campaign, which seemed to have more resources to support his projects. He printed and publicly distributed special "Father Columbia Butler and Reagan campaign publications," and he privately wrote Reagan, as did Butler, Nichols, and surely others. Reagan, however, could hardly have been clearer in his response. While he fully conceded that the Democrats had become "somewhat debauched by the same vices" as Republicans, Reagan insisted that "I do not wish to ally myself at this time with any movement which may antagonize the Democratic party."[9]

In spite of his 1880 experience—or, perhaps, because of it, Weaver also worked behind the scenes for Butler. Well aware that the Democratic Party had hobbled his own independent effort, he concluded that the Democrats might see enough of their views in Butler to permit him a fair shot at participation in the election. In any event, Weaver tried his own hand at persuading Reagan to consider the vice-presidential nomination. "I write you in the strictest confidence but upon a most important subject," he scribbled. The hopeful Weaver wrote that he expected the certain nomination of Butler by the Antimonopolists would be seconded by the national assembly of the Greenbackers on May 28. Butler's strategy also involved Reagan's cooperation, Weaver assuring Reagan that, once they had a coherent slate, "the Democratic Convention would certainly accept this ticket."[10]

Unfortunately, the Lone Star lawmaker would still have none of it. "I look to the Democratic Party as offering the best chance for the defeat of the Republican Party," Reagan wrote Weaver, "and for the correction of the maladministration and misrule which for a good while past oppressed the country." He believed that "the Anti-Monopoly element in the Democratic Party is probably larger than the entire Greenback Party." Indeed, he asserted that "the Anti-Monopolists, the Farmers' Alliance, the Labor Party and the Greenback Party have so much in common with the Democratic Party that it does seem to me wonderful, in view of the great results which might be achieved thereby, that they have not and do not consolidate themselves into one party."[11] The argument would reecho every four years.

The Antimonopolist-Greenback plans went forward despite Reagan's disinterest. It started with the Antimonopolist convention of May 14–15 at Hershey Hall in Chicago. Always eager to celebrate the community's hosting of a national convention, the local press described delegates from all over the country, loitering in the lobbies of the hotels and having exciting discussions and intrigues. The 163 delegates fell far short of the near thousand who had attended the national convention of the Greenback-Labor Party four years earlier. Of that 163, the host state of Illinois had forty delegates, and—with the neighboring states of Michigan (34), and Wisconsin (21)—totaled more than 60 percent of the convention. A handful or less represented other states, including those with the greatest recent history of mass insurgency. Butler's own Massachusetts sent a single delegate, as did New Jersey, and Pennsylvania. New York—the alleged center for Carsey's supposedly massive National Antimonopoly League—dispatched only ten.[12]

Like its predecessors, though, a small but well-organized current with resources found it easy to manage the proceedings, particularly so in this small "national convention." The idea that anyone associated with the Greenback movement on any level had become a contender for the Democratic presidential nomination proved far too irresistible to a figure such as Weaver or Alson J. Streeter, the Illinois Greenbacker, who served as the temporary chair of the Antimonopolist convention. As they discussed resolutions about money policy, women's suffrage, and labor reform, they hoped that antimonopolism would be the prelude to a vast reform of the Democratic Party and then of the nation.

As in earlier national Greenback conventions, those most blatantly concerned about the fate of the Democratic Party bolted to hold a convention of their own. Led by John G. Boyd of the New York Antimonopoly League, the "seceders" reassembled at the Briggs House in Chicago, where they argued that state conventions should precede any national nominating body and that any nominations made before those of the two parties would be "unwise, inexpedient, and contrary to the wishes of true anti-monopolists throughout the country." They complained that the nomination "reduced antimonopolism to "a stepping stone for Gen. Butler to the democratic nomination for president." Some participants in the meeting complained that Shupe and Charles Litchman, one of the Knights of Labor officers closely associated with Butler, had more or less public Democratic connections.[13] Of course, so did Carsey and Boyd, and those who had bolted from the convention were also operating in the interests of the Democrats, but the point of difference seemed to be a matter of degree and how public the associations tended to be.

The Antimonopolist nomination left the Greenbackers few options when they assembled in Indianapolis for a brief two-day convention on May 28. In a convention half the size of that of four years earlier, the fusionists and others seeking to cooperate with Democratic schemes carried disproportionate weight. It was revealing that William H. English, the previous Democratic candidate for vice president, gave the Greenbackers "the free use of his opera-house, etc." Certainly, veteran insurgents still sang the old songs in the lobby, but their very presence inside was now at the sufferance of a national leader of the Democratic Party. The Republican *New-York Tribune* described "the ring-streaked and speckled 'nature' of the motley throng." A solid majority of them voted to nominate Butler, though "about 100 delegates in an assembly of about 450 having refused to vote for him under any circumstances whatever."[14]

As had been frequently the case for other small insurgent national conventions, adjustments in representation provided ample grounds for dissent. The fact that so little substantive grassroots organization existed also made it easy for rival delegations to claim credentials for their state. Thomas A. Bland, an advocate of women's suffrage and Indian rights, represented the District of Columbia and also sought to obtain the credentials of South Carolina and wanted to be able to cast the vote carried weight as though it was that of the entire state's delegation. A particularly nasty clash occurred in the Maine delegation, where the head of the pro-Butler group warned that, if not seated, "we will put the wettest blanket on the Greenback party that is ever felt."[15]

Nevertheless, having Weaver preside helped to hold the convention together. The veteran Arkansas Greenbacker Charles E. Cunningham nominated Butler. A Maryland-born Missouri entrepreneur, Cunningham had gotten rich with a freight service to Mexico during the California Gold Rush of 1849, coupled with judicious investments in railroads and mining. He had spent the war in business in Warrensburg and St. Louis, Missouri, where he opposed both secession and emancipation, before heading to Little Rock. With more impressive credentials, Warren Chase of California, a veteran of forty years of radical activism, seconded the nomination. In the end, Butler got 328 votes, Jesse Harper got 98, Edward P. Allis 21, Solon Chase 2, and David Davis 1.[16]

Because of Congressman Reagan's disinterest in a vice-presidential nomination, the convention went for Absolom Madden West, the Mississippi "labor reformer," who enjoyed more prominence as a railroad developer. Others with equally clear Confederate credentials came to the fore as well. They included John R. Winston and Lee Crandall, as well as General John Tyler of Florida, the son of the president of that name and another ex-Confederate general said to have "declined more positions than any other American living."[17] West's record of having combated the earlier Greenback adoption of more radical measures made him a fitting pick to run with Butler.

Independent Political Action?

The script had accorded the most important act in the Butler campaign to the Democratic National Convention, which failed to follow the script. Butler got a seat on the platform committee when the convention opened on July 8–11 in Chicago.[18] He wrote a minority report, grandiosely declaring that monopoly created "two classes, the very rich and very poor, both of which are equally hurtful to a republic which should give to its people equal rights and equal privileges under the law." Corporations "for the purpose of performing public duties are public servants, and to be regulated in all their actions by the same power that created them at its own will, and that it is within the power and is the duty of the creator to so govern its creature that by its acts it shall become neither a monopoly nor a burden upon the people, but be their servant and convenience, which is the true test of its usefulness."

Correspondingly, Butler argued that workers had the right to "combine and organize for their own protection as capital may be incorporated and combined for its protection." He insisted, oddly, that "labor has a right to demand of the Government to establish tribunals in which these great controversies which may lead to revolution may be judicially and justly determined, with the fullest power to enforce their decrees." He sounded most like Carsey when he declared that "All the great woes upon our country have come because of imported labor."

Remarkably, after all this rhetoric, Butler wound up proposing only a vote on a resolution favorable to the tariff. He agreed that "all materials used in the arts and manufactures, and the necessaries of life not produced in this country, shall come in free" while "all articles of luxury should be taxed as high as possible up to the collection point. He insisted that "the people will tolerate direct taxation for the ordinary expenses of the Government only in case of dire necessity or war," making customs duties on imports particularly essential. Butler warned that the party faced a hundred districts across the country "where a change of 500 men one way or the other" would determine the outcome. Neither persuaded nor intimidated, the Democratic convention voted down Butler's tariff resolution and nominated Cleveland for the presidency and Thomas A. Hendricks for vice president.

The lamps had hardly flickered out at the Democratic convention before Carsey and his New York colleagues went to work on their own promised "national labor Convention," scheduled for Chicago at the end of July. If this convention had initially expected to ratify the Democratic nomination of Butler, it now had to throw cold water on the possibility that he might run on his own. As the "secretary," Carsey asked delegates to send their names to him at No. 42 Duane Street in New York City by July 25 and to forward any later notifications to the convention headquarters at the Briggs House in Chicago.[19] Unlike earlier efforts to deflect the impulse toward independent action, this one sought simply to disparage the entire project.

"All workingmen who are in favor of the protection of American labor from the unfair and unjust competition of pauper and convict labor" would be welcome. In addition to tariffs, though, the body urged a revival of shipbuilding and proposed a National Labor Bureau. More substantially, they offered a clear strategy: "To organize a balance of power; then to go before each convention with certain planks it was desired to have inserted in their platforms."

Before the scheduled opening of the convention, Carsey—now described as the "president" of the organization—stopped briefly in Albany before starting for Chicago, joined by one Henry Wolf. Interesting to note is that an individual of that name had, a decade earlier, led an English-speaking split from Chicago's "Workingmen's Party of Illinois." It had "no sympathy whatever" with the IWA and denounced "the communistic principles which were advocated by the German workingmen."[20]

The summer of 1884 found Wolf the secretary of Carsey's new national labor party. Staying behind, Keogh—already immersed in the Butler campaign along with Shupe—began to worry that Carsey might use the convention to break definitively with Butler and called a meeting of the labor party's national executive committee at No. 3 Prince Street in New York. It denied that "intelligent action" would be possible before Butler and Cleveland responded to their nominations, and it recommended postponing the labor convention until September 1. They not only sent their instructions to their representatives in Chicago but released it to the press, which the reporters took immediately to Carsey and Wolf. The two claimed to have received nothing officially and dismissed it all as an act of factional trickery.[21]

As it became apparent that it was not a trick, Carsey and his immediate allies pointed out that the members of the executive committee "are all here with the exception of Keogh, and they repudiate his action." They flatly refused the instructions from New York for an adjournment until October, saying no individual or committee has authority to postpone. They claimed to have "over one hundred delegates ready to meet at the Briggs House." Among them, adherents of both Butler and James Gillespie Blaine expressed confidence in a favorable outcome.[22]

Carsey also raised expectations for the convention. He anticipated "some 400 representatives of labor organizations from pretty much all the states" to join the hundred already waiting. The convention would engage in "a free, fair and open discussion. Blaine, Butler and Cleveland will have friends there, no doubt, but I am not here now to express any opinion. I have mine, and I propose to speak out in the convention, and not before. The gathering will be strong in men and I believe it will act wisely in the interest of the laboring classes."[23] They also mentioned the presence of trade union officers.

Hours later, though, the "professional labor reformers of New York," Carsey and Wolf, clarified the position of the convention without even convening it. On its behalf, the two issued an address to the national labor party praising Cleveland and recommending that the labor party "make no nominations for president or vice-president." Reporters thought the address came from the Democratic Party. "These two men ought to build monuments of brass to themselves," quipped one observer. "They are not workingmen, and have no authority to represent any labor organization."[24]

However true this characterization of Carsey may have been, he also had years of experience dealing with the press. Indeed, making himself and Wolf the story helped distract a bit from the realities of the convention, the very existence of which appears doubtful. The promised celebrities and the predicted four hundred delegates became accounts of "about 200 delegates." As the reporters got close enough for their own look, organizers started talking of about a hundred, which the *Chicago Tribune* reported as "between thirty and forty delegates." This number, too, proved to be an illusion. "For two weary days a close watch had been held by the Monday morning's contingent for recruits, but up to 9 o'clock Tuesday night not a solitary delegate had come in." A "strong Cleveland man" insisted on the value of the gathering to the press, but seemed to confirm that only Carsey, Wolf, and perhaps three other participants actually voted on the resolutions. The *Tribune* summarized the proceedings thus: "A convention with no delegates stared the committee in the face, and to save themselves they [the committee] proclaimed their objects already accomplished."[25] Such a course may have been new to Chicago, though it had become a regular part of Carsey's *modus operandi* back in New York City.

Of course, later media complaints that they had spent their resources on covering a non-existent convention hardly changed the fact that they had done so.

Moreover, the public criticism from the press invited Carsey to fire back. He now insisted that the convention had been called "simply to devise means to protect the laboring men, not to discuss politics nor to boom any candidate." He also declared that the platforms of both parties had been responsive to organized efforts by workers "and advises the workingmen to vote as they deem proper." They then voted to head home "and meet again in Chicago on June 13, 1888."[26]

To be fair, some reporters did press Carsey. After insisting that electoral deliberations had actually not really been the purpose of a "party" convention, he then plunged into one of his favorite subjects: politics. "The conference making the call for this convention was one of the most authoritative character and thoroughly representative," insisted Carsey, "as much so as any conference could be." "After a long trial in New York," he added, in speaking to the *Chicago Tribune*, "I can say independent action is a failure." "Repeated failures left us worse off each time," said the man who had done so much to ensure those failures, "and after ten years of it we gave up independent action." Reporters did not note that the most important experience Carsey had with independent politics involved their destruction.

Carsey also proposed that workers actually wanted to focus more on legislative and congressional elections. "I believe that fully 10 per cent of the votes in each district are in sympathy with us and that we possess the balance of power in each district," he said. This seemed to argue for using independent action or its threat to wring concessions from one of the dominant parties, but it was not used for that purpose. "Now if we organize not for independent action, but for the purpose of forcing the old parties into adopting our principles, we shall soon acquire all the influence in the national and state legislation," he said. "We need to put our reforms into practical operation far sooner indeed than we could be fighting for our own principles outside of the existing parties."[27] In the course of the 1884 campaign, Carsey's core politics became very evident.

Later, Carsey announced that their organization had simply endorsed Cleveland, even though the announcement detonated an explosive response within his tiny group back in New York. Keogh and "the national committee of the national labor party" condemned the action and authorized the expulsion of Carsey and, if he were a member, of the mysterious Mr. Wolf.[28] Unfortunately for Keogh, though, everybody present must have known how insignificant such a resolution would be.

Carsey and Wolf just shrugged off news of this revolt back home. No sooner had they got back to New York than they summoned a meeting to ratify their actions in Chicago.[29] On August 8, Carsey took the chair at Clarendon Hall and Wolf gave their report, making the astonishing declaration that "both parties had met the labor question fairly, and both platforms had a plank which satisfied the demands of workingmen." This, he argued, represented a realistic improvement over "the golden promise of Anti-Monopolism and Greenbackism." In particular, "the Boss Communist" Carsey took the floor to praise the

Democrats in particular for a platform "broad enough for the laborer and the capitalist to stand upon." The little convention they had held in Chicago had taken the proper course and "left members free to vote as they will." Oddly, though, Carsey also acknowledged that he had simply scratched out the name of one of the delegates to the Chicago convention who had argued for endorsing the Republican candidacy of Blaine.

While 1884 brought no serious shift among the New York Irish to Blaine and the Republican ticket, Patrick Ford, the editor of the *Irish World*, made a considerable effort to shift that important ethnic component of the Democratic base away from the party. In 1880, Ford had tried and failed to use Weaver and the Greenbackers to lure the Irish to independence. After his move failed, he tried in 1884 to lure New York Irish voters to the Republicans. Publications supporting Blaine subsequently published more than a hundred "prominent representatives of labor" said to have endorsed the ticket. In Carsey's circle, rumors that one of their number, James P. Archibald, had become inclined to the Blaine campaign became serious enough to make him emphatically and vehemently deny any affinity for the Republican candidate.[30] To state the obvious, of course, this represented the absolute opposite of the group's approach to the Democratic Party.

That critical August 8 meeting of the group dissolved when a young man named Christopher Malone took the floor to ask Carsey directly "if he ever was a member of a trades union." When Carsey claimed membership in Bricklayer's Union No. 4, Malone flatly denied it. An officer of the union, he offered to open the membership books of the union to prove it. Carsey responded by dismissing the very idea of trade unions as "nonsensical" and run "only for the benefit of a few blood-suckers, and that legislation was the only means of redress for workingmen."

When Malone repeated his offer to document his charges, the meeting passed a resolution to prosecute Malone for libeling Carsey and quickly adjourned. In short order, a small group pretending to be a mass labor organization threatened anyone who questioned the fiction with legal action. The struggle for labor reform had come to turn on people with press connections and the wherewithal to threaten legal action against those who challenged their version of events.

Freedom of speech had become the freedom to shape a public image and to take legal action against anyone who doubted the emperor's new clothes.

Rightly understood, Carsey's independent labor party proved not to have to be either independent, labor, or a party. As far as that goes, a national labor party did not even have to be national. Indeed, it did not have to be much of anything beyond how it chose to present itself.

Butler's Decision

Carsey's organization made its support of Cleveland public, even as Shupe and Keogh became central figures in the organization of a local Central Butler Club, even though their candidate declined to accept the nomination for weeks. The press asked, hopefully, whether "the General is playing with the nominations given him in good faith to make the best possible terms for Butler with the Democrats." "Had he not been disposed to run," replied one of his more trusting supporters, "we would have heard of it long ago."[31] Nevertheless, the candidate's silence followed by his later decision to run inspired considerable press skepticism.

What exactly Butler was up to in 1884 left later commentators and scholars no less befuddled than his contemporaries. The complexity of his character was such that some of the various contradictory explanations were necessarily mutually exclusive. Those who despised Butler liked to recall how, in 1860, he had tried to secure the Democratic nomination for Jefferson Davis, but he never winced at its recollection. When a heckler asked "how many times he voted for Jeff Davis," the general replied that he "voted for Jeff Davis when he was a Union man, and when he turned traitor, he fought him." The heckler responded that Davis had been "about as much a Union man and a friend of the union as you are a laboring man or a friend of the laborer."[32] Butler enjoyed the rough-and-tumble of mass electoral politics, and it remains hard to imagine that he spent much time seriously trying to define himself in a steadfast and ideologically coherent position within a radical tradition.

The simplest and most positive interpretation was that the campaign allowed Butler to raise issues in the electoral arena that would have otherwise remained undiscussed, at least not in any way different from the way the Greenbackers had done so. Very fundamentally, his candidacy had overwritten Greenbackism and taken management of their own future away from the Greenbackers even more ruthlessly than had Carsey. Also, Butler provided voice for the concerns of urban workers, droves of whom were joining the Knights of Labor, which regularly toyed with introducing class politics into the United States.

Nevertheless, Butler remained as elusive as Carsey about whether he would be speaking for an organized movement with a strategy and a direction. The *Idaho Avalanche* acknowledged that Butler claimed that he "desires to lay the foundation for a great party." The paper ceded him "many virtues, but he is a political rogue and his nature will not permit him to change." His campaign inspired another paper to recall the Pennsylvania miner who "caught a young rat in a mine at Honesdale and made a pet of it. The animal repaid the kindness by biting its benefactor with such severity as to cause his death." The moral it drew from this was the Greenbackers should have run one of their own again rather than "a bad rat" like Butler.[33]

Scholars seem to have reached a consensus that Butler functioned as an ally of the Republican campaign. Through June and July, Butler made no secret about having met with Republican officials. The *Boston Herald* reported the candidate's first joining President Chester A. Arthur's secretary of the navy William E. Chandler on board the *Talioposent*. Butler said that he had gone there to meet Lieutenant Adolphus W. Greely, "an old friend and constituent of mine" who had just returned from years in the Arctic. He also knew former congressman Samuel J. Randall, who was also present. Butler claimed to have been on his way to a veteran's reunion where he and Chandler also "made some speeches."[34]

Republicans initially had every reason to hope that Butler's campaign would be a significant help to them, at least in places. The GOP faced a particular challenge where it needed to offset potential losses to rural voters drawn to Greenbackism in the Midwest and from the "mugwump" revolt in their own ranks. The Republicans still felt secure in most of New England, while they realized that they would lose New York, as it had the last time a New Yorker had headed the Democratic ticket. If Butler could siphon off potential Democratic voters, however, particularly urban workers in the Midwest, it might allow the Republicans to keep Indiana and put other states in jeopardy. More important, Republican leaders had felt their base weakening in the Midwest and believed it far better for their disaffected voters to have a third-party alternative than to have them voting Democratic.

Chandler confirmed this arrangement in a letter to Blaine, describing Butler as possibly "an important factor. . . . His vanity, his desire to see how many votes he can get and his hope of getting enough electoral votes to hold the balance of power are all that I can think of to keep him firm." Leading Republicans agreed to subsidize Butler's campaign at the rate of about $5,000 a week, and, at one point, Butler wrote to Chandler, requesting more. The extent to which Blaine's campaign complied remains uncertain.[35]

Butler denied anything untoward in this agreement with the Blaine campaign. At one point, he explicitly claimed to have never taken any Republican money, but, at the close of the campaign, in Boston's Music Hall, he offered a backhanded admission that he had done so. "They say on the other side that money has been paid me to work in the interest of Blaine and the republican ticket," he declared. "Pardon me. If I had remained at my profession, I could have earned at the lowest estimate $5 for $1 that my enemies say I have received."[36] In the end, the promise of Republican funding may have been a factor in his decisions both to accept the nomination on August 6 and to begin his campaign with a foray into the Midwest.

As with all things Butler, though, the story was hardly so simple. His handpicked campaign manager, Colonel Noah Allen Plympton, sat on the Democratic state committee in Massachusetts and made his living in "the ranks of the old guard of Boston life insurance men." He worked for Penn Mutual Life until May 1883, when he left to spend a year as the examiner for the Massachusetts state insurance department. Butler had tried to bring him into the state government, but the Republicans had blocked his confirmation as the state insurance commissioner. Butler expected Plympton, who "spread the gospel of reliable life insurance protection," to provide loyal, dependable, and level-headed advice. Meanwhile, Butler supporters embraced Plympton as "the only true Democratic candidate."[37]

Butler's campaign experienced a remarkable transformation. He certainly sounded unabashedly radical, particularly when he addressed largely working-class audiences in cities such as Pittsburgh. Yet, halfway through his campaign, Butler turned away from those states where the Blaine ticket wanted him to draw off Democratic voters that might otherwise threaten Republican majorities.

Instead, Butler shifted his focus to New York, using the city as his base of operations. With the Democrats exercising a strong hold on the state and running a popular governor of the state for president made it virtually impossible to imagine a place north of the Mason-Dixon line where the Butler campaign could do less damage to the Democratic ticket. Similarly, the expenditure of Butler's time and energy in Cleveland's own state would assuredly contribute virtually nothing to Blaine's hopes in the Midwest.

Despite the chokehold the Democratic machines held on the city, Butler's supporters planned a massive campaign coupled to the extensive coverage by the *Sun*. They started with plans for an "open air demonstration in Union square will be of a magnitude not seen here since the huge popular rally in the same square at the opening of the war in 1861." They expected a variety of nationally prominent insurgent leaders, and rumors suggested that the elderly John C. Frémont, the original Republican presidential candidate, would make an appearance. In the end, thousands marched, including veteran radicals such as William McCabe of the Typographical Union, the Black socialist Frank Ferrell, the veteran of Reconstruction Louis F. Post, the freethinker Edward King, and the German socialists Alexander Jonas and Henry Emrich.[38]

Nevertheless, the National Antimonopoly Party dragged little beyond the shriveling remains of the Greenback-Labor Party back to the polls, where they registered a national showing of only 175,370. The Butler campaign, which had claimed hundreds of clubs in New York alone, actually delivered only a bit more than 17,000 votes there. Insofar as his campaign had hit the upstate communities favorable to Blaine, it had little impact, the *Sun* admitting that "very few votes for Butler came from Republican counties."[39] Finally, Butler himself expressed a smug satisfaction not with a genuinely independent effort but that he had helped elect Cleveland, the first Democrat able to occupy the White House since the Civil War.

Yet, whatever assistance the Butler campaign rendered the Democratic ticket, it had always come with a risk. Carsey—and those who had earlier encouraged his activities—saw Butler's course as fraught with threats to the party, intended or not. What if independent voting were to become a habit? What if the electorate rebelled on a scale comparable to what it had a few years earlier? What if those rushing to Butler's support were to take matters into their own hands and construct what would become an obstacle to Democratic electoral recovery? The ever-dependable Carsey quickly bounced back from the Chicago embarrassments and began whipping his organization into line, attempting to enter the Greenback state convention in Utica. When George Blair and other organizers rejected his credentials and those of eight others who "had come to Utica under the pilotage of W. A. Carsey, who was acting for Commissioner Thompson."[40]

Once more, Carsey and his circle responded by holding their own state convention there and returned to New York. At No. 42 Duane Street, they reassembled as the city's "Executive Committee," the first gathering since the "national convention" fiasco. With Wilson S. Wolf presiding, the committee approved Carsey's report of the proceedings "without discussion." It also declared a third-party movement unnecessary, as both the Democrats and the Republicans had incorporated into their platforms the basic positions of their National Labor Party, while neither the Greenbackers nor Antimonopolists adopted protectionist planks.[41] It soon left little doubt about their preferences between the two major parties.

At the start of September, Carsey publicly refuted Butler's complaint that the Democratic Party had been unresponsive to working-class concerns. To provide some background for his refutation, he headed a well-padded "delegation of workingmen" that approached the Democratic National Committee. In his acceptance letter, Butler referred to the Democratic convention's refusal to include his tariff resolution, declaring that the party had balked at including that "single demand of the workingmen." Carsey and his team took advantage of their meeting with the Democratic leadership to declare that the party had "listened to their arguments and inserted in the Democratic platform every measure demanded by those *bona fide* representatives of labor." It further declared that the Democrats had incorporated "every measure asked for by the League and the Labor party of this State" into the New York platform in 1882, and that the gubernatorial administration of Cleveland "can honestly claim the merit of inaugurating all the measures that have been taken up by other State Legislatures and passed to the great benefit of the working classes and incorporated in the national platforms of the Democratic and Republican parties."[42] In particular, though, the Democratic press across the country often reprinted Carsey's statement as a demonstration of an alleged workers' repudiation of Butler's campaign.

In the middle of the campaign, Carsey capped his efforts with a more general effort to redefine the Independent Labor Party or the New York Antimonopolist League or whatever else it would ever choose to call itself. On September 29, he assembled "about 50 persons" in the basement of Clarendon Hall for their own Antimonopolist convention. The convention explicitly cast its objective not in terms of electoral politics but in terms of efforts simply "to gain legislation in the interests of labor."[43]

Near the top of its list of antimonopolist labor reform demands the body placed "the right to play baseball in Central Park on Sundays and holidays." The game had become a personal obsession for Carsey, who still played as a catcher, and his organization also spearheaded efforts to open the parks to baseball and to secure the use of ball fields at night. Fudging his age to make himself a bit older, his son, "Kid Carsey" joined a local team, the Eccentrics, later signing with New Haven's Atlantic Association, and still later entering the major leagues on the Washington team.[44] The demand for greater working-class access to baseball fields may have addressed a popular concern, though not one that required any serious concession from the authorities.

On the field of politics, the elder Carsey had long experience in the fine art of stretching rules. He had spent years flitting about third-party efforts—alternately promoting and sabotaging candidates, platforms, and strategies and ever avoiding anything that might damage the Democratic Party or that might be seen as doing so by the party managers. Butler took the field to play Carsey's game on a national scale with his own ever-changing rule book. Carsey's responses to Butler—and soon to Henry George—would require a much more explicitly partisan Democratic orientation, albeit with a carefully constructed façade of labor reform and radicalism.

* * *

Where the 1880 Weaver campaign had aimed at building a third party, Ben Butler's 1884 presidential run offered a nominally third-party alternative ultimately as helpful to the Democrats as Carsey's various manipulations. Moreover, the Antimonopolists claimed the numbers, organization, and press coverage to simply eclipse Carsey's operation without deigning to notice. Those who established a Butler headquarters in Union Square proposed to translate Greenbackism into antimonopolism around the more limited goals of antimonopolism, swirling in "a great political cyclone in favor of the People's candidate." Nearby, an "Independent Labor Party" opened a headquarters at Clarendon Hall, where "the People's party" raised "the largest and handsomest Butler and West banner in this city."[45] At that point, then, the city had two independent labor parties, one supporting Cleveland and the other Butler.

Carsey's lilliputian group had taken its own course, as confusing in its way as had been Butler's. Shupe, Keogh, and others popped up regularly in the antimonopolist gatherings, especially in an "Independent-Labor Butler and West Club," while Carsey consistently stood by his earlier denunciation of the insurgent ticket. Simultaneously, Kelly, the veteran leader of Tammany Hall, seems to have made his peace with the national Democratic effort after a private meeting with Cleveland. By mid-October, Cleveland's former critics in the party had fallen into line, even as Butler himself reoriented his activities so as to assist Cleveland.[46] However different and mutually exclusive the strategies of Butler and Carsey may have been in their use of third-party politics, they converged to help elect the first Democrat since before the Civil War to the presidency.

On a deeper level, of course, the expansion of literacy, the new technologies of the press and telegraph, the proliferation of newspapers, and the rise of news syndicates or their practices had shaped the postwar course of mass politics in America. Organized and focused, the printed word demonstrated its power to create the mass perceptions of parties, issues, and candidates. In 1880, it had exercised enough power to define Weaver's Greenback campaign into nothingness, and, in 1884, the *Sun* alone demonstrated how it could conjure an antimonopolist electoral presence from nothing. This reality made it possible for a Carsey to lead a "party" representing "labor" that would be preoccupied with protectionist tariffs and foreigners rather than wages, working conditions, and the length of the workday.

It would also make the continuation of such a world problematic.

CHAPTER 5

The Path through Populism

From Henry George to William Jennings Bryan

The lessons of paternalism ought to be unlearned and the better lesson taught that while the people should patriotically and cheerfully support their government, its functions do not include the support of the people.

—Grover Cleveland [1893]

Ask not what your country can do for you, but what you can do for your country.

—John F. Kennedy [1961]

With the first postwar national triumph of the Democratic Party, William A. A. Carsey had given long revenge of loyal service to the now-solidly-resurgent party. Then well into middle age, his repeated requests for one of the various civil service jobs in the gift bag of the city's machine finally bore fruit. The city government appointed him first an inspector of sewers and bridge masonry and later assigned him to collect personal taxes from those in arrears.[1] In spite of this—or, more accurately, related to this—Carsey nevertheless continued to appear episodically before the public in the guise of a spokesman for labor.

Carsey's career as a designated spokesperson for the "working class" continued to require some deft maneuvering. The new wave of insurgency that arose in 1886, for example, had a specific appeal to workers and their organizations, though its leadership proved no more serious about building a permanent popular party than had been the Antimonopolists two years earlier. By the late 1880s, though, veterans of those earlier derailed attempts made serious renewed efforts to establish a broad new national insurgent coalition, although it, like its predecessors, fractured quickly, partly because of the efforts of Carsey and similar veterans of mass demobilizations. Finally, in the 1890s, Carsey became the only known member of the old American International Workingmens' Association (IWA) known to be present for the founding of the People's Party, and the only one who worked professionally to distract, mislead, and dissolve both.

Circumventing the United Labor Party 1885–87

By the fall of 1885, Carsey began presenting himself as the head of the Antimonopolist Party, even though that party had ceased to exist and Carsey had opposed it when it did. In his self-appointed capacity, however, he clarified an antimonopolism that demanded more government aid to the railroads in the name of benefiting the working people. After all, "the rich people who were interested in railroads had one in operation in front of their palatial residences." Carsey's organization required no independent political action and sent representatives to both the Republican and the Democratic state conventions "to ask that Anti-Monopoly principles be upheld in the party platforms."[2]

Yet there was a well-practiced method to Carsey's purloining of the Antimonopolist moniker. When he had taken up the Greenback designation, for example, he had done so to launch rabid public attacks on "bogus" labor and Greenback groups, doing what he could to fracture the movement for a new party before again shifting publicly or surreptitiously to the Democrats with as much as he could carry with him. Becoming a nominal Greenbacker to denounce Greenbackers had proven an effective way of dividing and diffusing it, and so doing the same with the Antimonopolist Party not only suited his immediate tactical goals, but, over the long run, helped to fuel the myth that somehow the broader Democratic Party reform current had taken up the genuine concerns of the independents, leaving behind only the apparently bull-headed and impractical.

Carsey's antimonopolist self-identification did not preclude his periodic appearance as the leader of his old National Labor Party, which seems to have actually supported Butler. Half a century later, a student of socialist history recalled a group prone to ideological hairsplitting to such an extent that one of its main leaders "now alone, soon developed schizophrenia, and split with himself."[3] This humorous bit of sectariana from the 1930s had already become a reality in the career of Carsey.

Carsey donned his labor party hat to describe the upcoming fall campaign of 1885 as "a contest between the plain people and the men who live by the plunder of your labor." His version of the class struggle explicitly asserted working-class interests as expressed through "the cause of Gov. [David B.] Hill and the State ticket." Other signatories to Carsey's statement may have been trade union officers, but many represented paper organizations under such rubrics as the "Protective Tariff Labor Union" of Fifteenth Assembly District.[4]

After his election, Governor Hill held a private meeting with Carsey and John W. Keogh with "about a dozen retainers" in the Knickerbocker Cottage on Sixth Avenue. Here was where they recast themselves as the Anti-Monopoly League of New York. They attempted, with little success, to get a Tammany thorn into the paw of Mayor William R. Grace, another of the city's oligarchs who enjoyed sufficient wealth to chart a course somewhat independent of that particular party machine. Carsey and Keogh focused on an examination of city works, street cleaning, and "alleged abuses in the Dock and Health Departments." They sent a delegation to City Hall to demand "the wholesale discharge of city laborers," but Mayor Grace declined even to meet with them, after which the group retaliated with a series of "protectionist resolutions."[5]

A few weeks later, in January 1886, "the Anti-Monopoly League" thanked Governor Hill "for his advocacy of labor measures in his message to the legislature." It also urged the governor to appoint Keogh harbor master and Carsey chief of the Bureau of Labor Statistics. In state politics, the organization publicly differed with the Democratic leadership only over its renomination of John O'Donnell as the railroad commissioner, a Tammany ally and something of a reformer in his own right. In February 1886, the *New York Times* noted Carsey's presence with the aging reform Democrat Nelson J. Waterbury at a party meeting in the Thirteenth Assembly District.[6] Nevertheless, Carsey would fade from such public Democratic meetings as the party's need for a seemingly independent labor voice became more important.

The 1886 upsurge of urban labor proliferated the red flags that Carsey and his group had already denounced. Most dramatically, the May outbreak of violence at Haymarket Square in Chicago reflected the demoralization of working-class electoral aspirations. For years, the authorities had simply counted out radical victories at the polls and disintegrated a promising socialist current there. This process coincided with the German repression of a promising social democracy in that country, and many radicals on both sides of the Atlantic adopted the rhetoric, if not fully the ideology, of anarchism. In 1886–87, the brutal suppression of the Chicago movement inspired a broad international reaction and third-party tickets in dozens of communities across the United States.[7] The third-party tickets often represented the residual organizations of the Greenbackers, but the movement also inspired new formations gathered around the Knights of Labor and the revived trade unions, preoccupied with practical action to establish the eight-hour workday.

In short order, a new movement sprang up on Carsey's doorstep, where repressive policies by the local authorities pushed labor organizations toward independent action around the newly arrived western social critic Henry George.[8] Born to the family of a religious publisher in Philadelphia, George had enjoyed a decent formal education and went to Australia and India as a sailor before settling into the printing trade in California in 1858, where he married. Success—even a minimal financial security—came slowly, and he toyed with prospecting in British Columbia or joining a filibustering adventure in Mexico. Instead, he stayed with the *San Francisco Times*, becoming the managing editor, before moving on to other papers, even editing his own, the *Daily Evening Post* and the reform Democratic *Reporter*.

Hard experience rather than theorizing made George's critique of capitalism practical and appealing to a broad public. Although formerly a Lincoln Republican, that party's fostering of railroad and mining corporations in the West pushed him back toward the Democrats. In 1868, his article "What the Railroad Will Bring Us" warned that the innovative technology would tend to make the owners exponentially wealthier and push workers ever deeper into poverty. Largely influenced by the transplanted old land reformer James McClatchy of the *Sacramento Bee*, he began to see the governmental management of a more democratic land ownership as the essential key to making any sort of democracy work. In 1879, George's *Progress and Poverty* expanded on his insight into the link between economic development and mass impoverishment, focusing on the use of rent to exaggerate and deepen economic inequalities.

Progress and Poverty quickly became a major bestseller, said to have eventually surpassed the sales of any other US book abroad. In 1880, George and his family moved to New York City, and his subsequent tour of Ireland and Scotland to promote his ideas made him a movement celebrity, particularly among the Irish. He encouraged the formation of Spread the Light Clubs to promote his ideas. This involved him with old internationalists such as Robert W. Hume and John Swinton, who by then were "utterly disgusted" with the Democrats as "a mere party of expediency." Other veteran land reformers who had also passed through the IWA joined in the 1884 effort to launch the more political American Free-Soil League. George, however, had kept his distance, openly supporting Grover Cleveland for president that year, and dismissing Butler as a "decoy duck" for the Republicans.[9]

When the city authorities moved against local strikers, the Central Labor Union asked George to accept an independent nomination for mayor. He agreed to do so, should the trade unions demonstrate enough support to ensure that he would not be waging yet another tiny *pro forma* labor campaign. They did so, developing a mass United Labor Party. The two dominant parties also offered strong candidates. The Democrats ran Abram S. Hewitt of Cooper, Hewitt, and Company, and Police Commissioner Theodore Roosevelt won the Republican nomination.[10]

As George's United Labor Party threatened to upend politics in the city, Hewitt and the Democrats relied heavily on Carsey and his operation. In mid-September, he, Keogh, and Theodore E. Tomlinson met state officials in Albany, carrying a letter of support from Henry Nichols of the old National Antimonopoly League. They agreed on a plan of action mapped by Governor Hill to recast the Democratic ticket as a labor reform campaign endorsed by various workers' organizations, including those invented and named by Carsey and his crowd.[11]

On September 22, Carsey knocked off work early as an inspector in the Department of Public Works to assist the Hewitt campaign in what the *New York Times* described as an effort "to try and split up the labor vote in the interest of the Democratic Mayoralty candidate." The United Labor Party's *Standard* rightly complained that the would-be "saviors of society" used "a certain employe [*sic*] in the public works, an inspector of sewer connections of the name of Carsey, to manufacture bogus trade unions and K. of L., assemblies for newspaper consumption."[12] This role must have become increasingly difficult for Carsey and should have fooled only those papers that had a vested interest in being fooled.

At a meeting on October 22, Carsey of the "Independent Labor Party" turned both barrels on the United Labor Party (ULP) campaign, blasting George as "a crank, come from no one knows where." While belittling Theodore Roosevelt, the Republican candidate, he also praised the Republicans generally, perhaps to avert any possible backlash against the Democrats for his actions. Although subsequently suspended from his position as inspector in Public Works for his overt political work, Carsey publicly declared his confidence that he would be reinstated.[13] How could he not be?

Aping the Central Labor Union's petition campaign, Hewitt solicited labor pledges to support him. He not only "issued blanks calling for signatures to a pledge to vote for him for Mayor," but began "quietly catering to the George people by having his 'workers' give it out that he really believes in nearly all that George teaches. The manufacture of bogus labor news has been stopped by order of the gentleman in charge of the literary bureau." As part of this disinformation effort, Carsey's Independent Labor Party and his Antimonopolist

League also produced "purely imaginary reports of the decline of the George movement."[14]

In the end, George and the ULP outpolled Roosevelt and the Republicans, but Hewitt prevailed through what George's supporters suspected to have been a miscount. Throughout, the antimonopolists—Carsey, John F. Henry, and their allies—did their best to exaggerate Hewitt's base by making astronomical claims about their own membership. Carsey said his league had 5,000 members in the city and 20,000 in the state. The only context for such claims might be the tall tales Walter H. Shupe told about his own Sons of Columbia. "Father Columbia" himself had emerged unscathed from his wild claims about the size of his organization (the reality of which faced an obvious test in the pathetic vote totals for Butler in the city).[15]

After Hewitt's victory, the press seemed more inclined to present the size and scale of such groups more realistically. The Republican *New York Times* noted that Governor Hill had given Carsey his job in return for his role as "the leader of one of the anti-monopoly bodies which makes themselves known during State and local elections. Nevertheless, in the aftermath of the election, the *Standard* thought Carsey's group would be "like the gangs of street laborers that got a job at the same time [and] must go until society is pushed into a corner again. He is discharged from the public works."[16] This last point, though, proved as misleading as Carsey himself had noted, because he went on to other government jobs.

Early in 1887, Carsey testified before a committee of the state assembly to present what he claimed to be a real workingman's position on "the labor problem." Supported by credentials no more reasonable than they ever had been, he denounced strikes in general, particularly that of the Knights of Labor against Jay Gould's railroads in the southwest. He claimed Terence V. Powderly, Samuel Gompers, and other leaders of striking labor organizations enjoyed large salaries and characterized one of the local leaders as "a very shallow man when he testified that the Government should take hold of the railroad, telegraph, and other business of the country." Unions went on strike, declared Carsey, only because their leaders had not been sufficiently bribed with "beer money." Echoing Governor Hill, he urged "compulsory arbitration" as an alternative to strikes. Also, in direct contradiction to his claims of affiliation with the labor movement, Carsey freely acknowledged that his current was "denounced by labor organizations, which had, he bitterly complained, reaped the advantages of its labors."[17]

Months later, Carsey, Keogh, and their colleagues took the "Anti-monopoly League of the state of New York" back into the spotlight for use "in cities where there is political agitation." Their circular placed select points of the declaration of principles of the Knights of Labor alongside the Democratic platform of the New York party and asserted that the Democrats had promulgated every plank. This, they argued, demonstrated that the Knights could gain everything they wanted by state legislation through the Democratic Party, acting as "the friend and champion of the rights of the working people."[18]

Meanwhile, the ULP that had gelled around George's campaign expedited Carsey's plan by sputtering into oblivion. Roosevelt had dismissed the George movement as simply the work of yet another interest group over which the two parties would compete. From George's perspective, the ULP had made its point, and its survival threatened to move it in directions that would misrepresent his views. In the end, George inadvertently validated Roosevelt's point by arranging for the party to both purge the socialists in the city and repudiate erstwhile allies upstate. The trickle of newspaper accounts that covered the dwindling meetings of separate United Labor Parties included notice of "a hurried meeting of the Committee on credentials" that recommended that "the credentials of George D. Lennon of the VIth District, who had been more or less identified with W. A. A. Carsey and his crowd, be not accepted."[19]

Other forces tore at the unity of the movement. Like George, the trade unionists had wanted to register a protest vote but had not signed on to launch an ongoing political party. Also, the Knights of Labor under Powderly shared Carsey's interest in protective tariffs, in direct contrast to George's advocacy of "free trade," to which some—but not most—Democratic leaders were predisposed. Also, that active intervention of the Vatican, which suspended and then excommunicated Father Edward McGlynn for his political activities, intimidated working-class Catholics, taking a heavy toll among the working-class Irish that had embraced the movement.

The ULP seemed to share the fate of Butler's Antimonopolist Party, but the former grew from a genuine labor upsurge. George, unlike Butler, made a serious effort to get the strongest third-party total he could, if even just as a single-shot protest vote, an effort reflected in its impressive turnout. At the same time, the ULP left a significant residue of sentiment favoring independent political action, partly in the analogous labor party efforts in cities beyond New York and also in the revitalized local Greenback currents.

Even in New York City, the purging of the socialists led to a serious effort to rebuild their own older party organization of the 1870s on their rapid growth as part of the George movement. As that broader movement withered, a Columbia law professor named Daniel DeLeon moved into the leadership of the organization that now called itself the Socialist Labor Party (SLP). Eschewing all association with such formations as the Greenback-Labor Party (GLP), the

ULP or the later Populists, DeLeon reorganized the SLP, which would survive for more than a century.[20] Socialists, reorganized as a party, would become a persistent consideration in any later independent political movements.

Addressing the Union Labor Party 1887–89

In February 1887, the remnants of the Greenbackers across the country, together with bits and pieces from various local labor-party movements, sent representatives to a convention in Cincinnati's Music Hall. Eager to avoid a repeat of 1884, when Butler's supporters held an early convention to present more serious insurgents with a *fait accompli*, this gathering took place more than a year and a half before the presidential election to declare themselves the Union Labor Party.

Alongside the founding convention of the ULP, Carsey chaired a meeting of the Antimonopoly League in the Queen City Hotel on February 21, with James E. Curtiss of Kansas serving as the secretary of record. Newspaper reporters became commonly inexact in giving names—middle initials even more so—and the census recorded nobody of that name in Kansas. The most likely individual referred to here may have been "James W. Curtiss," later a police commissioner in Buffalo. As a former resident of Kansas, Carsey might well have taken it on himself to assign proxy credentials for the state. The meeting explicitly "decided not to attend the Greenback Labor Conference for the reason that it is the purpose of the managers of that conference to arrange for the nomination of Presidential candidates, which is contrary to the policy adopted by the Anti-Monopoly League of supporting candidates and parties who will adopt anti-monopoly principles."[21]

Fragments of the now-fragmented Henry George movement in New York had their own reasons for balking at participation. *The Standard*, the organ of the largest remaining body of the Georgists, described the convention as

> a sort of omnium gatherum of all shades of "reformers," deriving what little representative character it had from the delegates of western greenbackers' and farmers' associations. There were some few representatives of isolated assemblies of the Knights of Labor, but the great bodies of organized workingmen, the central labor unions of the large cities and, with one or two local exceptions, the branches of the united labor party and the land and labor clubs now forming throughout the country refused to have anything to do with it.[22]

It singled out, with special annoyance, the presence of Carsey, Lennon, and their old antimonopolist ally Dr. Ferdinand Seeger. "In New York," quipped *The Standard*, "these three names would not be taken as representing three votes."[23]

The Standard used the presence of Carsey and his followers at the end of the process to discredit the entire enterprise, saying that they would simply mimic an insurgency for their own purposes. "There is little shrewdness shown in the employment of these men to plead a party's cause with organized workingmen," it declared.

> They are not members of any labor organization; they have been ruled out of the State workingmen's assembly, and their names have been bandied about in every party and every hall as self-constituted leaders who hold their influence on sale. So intangible is this influence that workingmen have ceased to resent their assumption of being possessed of any, but merely regard with amusement their remarkable effrontery and their successive alliances with aspiring but not wily politicians.[24]

More realistically, though, George and his immediate circles actually vied with Carsey as a means of mediating labor discontent into pressure on the Democrats.

George's followers in Philadelphia and elsewhere also used its suspicion of Carsey, Lennon, and A. H. Gallahue to justify its hostility to the new ULP, in which none of those individuals actually participated. "While fully sympathizing with the spirit of your letter," responded one of the Georgists to the new party, "and believing that the better element of the union labor party will undoubtedly unite with us next year, yet it is impossible for us to unite under your call, and even more impossible for us to consent to become fellow workers with such politicians for revenue only as Carsey, Lennon, Gallahue and others prominent in your party in New York state, who openly acknowledge that they are for sale to the highest bidder, and whose weight will be too heavy a handicap for you to succeed."[25]

The reorganizing SLP, though embroiled in a bitter dispute with George and the Single Taxers, had the same response to Carsey and his group. The Socialists correctly described Carsey as "the well-known 'bricklayer without a trowel,'" whose presence should be "enough to disgust any honorable person with the whole affair." They recalled his betrayal of the Antimonopolist and the United Labor tickets, noting that he had represented "a different labor organization every night in the week; figuring as the bricklayers, the boilermakers, the carpenters, an assembly of the K. of L., or a section of the Central Labor Union, to suit his varying tastes. When *John Swinton's Paper* also warned about the gullibility of taking an organization on face value, the press generally published his letters under various cognomens, announcing the desertion of organizations "which did not exist." In any event, these honestly radical papers used the shadow of the Carsey group to disparage the largest of the immediate insurgent threats, suggesting that one "might call the Union [Labor] Party the Carsey party."[26]

The SLP's *Workmen's Advocate* of the SLP rightly lumped them in with similar operations. It noted that "the Grand Council of the Independent Labor Party of the United States," met in Detroit to support the Republican presidential contender, Benjamin Harrison, calling it "a humbug. It is in the interest of a squad of political mercenaries who cannot poll one hundred votes the whole country over." The socialists found it "very much like the grand humbugs who organized "labor parties" in the interest of the "democratic" gang, mentioning George, Carsey, Kehoe, [Lee] Crandall and the rest." Edward Goldsmith, a Socialist from the city's tenth assembly district also dismissed the entire of the Union Labor Party in New York City as "a sham headed by men like Carsey, Kehoe, and Lennon, who are in for the capital that they can make."[27]

In fact, Governor Hill called Carsey and his people into a strategy meeting in an Executive chamber in Albany. He suggested that they should "clean out" the Union Labor Party. When that party held a state conference in Elmira in June 1877, Carsey, Gallahue and the rest showed up with credentials from the long-defunct Antimonopoly League. The *New York Times* quipped that "the tail of a very long Democratic codfish hung out in full view from under the anti-monopoly skirts of each of these gentlemen."[28]

By the start of 1888, Carsey and his followers openly claimed credit for having elected Hill governor, for having secured Hewitt's victory as mayor, and for thwarting the menace to civilization that Henry George had been. The *New York Times* reported a meeting on February 7, 1888, noting that their gathering at No. 116 West Thirty-Third Street "sometimes consists of six and at other times of three members, according to the exigencies of the times." Carsey, Keogh, and George Blair dominated the proceedings. When a reporter pressed him, Keogh admitted the entire operation to be "composed of only nine men." Further pressed, he asked, "Are all the citizens who vote the Democratic and Republican ticket actual members of these organizations?" Unimpressed, the reporter compared them to the notorious "tailors of Tooley street," the alleged authors of grandiose proclamations in the name of the entire British working class.[29] In this case, though, it did not represent a small labor sect, but a Democratic operation ultimately directed out of the governor's mansion.

This did not prevent them from continuing to perform functions beyond the realm of electoral politics. In mid-February 1888, Carsey reappeared as the president of the Antimonopoly League in more government hearings. The Senate Committee on post offices and post roads solicited testimony on the idea of government ownership of the telegraph. On behalf of the working class, Carsey assured the honored senators and the press that the most militant and clear-eyed of the toiling masses opposed the government purchase and ownership of the telegraph, "but was strongly in favor of the regulation of telegraph lines by the government." Two years later, Carsey made a belated curtain call on the same stage to repeat this argument in defense of the telegraph companies.[30]

In June, Carsey—at the time briefly a subway inspector for a private transit company—presided over what the press described as a meeting of four hundred at Clarendon Hall. The *New York World* reported that the meeting launched a "Subway Workmen's Association," though nobody tried to discern the proportion of participants present who actually worked for the subway. Brushing aside issues like pay, this reportedly mass meeting of alleged laborers and mechanics readily adopted Carsey's position protesting "the employment of foreigners on important State works."[31]

Meanwhile, Shupe issued accounts of his own greater successes. He announced the revival of his shipping service to Albany, under a labor syndicate of no less than 600,000 members and managing to claim that number without choking. "Last time Father Shupe undertook to blast monopoly sky high the highhanded despoilers scuttled his ship and drove it ashore, and finally squelched the monopoly by buying the steamer and taking it away from him." This time, he also planned to charge $1 for meals on the boat. "It is the intention of the anti-monopolist to make stops at nearly every village on the shores of the Hudson and thus pick up many a dime in this way." Although Shupe said he would divide a third of the profit among the crew, they seemed to be not sanguine about receiving a fortune at the end of the year."[32] Once more, this antimonopolism was of the kind that defined itself as simply opposed to the companies in competition with their own.

In the end, though, who could resist the rough-and-tumble of politics? On February 8, 1888, Carsey and his people decided to skip the upcoming May convention of the Union Laborites and schedule their own national convention on August 1 in New York. They convened it initially under the rubric of the Antimonopolist Party.[33] It likely inspired predictable reactions among those who actually had actually supported Butler in the previous presidential election, few though they had been.

Perhaps just to cover the bases, Carsey also later showed up in the national capital for another convention. An earlier conference of the Equal Rights Party called a convention on Washington's birthday. Belva Ann Lockwood, a local lawyer with a national reputation, had maintained the name, if not the organization, for more than a dozen years, beginning with Victoria Woodhull's abortive attempt to launch a presidential campaign. By 1884, though, she had sought agreement with a handful of Greenbackers and other reformers who supported women's suffrage and agreed to place a major emphasis on it. A reporter described the forty-five delegates attending the starting session as having pockets stuffed with tracts and one of them simply shrugged an admission that theirs would be a cranks' convention, another "sort of *omnium gatherum*, including all who are dissatisfied with the old parties." The reporter summarized their sense that "all the profits of labor instead of going to the corporations and capitalists should go to the government for the benefit of the whole people."[34] Yet the platform they adopted centered on Greenbackism, with little attention to suffrage or socialism.

Reflecting the scope of these new kinds of concerns, the convention almost immediately renamed itself the Industrial Reform Party (or sometimes just the Industrial Party in the press). Oscar P. McMains, the leader of the movement against the Maxwell Grants in New Mexico, sat among its founders. Robert S. Tharin, once a fiery southern white opponent of secession and the restoration of the planters to power had since become a loyal Democrat and had no reason to be there other than from motives similar to those that brought Carsey there.

With the platform out of the way, the even smaller attendance the second day decided simply to plunge right into nominating a national ticket, despite the misgivings of some delegates about whether it would be premature. Albert Ellis Redstone entered the convention as a New York native and was roughly fifty years of age. Although he had run for office as a Greenbacker, he became better known as an inventor and engineer. He had an industrial operation going in Indianapolis during the Civil War, which offered the War Department a pioneering design for a "land monitor." He afterward married and moved his family to California, where he became active in the local Workingmen's Party—that misnamed anti-Chinese organization—before continuing through the Greenbackers into the mysterious western "Red International."[35]

As Redstone's running mate, the convention selected one J. A. Colvin of Kansas as Redstone's vice-presidential candidate. It most likely referred to Jerome Ashby Colvin, a horse and mule dealer in Topeka then in his mid-twenties. If so, his brother-in-law, Charles Curtis, much later actually did become the vice president of the United States under Herbert Hoover.

After all this overreaching, an understandably flustered Lockwood decided again to run her own campaign once more. She initially picked Alfred Henry Love of the Universal Peace Union for vice-presidential candidate, but he had no interest in being any kind of governmental executive. And so Lockwood replaced him with Charles Stuart Weld, the son of the abolitionists Theodore Dwight Weld and Angelina Grimké.[36]

In mid-May, the Union Labor Party reconvened in Cincinnati to pick its national slate. The subheading of the article in the *Cincinnati Enquirer* declared, "Nearly a Thousand Delegates Now in the City." The *Commercial Gazette*, more accurately, described the arrival of hundreds of delegates, including "prominent Laborites, both Union and United, from all parts of the country."[37] In reality, the ULP—the followers of Henry George without Henry George himself—arrived to hold a rival convention alongside that of the Union Labor Party. The new party nominated two former leaders of the GLP, Alson J. Streeter, who had run for governor of Illinois eight years earlier, and Charles E. Cunningham of the Little Rock Party. Other old Greenbackers, such as General James B. Weaver, did their best to unite their old coworkers behind the Union Labor ticket, while General Butler very predictably did not.

To clarify, then, the national election of 1888 found opponents of the two-party system fielding competing tickets by the Union Labor, United Labor, Industrial Reform, Equal Rights, and Socialist Labor Parties, not to mention a certain American Party, which fielded a slate aimed at breaking the alleged power of freemasonry over politics.

Eager to do their bit, "the Carsey-Keogh Anti-Monopoly Party, which is composed of the afore-named worthies and a baker's dozen of other political strikers" gathered on September 18 at the Metropolitan Hotel to hold their own "national Convention." The *New York Times* reported that they had gathered "in force, and the entire party found plenty of lounging place in one room yesterday."[38] Their course could not have been more confusing to possible insurgents.

In the end, none of it mattered for the final outcome of the election. Cleveland's plan to reduce tariffs tarnished him with a pro-British reputation that particularly alienated the Irish in his own state, where he had never actually placated Tammany. Amid the usual volley of charges about fraud, Republican Benjamin Harrison defeated the Democratic incumbent Cleveland in the Electoral College, though not in the popular votes. The official returns reported well under 150,000 insurgent votes nationally. Of these, fewer than 3,000 voted for Robert H. Cowdery of the United Labor Party—the tiny Georgist splinter without George—and the vote was apparently even lower for the newly reorganized SLP, which nominated a slate of presidential electors pledged to vote "No President."[39]

In spite of Cleveland's defeat nationally, Governor Hill won reelection. His administration, though, faced a rising tide of reform sentiment. In 1888–89, the legislature passed two bills requiring the state to print an official ballot and Hill vetoed both. He denounced the proposal as a foreign innovation out of place in the virtually perfected US institution. By 1890, though, Hill was ready to compromise.[40] These preliminary measures led to a series of reforms that extended government management over the ballot, which included access to the electoral process by new parties. That rang the death knell for the relatively easy and democratic formation of such electoral currents.

Those very reforms ultimately marginalized the value of a "labor leader" such as Carsey, though their usefulness had already begun to fade and would continue to fade rather than end abruptly. The city directory described him as a builder in 1888 and 1889, but he more regularly filled a series of government positions. Finally, he landed a federal position in the Pension Office in Washington with a salary of $840 a month. In the process, in July 1890, Carsey filed his own pension claim as an invalid from injuries sustained during his service in the Civil War.[41]

Through all this, though, Carsey regularly commuted back to New York and continued to play a role in local affairs. When doing so, he identified himself not as a federal civil servant but as a "labor agitator." He headed a delegation of his colleagues to an April 1889 hearing in favor of the construction of elevated trains. There Gallahue spoke for "the Workingmen's Municipal Reform League," while Lennon described himself as a "radical," though the directories had him in "real estate." Both urged the government to clear the way for the construction of a special route for an express train to Harlem. (It might be relevant to note that Carsey, at this point, had a home on 146th Street.)[42]

With the division of the insurgent currents in 1888 and the defeat and disintegration of its largest component supporting the Streeter-Cunningham ticket, Carsey repeated what he did after the disintegration of Butler's campaign four years earlier. He and his group now began to function as "the Union Labor Party," which no longer actually existed and had not enjoyed their support when it did. Under this banner, Carsey made an issue of the state's use of contractors to circumvent the law mandating the eight-hour day for labor on public works. He suggested a committee reporting "to the proper authorities and have the wicked contractors severely punished." At the same time, his new Union Labor Party called for a county convention on October 24 and sent him, Lennon, and John Cavanagh to consult both the Democrats and the Republicans, presumably to find which would be the less overtly hostile to enforcement of a Democratic law.[43] There would be no serious doubt about whether they would find Governor Hill's party the more amenable.

In the end, the "party" held a County Committee meeting in lieu of that scheduled convention. It endorsed a ticket supposedly nominated by "the citizens mass meeting—something the local papers apparently never noticed. Carsey and other speakers offered mild criticism of the city government for its alleged use of "alien 'scabs'" on the subway. The Union Labor Party nominations included the more prominent candidates of Tammany Hall.[44]

Having successfully mobilized the righteous anger of the proletarian masses to blunt the drive for government ownership of the railroad and telegraph, thwart independent political action, and rally the international working class against the threat of alien scabs," Carsey rallied his forces for the final conflict.

One can only hear the flapping of wings, as the chickens began to come home to roost.

Among the Populists 1890–93

As Carsey and his cronies continued to function as representatives of labor, the press began balking more regularly at simply accepting that self-description. In part, the newspapers had to address the more discerning perspective of a growing working-class readership informed by a "new unionism" on both sides of the Atlantic. When Carsey and Lennon claimed the mantle of the workers when they invited the Board of Aldermen to "a mass meeting to be held at Cooper Union, to make proposals to the Congress" in late 1889, the Central Labor Union publicly objected to the assertion that the Union Labor Party represented a labor initiative. Lennon, it added, was a member of no labor organization "and has no authority to issue a call for a meeting, which it is asserted represents the union men of this city."[45]

Undismayed, the group modified nothing about its claims, even as it waged a truly remarkable 1890 fight to protect employers from having to pay wages to their workers every week. Bosses in the building trades, such as Carsey still was at times, had been particular offenders in delaying the payment of wages. Early that year, the *New York World* had taken up the issue, an effort endorsed by the Brooklyn Central Labor Union and other labor bodies, including the state American Federation of Labor. Proponents noted the opposition of "[William] A. A. Carsey and his clique of the so-called Union Labor party," correctly describing them as tools of monopolies."[46]

Matters came to a head on March 5, 1890, in "a veritable Donnybrook Fair" at Albany.[47] Carsey and his allies turned up at a hearing before the New York State Senate Committee on Miscellaneous Corporations to speak at legislative hearings to give voice to the apparently voiceless working-class aspirations to not be paid regularly. The amused socialists reported that "Carsey, Lennon and Gallahue, who appeared before the Senate Committee to oppose the bill, were denounced as a clique of frauds, who have no right to speak in the name of labor."[48]

When the group attacked State Senator George Roesch, he replied in "appropriate denunciatory terms of those labor dead beats and political tramps, W. A. A. Carsey and A. H. Gallahue, who were here to oppose it." Carsey responded by threatening Roesch with the righteous wrath of the people should he ever dare show his face again in New York City. Then, after the hearing adjourned, the fifty-year-old Carsey knocked down Curtis Dunham, a labor reporter for the *New York World*, whom Carsey alleged to have written a "defamatory story against him."

When an assembly member tried to get between the combatants, "a son of Carsey 's jumped from behind" and struck him. With Kid Carsey the ballplayer in the fray, "Old man Carsey" punched James A. Buckbee, a former nominee for railroad commissioner. Buckbee seems to have given as good as he got, as "for three or four minutes the corridor was a bedlam." Not bad for an old soldier pensioned as an invalid.[49]

Periodic exchanges of angry words and threats, coupled to intramural fisticuffs, had long been part of the price white subalterns paid to participate in the political process. At this point in history, however, the world had moved on to a point where law officers intervened. The next time Carsey returned to Albany from his federal job in Washington, police officers arrested him.

The *New York Times* prefaced its report of Carsey's breaking the law with a misdescription of him as "a labor agitator." On April 4, the accused presented himself before a judge with "two or three members of his notorious gang of bogus labor representatives" and pleaded that they were not ready for a trial. His bondsman, Keogh, asked that Carsey be released to his charge and the court postponed its preliminary hearing until Thursday.[50]

Carsey's allies did their best to mobilize as many as they could of those toiling masses who had been outraged at the attempt of the government to foist regular pay on them. The Central Labor Union responded by, once again, placing him and his group at arm's length. When Gallahue and others showed up with credentials from a dubious labor organization, one of the unionists denounced him and "that notorious boodler and juggler Wm. A. A. Carsey," suggesting that Carsey explain to "Gallahue and his companions of the hod hoisters why scabs and defaulters are not admitted to the C.L.U."[51]

When Carsey appeared before the bench on April 10, he had yet to formulate a better defense than an assertion that he had been "abused" for opposing "the Weekly Payment bill." The *New York Times* did report that the Executive Committee of the Union Labor Party met at 193 Bowery to declare their complete support for lower telephone bills, better mass transit, the tariffs, and "the action of W. A. A. Carsey at Albany." By then, though, the *Times* added that "the Executive Committee . . . composes almost the entire party here."[52] In the big picture, it seemed as though the working class found better things to do than to defend Carsey's attempt to protect it from getting paid every week.

All these events took their toll on Carsey and the old gang. For twenty years, he had elbowed his way into the nominal leadership of major third-party movements and worked for their demise. It must have been demoralizing to find themselves confined to the role of mere lobbyists. And facing legal action, to boot, must have been another blow.[53]

Their last hurrah of sorts was news of the explosive threat of a new mass insurgency from the West. Transplanted New Yorkers, among others, had organized a Farmers' Alliance in Texas that quickly acquired a mass membership, a cooperative ideology, and a militant willingness to confront the Democratic authorities. It spread into Kansas, where the remnants of the GLP and ULP rallied to the Alliance cause and confronted the Republicans who dominated government there.[54] Starting in Kansas and Texas in 1890, the Farmers' Alliance formed the core of a new People's Party.

In December 1890, Carsey and Gallahue headed for Ocala, Florida, for a convention of the Farmers' Alliance called to put together a set of demands. Among others, the Alliance welcomed "W. H. Carsey" of Washington, DC, representing the "Anti-monopoly League" and Gallahue from a "New York Workingmen's Reform League." Eager to hear representatives of the working class, the convention permitted each of them to speak "for half an hour or more." One account indicates that Carsey and Gallahue urged the Alliance to admit urban workers and kindly offered their services to implement the process on their behalf.[55]

Of course, some militant Populists with good ears and ties to the radical and labor movements back east caught on to the game rather quickly. *The American Nonconformist and Kansas Industrial Liberator*, a major voice of the insurgent wing of the party, noted the presence of "one W. A. A. Carsey, the bogus working man of New York City, who was hired to oppose the weekly, wage payment bill at Albany last winter." "The honest workmen of the city and state, who have long known Carsey as a vulgar fraud and corrupt ruffian, will make a note of the fact they are scattered throughout the entire land." It grouped him with "the political pimps and cesspool cleaners, for the two old parties that oft times join the Alliance and other reform organizations for the purpose of deceiving and misleading the honest people, that they may have trading stock to transfer to either of the old parties at election time." Nevertheless, the Republicans had reasons of their own later in the year to treat the protariff Carsey to a meeting for what might later be called a photo op with President Benjamin Harrison.[56] None of this meant anything in terms of the group's automatic affinity for the Democratic ticket.

Perhaps in response to the circulation of warnings about using credentials from the Antimonopolists, Carsey and his allies convened as the Executive Committee of "the Union Labor Party." It met at Military Hall in the Bowery "to elect delegates to the Cincinnati Convention of the Farmers' Alliance and other organizations" slated for May 1891. The *New York Times* reminded readers that the party "consists of W. A. A. Carsey, McGallahue [*sic*], and about a dozen lesser lights."[57] Nevertheless, Carsey's minuscule party sent a delegation that tried hard to blend into the crowds at a large convention.

By then, though, Carsey and the delegation of his minuscule "party" were hardly alone in trying to blend into the crowds at that convention. The Socialist Labor press mentioned "Major Carsey" among other "scarred veterans" with invented or exaggerated military titles. It asked "what may we not expect from that patriotic, honest and disinterested body? By the way, which of the two old parties is paying for the trip of those independent bushwackers?"[58]

Carsey, Gallahue and other "independent bushwackers" also turned up at the February 1892 convention in St. Louis, which voted to call a nominating convention in Omaha in July. This time, though, Powderly of the Knights of Labor recognized them. From the chair, he singled them out "as two pretended delegates on the floor, who were hostile to the movement and were there only to do it harm." He denounced them "as traitors to the cause of labor and demand[ed] their expulsion."[59]

Once back home, Carsey and his circle exacted their modest revenge on Powderly by holding their July 1892 meeting "at their rooms in Clarendon Hall"—this time acting as the "Knights of Industry." They not only passed resolutions on the strikes at Homestead and Coeur d'Alene but addressed issues that came up at the recent Democratic National Convention. Carsey's old manager, Governor Hill, had challenged Cleveland for the presidential nomination, which made it possible for Carsey to strike two birds with one stone. The meeting attributed the lowering of wages to lower tariffs on steel and lead "and the competition of cheap foreign labor," blaming both on Cleveland.[60]

Through all this, Gallahue assisted those Republicans eager to renominate Benjamin Harrison. Gallahue presented himself at the Republican National Convention in Minneapolis as the leader of the "Workingmen's Municipal Reform League of New York City." With him he brought a committee of "the Associated Trades of New York City" claiming to represent eight thousand workers in eleven labor organizations at the Republican National Convention in Minneapolis.[61] Clearly, Republicans proved themselves to be as remarkably desperate as they were entirely ignorant of the labor movement.

In the course of all these activities, an intriguing little Populist Party emerged in New York City with a county convention on October 10 in the small assembly hall of the Cooper Institute. The body well represented the radical wing of the local workers' movement, and they nominated Henry A. Hicks, a leader of the Knights of Labor, for mayor. In addition to various former members of George's United Labor Party, such as Timothy Putnam Quinn, the socialist leader of District 49 of the Knights. The locals though, had already gotten the number of Carsey, Gallahue, and "the bogus labor men."[62]

Populism reached its apex in the 1892 presidential election, with a ticket headed by the old GLP warrior, James B. Weaver of Iowa, coupled to James G. Field of Virginia, expressing the discontent of the West and South with the course taken by the Republicans and Democrats. The party totaled more than a million votes; carried Kansas, Colorado, Idaho, and Nevada; and won Electoral College votes from North Dakota and Oregon. The strength in the Far West reflected the increasing influence of mine owners interested in promoting "free silver," which, after the election, began to crowd out the concerns of farmers.

Meanwhile, Carsey and his little New York City operated independently to jockey for some kind of national recognition and respectability in a western and southern movement. As late as the spring of 1893, *The Progressive Farmer* of Winston, North Carolina, acknowledged receipt of five subscribers from "W. A. A. Carsey, President of the Knights of Industry, New York City." Kansas Populists, some of whom must have recalled his time there, proved more skeptical. When the Republican press in Kansas once more cited protariff resolutions by Carsey's "workingmen," a Farmers' Alliance paper responded with information that came directly from a New York correspondent, who wrote,

> The organization in question, if it can be called an organization, consists mainly of W. A. A. Carsey, John Kehoe and a fellow named Gillhooly [*sic; meaning* Gallahue]—all three labor "fakirs" and campaign strikers, fellows who for a consideration, boom "protection" or "free trade" according as they are paid by the unsophisticated politicians who imagine these gentry have any following among the working people here. We have in this city quite a number of such "striking organizations" both Democratic and Republican; they pass resolutions to order, or pass them before they receive orders, and then try to sell them. These "organizations" sprout up during a campaign, especially a presidential one, regularly every time.

Workers in New York, the writer assured them, "take no stock whatever in this protection or free trade clap trap. Those who do so, do so for income only."[63]

The triumph of "free silver" among the Populists upended whatever stability existed among its adherents in New York City. "Little was heard but recrimination" when they met to discuss which groups had the best claim on representing the community in the national bodies of a reordered party. Carsey, Keogh, and the "crowd from the Anti-monopoly League" sought to resolve the problem in a shouting match with genuine radicals such as Colonel Richard J. Hinton, who may have known Carsey from their days in the International, if not their wartime service. After a brawl broke out, the police intervened to break it up. That summer, though, organizers of the People's Party told the New York *Evening World* that "the New-York delegation, which will be headed by W. A. A. Carsey and James [*sic*] Kehoe, will be refused admission" because all the other contending factions saw them as "traitors to the party."[64]

Nevertheless, Carsey, his group, and similar bodies always had the option of simply changing the label under which they functioned or launching secret societies of dubious substance and strength to pursue their goals. "The political sky in this country is dotted with a great many clouds," fretted a Republican paper. "From which of all these will come the rain is hard to tell." "We hear talk of Citizens' Alliances, Knights of Reciprocity, Farmers' Alliances, Knights of Labor, and what not, in addition to the regular Republican and Democratic parties." The press reported the existence of a Republican secret society launched by critics of the Harrison administration and "other orders of a similar character that are hostile to Mr. Blaine." The latter, allegedly inspired by Kansas Republican congressman, got seated at Populist conventions and may, or may not, have been a Democratic cat's-paw. The Knights of Reciprocity represented a self-declared "new political organization" of "an oath-bound secret organization and is composed of laboring men in the protected trades, farmers who are tired of the Alliance, and all others who believe in Blaine and a protective tariff." Its membership ran to 3,000 in Chicago and 75,000 in the rest of the country, operating in the east as the "Continental League."[65] Whatever the realities, Populist bodies seated representatives from the Knights of Reciprocity alongside those from the Knights of Industry and associations of even more dubious provenance.

The Panic of 1893, which ultimately starved the Populist insurgency, permitted a last gasp to careers such as Carsey's. Hard times exaggerated the nature of a US work force characterized by its extensive mobility, not vertically but horizontally. Indeed, the actual difficulties of upward mobility kept churning much of the labor class into constant motion, roaming from place to place in search of a better life. Horizontal mobility made it relatively easy for figures such as Carsey to claim to speak for the invisible laborers, "the silent majority," the working class. However briefly, the onset of economic crisis intensified these features.[66]

In New York City, Carsey, Gallahue, and their friends had a last chance to don the garb of labor leaders to represent working-class interests in a dispute between rival rapid transit companies. Essentially, this recalled the "anti-monopolism" of Shupe's effort to remove the charter of a competing firm. This time, though, the Knights of Labor protested when Gallahue claimed to represent them, and the Central Labor Union denied any role in the dispute between the workers and the firm at the Sea Beach railroad Slip to the Staten Island Ferry. The *New York Times* also covered the group when, as the "National City Industrial Alliance," it met with the mayor to advocate for the municipal encouragement of boardinghouses, and when it gathered at the Cooper Institute to renominate Controller Theodore W. Myers. It also reported that it "claimed 6,000 votes" but added that the "alliance" "consists of about sixteen men" who "are not recognized as workingmen by trades unions." "In case of labor troubles," it added, "the group has been known to approach employers and offered to get up mass meetings of workingmen to support their position. At such times, the members of the Industrial Alliance usually assume some name that resembles some well-known union." They specifically mentioned Carsey, Gallahue, and others "who for years have never done any actual work. They have posed as professional labor agitators and are nothing less than political strikers."[67] At long last, history had passed by them far enough to transform them from ostensibly calloused leaders of the toiling masses and political activists into partisan functionaries and government bureaucrats.

Or, more clearly, time had uncovered what they had been for decades.

The reelection of Cleveland, the destruction of the Populist alternatives, and the Panic of 1893 closed that stage of US political history that had given rise to the careers of Carsey and his contemporaries. The new wave of progressive reform began with trickles before becoming a transformative torrent that entirely restructured everything from civil service and government work to party structures. These new reforms centralized the electoral process, imposing ballot lines and ballot status. The government, meaning the dominant two parties, assumed the power to regulate possible insurgent efforts far more effectively without needing to rely on the ongoing presence of figures such as Carsey, Shupe, Keogh, or Dyer D. Lum.

Moreover, the proliferation of newspapers that became doomed to play the same game Carsey had played for decades had come to an end. Simply put, Carsey's ability to give a "labor" voice to conservative interests outside New York became less effective as Populist editors in Kansas could check his credentials. Groups such as the Knights of Labor had also lasted long enough to develop an institutional memory, on which Powderly could draw to expose Carsey and his allies as "bogus" labor reformers. As time went on, the playing field for Carsey's game shrunk and would never run into as many innings as it had. If it never entirely faded away, its general utility as an ongoing tool for any party organization withered.

* * *

A complex figure, Carsey's ally Lum sensed the politics with which they were familiar slipping away. He had lost the trust of the movement from his partisan-funded activities to discredit the 1880 Greenback-Labor campaign. The old excuse that he had rejected some alleged lack of radicalism on Weaver's part crashed with his embrace of the Butler campaign, after which he assisted the suicide of one of the Haymarket leaders. By the 1890s, Lum found himself "known in some quarters as an anarchist dilettante and in others as a boodle politician of the most corrupt character," after which his drinking got understandably worse. He slumped into an even greater depression after Butler, his occasional benefactor, passed away on January 22, 1893. On April 3, Lum died alone in the Summit Hotel on Canal Street in the Bowery, his body identified by the anarchists Justus Schwab and Johann Most.[68]

A few weeks later, it all came crashing down dramatically on Carsey one spring evening when he stopped off in a bar on Ninety-First Street and Ninth Avenue. Elements of the Grand Army of the Republic, the organization of Union veterans of the Civil War, had gone into open revolt over the appointment of nonveterans and even former opponents of the war to the Pension Office without hearing objections from the veterans' group. In the saloon, an old soldier from Elmer E. Ellsworth's Zouaves and a member of the particularly irate Noah L. Farnham Post of the Grand Army of the Republic bitterly and loudly contrasted the experience of the veterans with those of the pencil-pushing functionaries in the Pension Office. Taking umbrage, Carsey barked back, "I am no light-service man." Then the two old men then began whaling on each other, the press noting that it left Carsey with swollen cheeks, a reddish-marked jaw, and split lips.[69]

Carsey could share Lum's awareness of the obsolescence of their kind of politics and remain durable enough to take the punches as he fought to retain a persistent relevance and achieve certain vindication for his career.

EPILOGUE

Carsey's Progeny

The Forgotten Grandfather of American Progressivism and the Political Unmaking of an American Working Class

The real difficulty is with the vast wealth and power in the hands of the few and the unscrupulous who represent or control capital. . . . This is a government of the people, by the people, and for the people no longer. It is a government of corporations, by corporations, and for corporations.—How is this?

—Former President Rutherford B. Hayes [1888]

Corporations are people, my friend.

—Mitt Romney [2011]

Twenty years after William A. A. Carsey had helped to demobilize the Populist movement, he surely took joy at his son's success as a sports promoter after a career in baseball. In the summer of 1913, the interest in female ballplayers stirred by the Chicago Bloomer Girls' upset victories struck the fancy of "Kid" Carsey, who promised to bring them to Washington for a game on July 30. He scheduled Union Park as the venue, "where the colored people go to play ball and to watch the game." The crowd of thousands that filled the bleachers reportedly became increasingly suspicious of the players, until a little boy dashed out behind the third baseman "and gave her golden locks a vigorous pull." It exposed "a chunky young man with an elaborate make-up, ending just above the eyebrows," and the team made a mad dash for the clubhouse "through a storm of bottles and bricks." The riot that followed led to numerous arrests, leaving three policemen and an uncountably larger number of Blacks injured. Although the cops "broke their clubs on the first few," much of the crowd surged from the seats toward the cashbox in hopes of getting their money back. Those that reached that goal found that no refund would be possible, because the promoter had already disappeared from the field with the money half an hour earlier.[1] The Kid had learned the game from one of the best.

Carsey's life and accomplishments, as discussed in this study, have been those of his public *persona*, taking the liberty to leap over the sometimes-frustrating gaps in the documentation. The world into which he had been born experienced the rise of mass politics, an expanded suffrage, and the emergence of a partisan politics permeating civil society, all systematically recited in secular homilies about the development of a more representative political system and a more popularly based two-party system. Carsey's work performed a regulatory function vital for ensuring that the expansion of political participation would not backfire, that most of the population would not be able to find the means to use the political system to foster their interests and challenge the social and economic structures of power. Repeatedly over a crucial period, he had fought to present himself as a spokesperson for insurgent political movements in pursuit of an avowed strategy that essentially short-circuited those efforts and sweep whatever remained into the Democratic electorate or out of the electoral process entirely. On one level, we should probably understand those gaps in the detailed accounts of Carsey's career not as a reflection of its unimportance or failures but of his success in the messaging of his priorities.

* * *

The historiographic shadow of Carsey is sharply and easily defined. Later scholars tend to be no more critical of accounts than contemporary newspaper readers, nor have they shared enough context information in terms of gaining the contextual information to recognize what they read. Joseph Dorfman's monumental five-volume post–World War II work on the *Economic Mind in American Civilization* dismissed Populism as inherently conservative, partly basing his opinion on the positions taken by Carsey the Democratic operative.[2] Nor was Dorfman alone in citing Democratic spokesmen to define what workers wanted and why.

More broadly, Carsey's career touched on some of the various reasons the American working class has not found a distinct political voice, much less a political party, elusive, largely rooted in the very nature of the US two-party system. The nature of that system and a civic culture—shaped by the institutions of government, media, and education—inculcates a virtually unchallengeable acceptance of its permanence. The arrangement required no more of a conspiracy than the one that enabled land speculators in the West to foster the ethnic cleansing of native peoples or the one that mandates the fossil-fuel industry to sell gasoline. Such functions baked into the institutional hegemony of a two-party system governs the way in which it deflects expressions of disaffection and insurgency into manageable channels. That process not only created (and, ultimately, somewhat outdated) a political space for roles like that of Carsey, whose career may well have been unique primarily for its duration.

The postwar reconstruction of the party system required new mechanisms and personnel to mediate the expectations of voters and the needs of the movers and shakers within the party structure. The weight of the system alone created a predisposition within any insurgency for some individuals to attempt to be a power broker. Proponents of fusion among the Greenbackers and Populists may have sincerely hoped to promote movement goals but saw their realization as requiring the success or defeat of one or another of the two major parties and, hence, the destruction of their own independent movement.

Carsey's efforts to redirect and diffuse working-class discontent initially centered on encouraging discontented workers to move into the West, supposedly the once and future "safety valve" for social conflict, and on ensuring unbroken successes in the course of capitalism. His experience indicated that whatever realities may have fueled this timeworn cliché had begun sputtering out of steam. To the credit of Carsey and his advisers, he reshaped his career to acknowledge the illusory nature of that safety valve and the need to address the subsequent growth of the working class. In particular, they became concerned with the extent to which such a movement might interfere with the systemic, regularized ritual of electorally legitimating the power structure.

In a sense, the growth of a national news pool both made this kind of career possible and ultimately proved its undoing. By the 1890s, Carsey could no longer present himself as a representative of a mass New York City labor movement in Indianapolis because news syndication and newspaper exchanges would place such a portrayal before a workers' movement large and coherent enough to expose his claims with finality. To be sure, Carsey persisted in his efforts to speak for the eastern working class in a mass, diverse, and complex Populist movement, but his efforts were of decreasing effectiveness.

Within the major parties, then, these conditions shaped a new partisan strategy that involved the manipulation of those insurgent impulses in the interests of the party. Carsey's career is so clearly identifiable for us—primarily because he had been at it long enough to have made an impression. The length of his career itself created a variety of problems and had to formulate an array of tactics in response. During this time, he encouraged a proliferation to third-party efforts to blunt insurgent impulses and minimize their possible impact as independent forces. Beneath this range of tactics was a consistent underlying strategy of shaping the best outcome for the New York factions of the Democratic Party he served.

The nature of the party system gave rise to two, three, many Carseys briefly making their appearance, several whom we have encountered, such as Walter H. Shupe and others. As they worked on behalf of various New York political leaders—from Peter Cooper to Governor David B. Hill—the different needs of various Republican and Democratic factions facing threatened insurgencies elsewhere responded with their own contemporary Carseys. Dyer D. Lum, Charles Litchman, and others in the Boston area operated on behalf of Governor Benjamin F. Butler. Like Carsey and his lieutenants in New York, Butler's people in Massachusetts established credentials in real movements for labor reform and Greenbackism before coaxing insurgents into the institutionally suicidal strategy of fusion with the Democratic Party, or simply taking leadership of an independent movement and pulling the rug out from under it at the last minute. Lum's realization of his own manipulation or depression over its results may have hastened his self-destruction. One suspects that a bit of digging could identify comparable figures operating in most large American communities experiencing comparable stages of party development.

Moreover, as the case of A. H. Gallahue's intervention with the Republicans demonstrated, once one had marketable credentials, who the purchaser is may have less importance than the general contribution to the higher needs of the two-party system. Perhaps the most significant Republican operative, Charles A. Henrie, also became the best-known "anarchist" in Kansas. In that capacity, he scoffed at the reformists urging changes like the establishment of a state bureau of labor. After being exposed as an agent of the GOP, he sought and won appointment to the state's new Bureau of Labor. After later running several small-town Republican papers across the West, this forgotten pioneer of modern misspokesmen for labor radicalism went to work as an adman for a used-car business in Wichita before retiring in Oklahoma.[3]

William H. Vanderbilt, the oldest son of Commodore Cornelius Vanderbilt, offered a frank response about the political movement against monopolies. Acknowledging some to be serious about the subject, the New Yorker may have had Shupe and Carsey in mind when he described its initiators as "a set of fools and black-mailers." Of the latter, he said, "when I want to buy up any politician, I always find the Anti-Monopolists the most purchasable. They don't come so high."[4]

Regrettably, we can only speculate about how Carsey himself evaluated his career as he looked back on it. Probably, he shared the assumption that, beneath the tumult of an immediate election, the party labels represented different eternal impulses. And the rivalry of the two parties represented a continual struggle to resolve those differences.

At the same time, Carsey witnessed and felt the changes that continually remade the Democratic Party—not only momentous events like the Civil War or the party's postwar crisis, but the generational loss of old leaders. Old St. Patrick's, where he had himself been baptized, filled graves that marked something of an end to the rough-and-tumble political universe that had made him. It is not hard to imagine that Carsey there at the June 1886 funeral of John Kelly, the leader of Tammany Hall, or at that of Charles O'Conor two years later.

Carsey and the New York Democratic leaders of his generation particularly deplored the national changes that undermined the power their state organization enjoyed through the Gilded Age. The return of the overwhelmingly Democratic former Confederate states into national politics weakened the strength of the New York organization. More important, the subsequent expanding strength of the midwestern and western organizations provided the base for a quite different kind of national spokesman, William Jennings Bryan.[5] The son of a Democratic lawyer and landholder in rural Illinois, he experienced a religious conversion experience at fourteen, attended college, married, and studied law in Chicago before going to work for a family friend, Lyman Trumbull. In 1887, Bryan and his wife moved to Nebraska, where he built his reputation as a Democratic orator, later carefully straddling the fence between the party and the rising Populist insurgency. In 1890, he became part of a Democratic wave that captured the US House of Representatives.

In 1892, the yet dominant New York organization again secured the presidential nomination of Cleveland against the incumbent Republican President Benjamin Harrison. This capped the successive postwar Democratic candidacies of Horatio Seymour, Horace Greeley, Samuel J. Tilden, Winfield S. Hancock, and Cleveland himself. In this last case, Bryan supported the Populists, something that would have been unthinkable to Democrats in New York. The financial Panic of 1893, however, further strengthened westerners in the party advocating a strong government, capable of regulating the railroads, money supply, and corporations. This sentiment provided the foundation for Bryan's unsuccessful bid for the US Senate, but he eyed a larger prize.

On July 7, 1896, US Senator Hill chaired the Democratic National Convention that met in Chicago's Coliseum, and his credentials body recommended the exclusion of the Nebraska delegation Bryan led.[6] After several days of floor fights, the convention seated Bryan's delegation and put him on the platform committee, where he inflicted another defeat on Hill, who led an unsuccessful effort to get the party's endorsement of enacting the gold standard. On the morning of July 9, Hill presented his minority report from the platform committee to the convention. In one of the most dramatic events in the history of US politics, Bryan responded for the majority:

> Having behind us the producing masses of this nation and the world, supported by the commercial interests, the laboring interests, and the toilers everywhere, we will answer their demand for a gold standard by saying to them: You shall not press down upon the brow of labor this crown of thorns. You shall not crucify mankind upon a cross of gold.

A stunned silence followed. Before he made his way back to the seat, though, the hall exploded. Delegates shouted themselves hoarse, threw their hats into the air, and gave a noisy demonstration of their appreciation that lasted for half an hour.

Bryan's nomination for president the next day hit the tough-minded New Yorkers like a kick in the stomach. Since the Civil War, the largely New York leadership of the party periodically embraced some of the reform rhetoric hostile to the railroads, banks, and the emerging corporate capitalist world. But western silver concerns, the Populist rhetoric, and the evangelical overtones simply left Cleveland, Hill, and papers such as the *New York World* absolutely cold. Well aware of this, the Republicans even funded a Carseyesque independent campaign by Gold Democrats, who had their own Butler-like convention in Indianapolis.[7]

Indeed, from the perspective of the New Yorkers, Bryan's election as president would have not only initiated a radically unique presidency but established a hugely different leadership of the national Democratic Party that would have persisted indefinitely into the future. From Carsey's perspective, Bryan provided an ultimately timelier model for turning movements for independent political action inside out. His candidacy effectively shattered the People's Party, which—allowing for a few of the most stubborn components—abandoned their "middle-of-the-road" independence between the two parties. The Boy Orator of the Platte took his strategy directly to the New Yorkers on August 12, delivering his formal acceptance speech at Madison Square Garden. Even this style of campaigning, however, smacked of the aggressive kind of electioneering pioneered by James B. Weaver and Butler. With minimal funds reluctantly provided by a suddenly frugal national leadership, no reliable organization, and a press either uninterested or hostile, Bryan labored tirelessly, speaking as many as twenty to thirty times a day, covering twenty-seven states, and directly reaching millions of voters.

Despite Bryan's defeat in 1896—one of the most important in presidential history—the subsequent rebalancing of the parties created a situation in which anything affecting one party would more directly change the other. That year's election completed the Republican transition from the log cabin of Lincoln and its concerns to the businessman's mansion. As Carsey had envisioned for the Democrats, William McKinley's campaign used the tariff to rally most of the middle-class and wealthy voters in the cities and towns with urban laborers, as well as the more commercially successful farmers.

Nevertheless, the Bryan wing of the Democratic Party continued to exercise power within the national party, much to the chagrin of the New Yorkers. When the McKinley administration took the country into a war against Spain in April 1898, Bryan dutifully supported the invasion of Cuba as a means of securing Cuban independence, but the actual course of the war alienated him. Most of the US Anti-imperialist League supported him in 1900, when he once more became the Democratic standard-bearer against McKinley and McKinley's vice-presidential candidate, Theodore Roosevelt. Although TR had got fewer votes for mayor than the United Labor candidate back in 1886, he had more recently recast himself as a cowboy and a war hero who spoke with an increasingly critical voice against unrestrained and unregulated corporate power. He and McKinley, who would be the last in a run of Civil War veterans in the White House, won the election, launching his second term in March 1901. His September assassination landed Roosevelt in the White House.

The new century brought a new Progressive agenda into the government. It did not reflect a popular mandate that one party won over the other but resulted from the common adoption of new standards of scientific management by elements of both parties. The bipartisan Progressive predisposition to regulate also extended into electoral practices, establishing a government monopoly over the printing of the ballot. It was a monopoly that imposed the regulation of ballot access and produced a lockstep cultural embrace of the self-restrictions of two-party politics.[8] Simply put, it left the participation of any alternative to the two dominant parties dependent on their approval.

In the face of this kind of sea change in the Democratic Party, Carsey surely shared the concerns of Hill and his fellow New Yorkers in these national power struggles, even as he enjoyed life in the capital through the late 1890s. While there, Wilfred "Kid" Carsey got his best shot at baseball stardom, breaking records with his pitching before going into a sharp and erratic decline. The return of the Republicans to national government in 1901 and the continual strength of Bryan's wing within the Democratic Party brought the Carseys back to New York.

The turn of the century found Carsey living in the Bronx while working in the city's Bureau for Collection of Arrears of Personal Taxes. He also found work as an architect for minor construction projects in the city and moved his family to Chestnut Ridge in Ramapo, New York, Shupe's old stomping grounds. He seems to have maintained a home in Pequannock Township, New Jersey, but took his family back to Manhattan in 1903, likely so that he could better "attend to his duties as Inspector of the bridge now being constructed, from the foot of East Fifty-Ninth Street, New York, across the East River to Blackwell Island." Age took its toll on him over the next decade. Through 1912 and 1913, he took long leaves from his job as a city inspector of masonry, presumably because of his age and declining health.[9]

The surviving record adds glimpses of personal tragedy. Their daughter, Lola Carsey Scott, committed suicide in 1905. Two years before, she had run off with a plumber, abandoning her marriage in Westchester. She killed herself by gas asphyxiation in a house at 3439 Broadway in Manhattan. The plumber identified her, telling the *Herald* that she had been the daughter of Carsey, who was taking charge of the burial, and she was described, with less accuracy than desirable, "secretary for the late Peter Cooper."[10] Around 1910, Carsey took up residence on Division Avenue in Brooklyn.

Around then, Democratic politics still dominated Gotham without having assimilated any of the substantive triumph of Populist ideas among them. In fact, Hill and Carsey's old New York crowd regained control of the nomination at the 1904 national Democratic convention. While dropping the gold standard and including some rather mild and well-mannered criticisms of corporate power, the party nominated Hill's old campaign manager, Alton B. Parker, for president. In the end, though, TR's shift to the left contributed to the biggest Republican victory since the Civil War, which rather seemed to vindicate Bryan and the reformers among the Democrats. Perhaps for that reason, the 1908 Democratic nomination once more went to Bryan, though the course of the Republican nominee, William Howard Taft, consolidated the hold of "Progressive" reform among the Republicans.

The high stakes of the 1912 presidential election drew Carsey's New Yorkers into another bid to retake the party. The growing rift among the Republicans between Taft and TR created a bolt by the latter, who took an independent nomination from the Progressive Party. The leading Democratic contenders were the Speaker of the House James "Champ" Clark of Missouri and Woodrow Wilson, the bookish Virginia-born southerner who had come north, become president of Princeton University, and then become the governor of New Jersey with close ties to the Progressives and nominal Progressives in New York City. At the convention, Tammany Hall tried to pull the New York delegation to Clark, but Bryan threw his support to Wilson, who secured the nomination. With TR taking an independent nomination from the Progressive Party, the division of the Republican vote with Taft paved the way for Wilson's election, the second Democrat to win the White House since the 1850s. The first had been the 1884 victory of Cleveland made possible by that earlier split among the Republicans, with the exodus of the Mugwumps.

On June 1, 1914, Carsey died at his home of asthma, ending a remarkable career. The *Brooklyn Daily Eagle* noted the passing of the seventy-two-year-old "former builder of Manhattan." A brief obituary notice described him as having been an inspector in the local Department of Bridges and a builder. It reported he had been in the First and Eighth Kansas during the war and also held membership in the Jefferson Democratic club and the Wyoming lodge of the Freemasons. The statement that he had been on the General Committee of Tammany Hall, however, tends to raise doubts.[11] For most of his time, Carsey had been a loyal foot soldier of the organization and had rendered his best service to it behind the scenes.

Carsey's passing cast a longer shadow than his life, of course. The notice announcing his funeral services added that he left a widow, Adele Z., two sons, Arthur and Wilfred, and a daughter, Muzette. Adelle filed for her widow's benefits two weeks later. She lived another ten years, dying in Pittsfield, Massachusetts, in May 1924.[12] Wilfred Carsey, his career damaged by neither brawls with legislators nor the Bloomer Girl scandal, lived past the age of ninety to die in Florida in 1960.

Beyond his family, though, Carsey's career had a lasting impact on the brave new political world that unfolded after his death. Certainly, the ambitious would continue to do what they could behind the facades of various shoddy organizations to successfully diffuse the hopes of citizens interested in any kind of reform that might threaten the standards of the ruling hierarchy. It is significant to note that the legacy would be no more partisan than Progressivism itself. Also, it emerged in response to popular mass movements among patrician political leaders such as Roosevelt, Wilson, and elite white gentlemen. In the process, images came to matter more than substance, a studied obscurantism more than transparency, and deference ever more useful than accountability.

The parties themselves continued to function as shifting coalitions scrambling to keep their balance amid ever-changing circumstances. They seemed to change almost completely over time so that they could leave nothing of their old selves but the shadow. Rhetoric and labels aside, the distance between the Democrat of 1912 and one of 1860 or of 1940 was probably not much greater than that between different internal wings of those parties in the same years. Indeed, the Republican of 1912 was surely closer to the contemporary Democrat than to either of the parties in the Gilded Age.

Put another way, the history of political parties recalls the musings of Heraclitus about how the flow of ever-new waters makes it impossible to step into the same river twice. A political party, like the physical contours of a river system—the channels, the relationship of tributaries, et cetera—are not as ephemeral as what moves through it. Regardless of rhetoric and platforms, the nature of the caucus party system treats citizens as civic consumers of promised policies or, at least, comforting social images.

Over the years, advocates of change increasingly tended to pin their hopes on a Democratic success. Wilson picked Bryan as his secretary of state, and the two cooperated to reduce tariffs and expand the scope of the new regulatory economic and social reforms. But the basis for more substantive hopes waxed and waned, mostly the latter. The shifts took place alongside ongoing efforts to blight any attempt for working citizens to find their own independent and distinct organizational voice.

This key partnership of Wilson and Bryan also sowed the seeds of a new bipartisanship. Despite Bryan's intellectual resistance to rising imperialist sentiments in the government, war became the engine of those centralizing currents. He reluctantly guided his department through US interventions into Haiti, the Dominican Republic, and Mexico. In 1914, when the world war broke out in Europe, Bryan helped keep the United States neutral and even tried to mediate an end to the conflict. When the drift to US involvement intensified in 1915, Bryan resigned. When the Wilson administration took the United States into the war in 1917, Bryan publicly closed ranks. So did the Republicans. The ascendancy of the United States as a world power created episodically central questions of war and peace that seemed to draw the parties closer together.

Despite these changes, the civic culture naturally generates as many Carsey reenactors as the party system required. An officer of the Socialist Party in St. Joseph complained in 1908 that "several political crooks carrying red cards and they had a contingent of two that did not belong to the local but came every meeting to make trouble." They tried to draw party members into their own "Debs club," which had neither dues nor membership meetings, which meant the operatives could simply do as they pleased under that rubric. As the presidential election approached, leaders of this "Debs club" sought to browbeat their erstwhile comrades into supporting Bryan, though, by then, they functioned under the rubric of the "Social Democratic Club." "I gave the ringleader of the gang a good punching about five weeks ago," wrote a comrade from St. Joe.[13] In reporting this, the *Appeal to Reason* added that almost all locals faced similar problems.

Nevertheless, the US entry into the world war allowed the Democratic administration to do several things otherwise denied it, including the conscious cultivation of the nationalism Carsey had long advocated. The government waged its own version of a *Kulturkampf* against immigrant identity and "hyphenated-Americanism." In the name of fighting German authoritarianism, it also embraced tightly the German precedent from forty years before to outlaw the legal and law-abiding political party of the Socialists. This squelching of the last real mass residue of the insurgent efforts of the Gilded Age to establish a permanent new party might have largely eliminated the call for anyone with the specific skills of Carsey or his younger successors "in almost all the locals" of insurgent movements.

Also, the Progressive imposition of the new bipartisan regulation of the ballot did nothing to quell discontent, but it deprived citizens of the opportunity to make issues publicly noticeable by peacefully assembling for the redress of grievances through the ballot. The Socialist Party briefly resurfaced in the 1930s but ultimately embraced self-destruction in deference to the Democratic Party. Indeed, despite its rabid vilification and even outlawing, the Communist Party wound up following the same course. Instead, the norm became individuals emulating what TR had done in 1912, La Follette in 1924, and Henry A. Wallace in 1948—one might perhaps add Ralph Nader in 2000. The Socialists made impressive one-off protest campaigns, but none aimed to build a serious new mass party of the people. None, though, have seriously taken up the project of building a new mass party of working people, and the flow of "Progressive" reform coursed safely between the regulatory guardrails of the two-party system. Then again, the first officially orchestrated national Red Scare used government employees to do quite different things than had Carsey, who sabotaged, misrepresented, and excluded radical voices for the public platform.

In the end, the twentieth century brought the US system farther than ever from the more democratic membership-based branch party model. US parties did structure a series of carefully managed primaries to allow the consumer-citizen to identify the most marketable candidate, while winnowing out the unacceptable options.

More fundamentally, perhaps, technological development changed the character of US politics, seemingly to surpass the usefulness of Carsey's contributions. Mass communications made access to the public platform increasingly expensive. Campaign costs have not only exploded, mostly imposed by the requirements of advertising on mass media. Viewers of mass media will also note that this industry also arrogates to itself the power to decide which candidates are serious enough to merit more coverage and even gauges that seriousness in terms of campaign coffers. Then, too, the commercial nature of politics ensured not only that money would generally prevail but that the lion's share of those escalating amounts would flow to an unregulated and increasingly profit-motivated media.

The 1987 elimination of the nearly forty-year-old fairness doctrine that effectively sanctioned any kind of misrepresentations or outright lying not only freed media of any responsibility to the public to cover any forces that might challenge the two-party system but fundamentally changed the nature of the climate in which those parties would operate.

In terms of power and its perception, print media had gilded the age of Carsey, but its development made it increasingly indistinguishable from its makers, subjects, and consumers. Among Ben Butler's descendants was the pioneering "participatory journalist" George Plimpton. One of Henry George's daughters married the nephew of Cecil B. DeMille and had two daughters, the choreographer Agnes de Mille and the actress Peggy George. A grandson of "Kid" Carsey, John Jay Carsey, and his wife Marcy Peterson Carsey became television producers and writers who had a hand in some of the best and most popular programs of the late twentieth century. New media technologies also manufactured new kinds of celebrity, starting in sports and finally contributing to a two-party electoral process that can function as simply a matter of picking teams, an observation that the old ball player Carsey would have fully appreciated.

The growth of these new industries deepened trends already evident in Carsey's day. Newspapers had always been a profit-driven, privately owned industry, though modern technologies spawned more elaborate appendages concerned with the kind of advertising, salesmanship, and public relations centered on image-making. Newspaper editors and reporters could complain that Carsey and his circle engaged in "the manufacture of bogus labor news," but as their potential audience became larger and advertising revenue more lucrative, information media found ways to monetize bogus stories of all sorts.

Carsey's contributions went deeper than the broad visible universe of old-fashioned pols, patricians, or bureaucrats—or even just television celebrities. Born into a world of the penny press, a media revolution made his career possible. By the time his family had left the city for Kansas, newspapers such as the *New York Tribune* already had massive steam-powered presses that cheaply printed a mass-circulation publication with a national readership served by locomotive deliveries. By the time Carsey had returned to the city and launched his strange career, the telegraph lines that went up alongside the tracks and their projected routes made it possible for the press to claim an unprecedented access to an ever more literate public readership. The telephone would follow shortly. More important, it permitted newspapers to replicate anything of interest that might turn up in their exchanges, ultimately leading to press associations and syndicates.

The early manifestations of these innovative technologies permitted the smoke and mirrors necessary for the wispy mass organizations of Carsey and Shupe to engage in controversies that also had meaning only through their systemic treatment as such. Carsey and Shupe could issue strange pronouncements in the name of many imagined thousands of his followers. Members of the news media might well have chuckled as they passed these on to their readers, but pass them on they did. The dancing shadow of those nonexistent mass secret societies of the Gilded Age paved the way for other flickering images that came to define our understanding of the social world.

Indeed, something of Carsey's fading fingerprints may remain most visible at the foundations of "astroturfing." Over the long run of our history, a proliferation of trusts, think tanks, foundations, nongovernmental agencies, lobbyist bodies, not-for-profits, and other organizations positioned themselves as advocates of grassroots interest in the promotion of meaningful change or, at least, the arbiters of what that change should mean. News media still report on the wishes of the ever-wispy "Tea Party" decades after David H. and Charles G. Koch began financing it and years after they found it in their interest to engage in the kind of street theater and image making that has provided a kind of media wallpaper. Media claimed these attempts to mimic mass mobilizations and popular self-organization to be a movement and have been dutifully described them as such in the media.[14] Buoyed by acronyms and initialisms and fueled by lobbyists, the news industry shapes a civic culture in which the unprecedented polarization of wealth, large-scale corruption, US acts of war against smaller nations, police violence particularly against unarmed Black citizens, and the gradual, globally suicidal assault on the natural world and the stability of the climate remain fleeting or marginal.

Subsidized mass organizations that have no real existence as such—save in the columns of the press, as an ethereal talisman for lobbyists and the media focus on those concerns—recall a different but clearly similar Gilded Age. With the expansion of the news media industry, it absorbed what had been more marginal and peripheral into its heart. The work of Carsey at the edges became the professions of Lee Atwater, Michael Deaver, and others. It allows their employers to speak for the same invisible laborers for whom Carsey spoke: Richard M. Nixon's "silent majority" or Donald J. Trump's bleached masculine image of the "America" he would put first.

The century after Carsey's death saw growth of the mechanisms of conscious misrepresentation into the mass production of disinformation, the strategic cultivation of mistrust, an ideology of deliberate dysfunctionality, and pervasive civic demoralization. The appearance of these things requires no conscious conspiracies by individual bad actors but represents the functions inherent to a winner-take-all two-party system within an electoral structure with various deliberately embedded antirepublican and antidemocratic features.

* * *

In the end, Carsey's importance in US political history rests less on any foreshadowing of Progressivism than on his persistent service to the stability of party politics in a changing postwar power structure. From its birth, any insurgent movement conjures would-be power brokers ready to serve as its pallbearers, even more so as the movement threatens to be successful. And the nature of the system so thoroughly presents the institutionalized two parties as immutable realities that it sweeps along the pragmatic, and even those who are willing to defer to the pragmatic solution. Carsey and his kindred politicos understood of the ability of the media to not only define but generate illusions of political reality.

Carsey's progeny blazed the trail from the Gilded Age into the current fray of electoral politics. They did not act within a deterministic framework. They made conscious decisions every step of the way but did so within a framework of well-practiced habits and predispositions. As long as preserving an ordered normalcy has priority over dealing with any of the problems endemic to that normalcy, US civic culture will fail to address the legacy of William A. A. Carsey, one of America's Forgotten Refounders.

Notes

Introduction

1. "Carsey Had Had a Fight," *New York Times*, May 27, 1893, 3.

2. Werner Sombart, *Warum gibt es in den Vereinigten Staaten keinen Sozialismus?* (Tübingen, Ger.: J. C. B. Mohr, 106), published in English as *Why Is There No Socialism in the United States?* trans. and ed. Patricia M. Hocking and C. T. Husbands, with introduction by C. T. Husbands and foreword by Michael Harrington (London: Macmillan, 1976). Eric Foner, "Why Is There No Socialism in the United States?" *History Workshop*, no. 17 (Spring, 1984): 57–80; Theodore J. Lowi, "Why Is There No Socialism in the United States? A Federal Analysis," *International Political Science Review / Revue internationale de science politique*, 5: no. 4, *Pluralism and Federalism* (1984): 369–80; Daniel Gaido, "'The American Worker' and the Theory of Permanent Revolution: Karl Kautsky on Werner Sombart's Why Is There No Socialism in the United States?" *Historical Materialism* 11, no. 4 (Spring, 2003): 79–123); David Montgomery, "Why Is There No Socialism in the United States? Conference in Paris," *International Labor and Working-Class History*, no. 24 (Fall 1983): 67–68. See also Reiner Grundmann, "Sombart, Werner," *Wiley Blackwell Encyclopedia of Social Theory*, ed. Bryan S. Turner (New York: John Wiley and Sons, 2017), https://onlinelibrary.wiley.com/doi/book/10.1002/9781118430873.

3. Robin Archer, *Why Is There No Labor Party in the United States* (Princeton, NJ: Princeton University Press, 2010). For the context of this question as played out during Carsey's career, see Leon Fink, *Workingmen's Democracy: The Knights of Labor and American Politics* (Urbana: University of Illinois Press, 1983); and Kim Moody, *Tramps and Trade Union Travelers: Internal Migration and Organized Labor in Gilded Age America, 1870–1900* (Chicago: Haymarket, 2019).

4. Moody, *Tramps*, 153–54.

5. Alan Wolfe, "Why Is There No Green Party in the United States?" *World Policy Journal* 1 (Fall 1983): 159–80.

6. Daniel Béland and Alex Waddan, "Why Are There No Universal Social Programs in the United States?" *World Affairs* 180 (Spring 2017): 64–92.

7. Carolina Santana Sabbagh, *Astroturfing: The Unrestricted Drowning of Political Dissent* (Cambridge, MA: Harvard Law School, 2016).

Prologue

1. "The Internationals Interfere," *New York World*, December 30, 1872, 8.

2. "William A. Carsey," *Brooklyn Daily Eagle*, June 2, 1914, 2. Their general absence from the city directories indicates Carsey had not been the head of his own household. For general overviews, see Junius Henri Browne, *The Great Metropolis: A Mirror of New York* (Hartford, CT: American Publishing, 1869), and Edward Spann, *The New Metropolis: New York City, 1840–1857* (New York: Columbia University Press, 1981).

3. Robert McNamara, "New York's Great Fire of 1835," ThoughtCo, updated August 31, 2021, thoughtco.com/new-yorks-great-fire-of-1835-1773780.

4. On Charles Shields versus William Carsey, Margaret Carsey, Margaret Ann McGowan, Michael McGowan, William Adolphus Carsey, Catherine Ellen Carsey, and Gerard Stuyvesant, see the item "Supreme Court—City and County of New York," *New-York Tribune*, December 3, 1858, 3. When Carsey is given a middle name, it is usually Augustus. This legal document makes it seem reasonable to conclude that the other A was Adolphus, though he did name one of his sons Arthur.

5. "Police Intelligence," *New York Daily Herald*, July 11, 1849, 2; "'The Confidence Man' on a Large Scale," *New York Daily Herald*, July 11, 1849, 2; "Police Intelligence," *New York Daily Herald*, July 14, 1849, 1. Herman Melville, *The Confidence Man: His Masquerade* (New York: Dix, Edwards, 1857), contributed to popularizing the term nationally. See also Wilbur Miller, ed., *The Social History of Crime and Punishment in America: An Encyclopedia*, 5 vols. (Thousand Oaks, CA: Sage, 2012).

6. 1850 US Census, "William Caffey," age 52 (but just as easily 55), born England, New York Ward 17, New York, New York, wife Margaret "Carrey," 35, daughter Margaret Carrey, 13, William A. Carrey, 9, and Catherine E. Carrey, 1. The lawsuit referred to him as "William Adolphus" which is therefore the most likely representation of the second A in "William A. A." This second middle name may have represented a confirmation name given him later by the church or it may have simply been one he adopted and used.

7. This interesting neighborhood itself has inspired work from Herbert Asbury, *The Gangs of New York: An Informal History of the Underworld* (New York: Garden City, 1927), to Tyler Anbinder, *Five Points: The 19th-Century New York City Neighborhood That Invented Tap Dance, Stole Elections, and Became the World's Most Notorious Slum* (New York: Free Press, 2001), and will surely continue to do so.

8. Alexander Keyssar, *The Right to Vote: The Contested History of Democracy in the United States* (New York: Basic Books, 2000).

9. On the political history of the city at this time, see Jean H. Baker, *Affairs of Party: The Political Culture of Northern Democrats in the Mid Nineteenth Century* (Ithaca, NY: Cornell University Press, 1983); and Amy Bridges, *A City in the Republic: Antebellum New York and the Origins of Machine Politics* (Ithaca, NY: Cornell University Press, 1987). See also Robert D. Sampson, *John L. O'Sullivan and His Times* (Kent OH: Kent State University Press, 2003), and Anthony Gronowicz, *Race and Class Politics in New York City before the Civil War* (Boston: Northeastern University Press, 1998).

10. William M. Ivins, *Machine Politics and Money in Elections in New York City* (New York: Harper's Handy Series, 1887); Terry Golway, *Machine Made: Tammany Hall and the Creation of Modern American Politics* (New York: W. W. Norton, 2014. See also Jeffrey D. Broxmeyer, *Electoral Capitalism: The Party System in New York's Gilded Age* (Philadelphia: University of Pennsylvania Press, 2020). On the problem of "horizontal" mobility in class formation, see Kim Moody, *Tramps and Trade Union Travelers: Internal Migration and Organized Labor in Gilded Age America, 1870–1900* (Chicago: Haymarket, 2019), 158–61.

11. Byrdsall to Calhoun, August 2, 1842, in *The Papers of John C. Calhoun*, ed. Robert L. Meriwether and Clyde N. Wilson, 20 vols. (Columbia, SC: University of South Carolina Press for the South Caroliniana Society, 1959–89), 16: 421–22, and Byrdsall's letters of October 11 and November 6, 1842, 491–92, 530–31. See also the clippings and reports to Calhoun on developments at New York on 397–98, 402–7, 445–46, 468, 560–61, 562–63, and 657–50. Byrdsall claimed southern nativity before the war but acknowledged his English birth in 1870, confirmed in the Ancestry Passenger and Immigration List, which describes his naturalization on April 14, 1840. See Kenneth Scott, *Early New York Naturalizations, Abstracts of Naturalization Records from Federal, State, and Local Courts, 1792–1840* (Baltimore: Genealogical Publishing, 1999). For a Republican version of this relationship between a local machine and national power, see David Jordan, *Roscoe Conkling: A Voice in the Senate* (Ithaca, NY: Cornell University Press, 1971).

12. "Canterbury Hall Burned Down," *New York Times*, March 25, 1861, 8; Donald MacLeod, *Biography of Hon. Fernando Wood, Mayor of the City of New York* (New York: O. F. Parsons, 1856); Samuel Pleasants, *Fernando Wood of New York* (New York: Columbia University Press, 1948); and Jerome Mushkat, *Fernando Wood: A Political Biography* (Kent, OH: Kent State University Press, 1990). On the eve of the war, Wood suggested the secession of New York City, and critics blamed him—rightly, I think—for instigating the wartime Draft Riot along with Governor Horatio Seymour.

13. In 1865, William Carsey was a sixty-seven-year-old laborer living with his wife and a daughter born in New York about 1849 at Fort Leavenworth Military Reserve (July 11, 1865, Kansas State Census Collection, 1855–1925).

14. "William A. Carsey," *Brooklyn Daily Eagle*, June 2, 1914, 2; *USA Official Register of the United States, Containing a List of the Officers and Employees in the Civil, Military, and Naval Service Together with a List of Vessels Belonging to the United States; US Register of Civil, Military, and Naval Service, 1863–1959* [database online] (Provo, UT, Ancestry.com Operations, 2014), vol. 1, 670. Carsey's war record is transcribed incorrectly as "William

E. Corsey," a resident of Leavenworth. Note that there was also a "William Casey" from Leavenworth who enlisted on May 31, 1861, in Company H of the same regiment before deserting on June 24, 1861, at Wyandotte.

15. "Carsey Had Had a Fight. He Looked Queer as He Appeared before the Rapid-Transit Commission," *New York Times*, May 27, 1893, 3.

16. "Base Ball! The Great Game for the Championship, between the Kaw Valley, of Lawrence, and the Frontiers of Leavenworth," *Daily Kansas Tribune* (Lawrence), March 16, 1868, 3; illegible title, *Leavenworth Daily Commercial*, May 15, 1868, 4; and William Carsey, 75, born about 1795 [but probably 72 and born 1798] England, and living with the Wever family in Leavenworth Ward 4, Leavenworth, Kansas (US Census of 1870). See also Jeremy Drouin, "Did Wild Bill Hickok Ump a Baseball Game in Kansas City? KCQ Steps to the Plate to Investigate," Kansas City Public Library, September 25, 2020, https://kclibrary.org/blog/did-wild-bill-hickok-ump-baseball-game-kansas-city-kcq-steps-plate-investigate.

17. The census records and an obituary indicate that William A. Carsey had been born in October 1842, lived at those times in the Bronx, married 1870 to Adele Z. Carsey in New York, his father was born in England and mother in Ireland. They eventually had three children together. He then had one son from another relationship ("William A. Carsey," *Brooklyn Daily Eagle*, June 2, 1914, 2).

18. "Base-Ball—Mutual vs. Social," *New York Times*, June 8, 1870, 2; "Base Ball," *Lawrence Daily Kansas Tribune*, March 2, 1871, 3; and "Stirred Up," *Daily Kansas Tribune* (Lawrence), March 10, 1871, 3.

19. Stephen V. Rice, "Kid Carsey," accessed May 12, 2023, posted by the Society for American Baseball Research at https://sabr.org/bioproj/person/kid-carsey/.

20. "Meeting of the Federal Council of Internationals," *New York Herald*, October 7, 1872, 3; item, *Atchison Daily Champion*, June 3, 1865, 3; "Old Topeka Students," *Topeka State Journal*, October 14, 1916, 11; and "Rare Specimens," *Nashville Tennessean*, October 14, 1873, 4. See also "Death of Peter Heil," *Topeka State Journal*, April 21, 1919, 6. "A large number of German citizens of Lawrence, Kansas, have received circulars requesting their influence with the Internationals of the Old Country in connection with a political movement there" ("News Items," *New York Herald*, September 23, 1872, 7).

21. "International Working-Men's Association," *Nashville Union and American*, August 21, 1872, 3. See, too, Edward J. Harcourt, "Who Were the Pale Faces? New Perspectives on the Tennessee Ku Klux," *Civil War History* 51 (March 2005): 23–66; and Virginia Gooch Watson, "The Order of Pale Faces," Williamson County Historical Society Publication no. 1 (Fall 1970): 37–96, particularly 43, 133. See further "Election of Officers," *Nashville Tennessean*, July 4, 1871, 4.

22. Roeliff Brinkerhoff, *Recollections of a Lifetime* (Cincinnati, OH: Robert Clarke, 1904 [c. 1900]), 87; George W. Hawes, *Ohio State Gazetteer and Business Directory for 1860–61* (Indianapolis: Hawes, 1860). See too the notices in the *Sandusky Daily Commercial Register*, January 1, 15, 21, 23, 28, 1861, 1; Daughters of the American Revolution, *Lineage Book* (Washington, DC: DAR, 1895–1921): 131 (1917), 126; 151 (1919), 92. Also see the

obituary, "Walter H. Shupe," *New Philadelphia* [OH] *Democrat and Times*, July 2, 1903, 4. Shupe and his family left the writer of his obituary to speculate whether they had been part of that German Separatist community there, demonstrating his silent disinterest in disclosing much of his own history. See also *Cleveland Morning Leader*, November 22, 1860, 1. Shupe was injured in the bridge collapse on May 11, 1858, over Sauquoit creek as the Cincinnati express passed over it. *Annual Report of the Railroad Commissioners of the State of New York, and of the Reports of the Railroad Corporations, Made to the Board, for the Year Ending September 30, 1858* (Albany, NY: C. Van Benthuysen, 1856), 156.

23. "The Cleveland Convention," *Black Hawk* [Colorado] *Daily Mining Journal*, June 2, 1864, 2; "The Cleveland Mass Meeting," *Mineral Point* [Ohio] *Weekly Tribune*, June 8, 1864, 3; "The Cleveland Mass Meeting," *Wood County* [Ohio] *Reporter*, June 9, 1864, 3; Edward McPherson, *The Political History of the United States of America, during the Great Rebellion* (Washington, DC: Philp and Solomons, 1865), 410–11; Franklin P. Stearns, *The Life and Public Services of George Luther Stearns* (Philadelphia: J. B. Lippincott, 1907), 326.

24. *Historical Record to the Close of the Nineteenth Century of Rockland County, New York*, ed. Arthur S. Tompkins (Nyack, NY: Van Deusen and Joyce, 1902), 261.

25. "Masonic Mission," *Washington* [DC] *National Freemason* 2 (September 1864): 57. See, too, untitled item in *New York Herald*, February 11, 1865, 7, and, for the Mackey fund, *New York Herald*, March 26, 1865, 7; "Our Visit to the Army," "Masonry in the Army," and "Masonic Mission," *Washington* [DC] *National Freemason* 2 (November 1864): 88–89 (December 1864): 107, and (January 1865): 122.

26. *Philadelphia Times*, April 7, 1890, 4.

27. William Wattenberg, "Progress of the Press in the Past Forty Years," *Fourth Estate*, 2nd ser., no. 1451 (December 17, 1921): xx. On Shupe at Nanuet in Rockland County, see *The National Legal Directory* (St. Louis: Hubbell and Craven, 1870), 74.

28. Austin Abbott, *New Cases: Selected Chiefly from Decisions of the Courts of the State of New York*, 32 vols. (New York: Ward and Peloubet, 1877–96), 9 (1881): 331, part of the coverage on 331–59.

29. See Henry Clay Dean, *Crisis of the Civil War, and Curse of the Funding System* (Baltimore: for the author, 1869), for a good example of such a position by a prominent wartime Copperhead. See also David Quigley, *Second Founding: New York City, Reconstruction, and the Making of American Democracy* (New York: Hill and Wang, 2004).

30. Robert W. Burg, *The Corruption of Liberal Republicanism, 1864–1877*, PhD diss., Purdue University, December 2005.

31. Gordon B. McKinney, "The Politics of Protest: The Labor Reform and Greenback Parties in New Hampshire," *Historical New Hampshire* 36 (1981): 149–70. See also several editions of the *Concord Labor Reform Dispatch* between February 1 and February 25, 1870. State Central Committee meetings are held at the state historical society (David Montgomery, *Citizens Workers: The Experience of Workers in the United States with Democracy and Free Markets during the Nineteenth Century* [New York: Cambridge University Press, 1992]).

32. "Official Proceedings of the National Labor Reform Convention Held at Columbus, February 21 and 22, 1872," *Workingman's Advocate*, March 2, 1872, 1, 4.

33. The governors were Republicans John W. Geary, Edward F. Noyes, and John M. Palmer and the Democrat Joel Parker.

34. *Workingman's Advocate*, March 2, 9, 1872. One of the best discussions of this part remains that in David Montgomery's *Beyond Equality: Labor and the Radical Republicans, 1862–1872* (Urbana: University of Illinois Press, 1981). For the Greenback ideology, however, one should turn to Solon J. Buck, *The Granger Movement: A Study of Agricultural Organization and Its Political, Economic and Social Manifestations, 1870–1880* (Cambridge, MA: Harvard University Press, 1913), and Chester Destler in his *American Radicalism, 1865–1901* (New London: Connecticut College, 1946).

35. Letter from O'Conor, slavery not abolished constitutionally, Union League Club of New York, *Report of the Proceedings of the Conference at Richmond, June 11th and 12th, 1867* (New York: Club House, Union Square, 1867), 9–10; Seymour Mandelbaum, *Boss Tweed's New York* (New York: John Wiley and Sons, 1965); and Leo Hershkowitz, *Tweed's New York: Another Look* (Garden City, NY: Anchor, 1977). See also Mark Summers's studies of corruption and perceived corruption: *The Plundering Generation: Corruption and the Crisis of the Union 1848–1861* (New York: Oxford University Press, 1987), and *The Era of Good Stealings* (New York: Oxford University Press, 1993).

36. "The Louisville Convention" and "Louisville Convention," *Terre Haute Daily Wabash Express*, September 4, 1872, 3, c3, September 5, 1872, 3, c1; "The Strayed Out Convention at Louisville," *Indianapolis News*, September 4, 1872, 1, 592.

37. Mark A. Lause, *Free Labor: The Civil War and the Making of an American Working Class* (Urbana: University of Illinois Press, 2015), 39, 107.

38. Advertisement in the *Sun* [New York], February 10, 1873, 4. See also Jon Scott Logel, *Designing Gotham: West Point Engineers and the Rise of Modern New York, 1817–1898* (Baton Rouge: Louisiana State University Press, 2016).

39. *Historical Record . . . of Rockland County, New York*, 549.

Chapter 1. Paper Party Power Broker

1. "An Impeachment Trial," *University Chronicle* [University of Michigan] 3, March 27, 1869, 4.

2. "A New Party," *New York Herald*, November 2, 1875, 3, with his description in "A Boss Communist" [from the *Washington Post*], *Memphis Public Ledger*, June 19, 1878, 2, c3.

3. Mitchell Snay, *Horace Greeley and the Politics of Reform in Nineteenth-Century America* (New York: Rowman and Littlefield, 2011).

4. David Black, *The King of Fifth Avenue: The Fortunes of August Belmont* (New York: Dial, 1981); Stephen Birmingham, *Our Crowd: The Great Jewish Families of New York* (Syracuse, NY: Syracuse University Press, 1996).

5. Gustavus Myers, *The History of Tammany Hall* (New York: Dover, 1971); M. R.

Werner, *Tammany Hall* (Garden City, NY: Doubleday, Doran, 1928); William Riordan, *Plunkitt of Tammany Hall: A Series of Very Plain Talks on Very Practical Politics* (New York: McClure, Philips, 1905); Oliver E. Allen, *The Tiger: The Rise and Fall of Tammany Hall* (Boston: Addison-Wesley, 1993). A useful reference is Marin W. Littleton, *The Democratic Party of the State of New York*, ed. James K. McGuire, 3 vols. (New York: United States History Company, 1905).

6. Dennis Lynch, *"Boss" Tweed: The Story of a Grim Generation* (New York: Arno, 1974); Kenneth Ackerman, *Boss Tweed: The Rise and Fall of the Corrupt Pol Who Conceived the Soul of New York* (New York: Carroll and Graf, 2005); William Ivins, *Machine Politics and Money in Elections in New York City* (New York: Harper and Brothers, 1887); C. K. Yearly, *The Money Machines: The Breakdown and Reform of Governmental and Party Finance in the North, 1860–1920* (Albany, NY: SUNY Press, 1970); Sven Beckert, *The Monied Metropolis: New York City and the Consolidation of the New York Bourgeoisie, 1850–1896* (New York: Cambridge University Press, 1993); Jeffrey D. Broxmeyer, "Politics as a Sphere of Wealth Accumulation: Cases of Gilded Age New York, 1855–1888," PhD diss., City University of New York, 2014; Robert Gabriel Nelson, "The People's Capital: The Politics of Popular Wealth in the Gilded Age," PhD diss., University of California, Berkeley, Spring 2019. The Tweed Ring may have siphoned off as much as $200 million from the public treasury before its destruction (Mark Wahlgren Summers, *The Gilded Age*, or, *The Hazards of New Functions* [Upper Saddle River, NJ: Prentice Hall, 1997], 182).

7. Speech at Meeting, Cooper Institute, November 2, 1864, *Letters, Speeches and Addresses of August Belmont* (New York: privately printed, 1890), 148; Thomas Hughes, *Life and Times of Peter Cooper* (London: Macmillan, 1886).

8. See Thomas Reeves, *Gentleman Boss: The Life and Times of Chester Alan Arthur* (Newtown, CT: American Political Biography Press, 1975). See also Ari Hoogenboom, *Outlawing the Spoils: A History of the Civil Service Reform Movement, 1865–1883* (Urbana: University of Illinois Press, 1968).

9. "Industrial Justice," *Woodhull and Clafflin's Weekly*, April 26, 1873, 3; US Congress, *Report of the Tariff Commission, Appointed under Act of Congress Approved May 15, 1882*, 2 vols. (Washington, DC: Government Printing Office, 1882), 1: 343, and his full testimony on 341–44. Others were George Blair, John Halbert, T. J. Kingett, G. W. Madox. See also Samuel Bernstein, *The First International in America* (New York: A. M. Kelley, 1962), 246, though Timothy Messer-Kruse has a much better assessment in *The Yankee International: Marxism and the American Reform Tradition, 1848–1876* (Chapel Hill: University of North Carolina Press, 1998).

10. "Death by Fire," *New York Times*, December 26, 1872, 3; "The Death-Trap," *New York Times*, December 27, 1872, 2; "The City's Shame," *New York Herald*, December 29, 1872, 3; "The Centre Street Fire—a Cruel and Disgraceful Outrage," *New York Herald*, December 29, 1872, 8; *New York City Directory, 1870–'71* (New York: John F. Trow, 1871), 898.

11. "The Centre Street Cruelty" and "The Internationals and the Outrage," *New York*

Herald, December 30, 1872, 6; "The Internationals Interfere," *New York World*, December 30, 1872, 8.

12. "Free Cuba," *New York World*, January 13, 1873, 1.

13. Samuel Rezneck, "Distress, Relief, and Discontent in the United States during the Depression of 1873–78," *Journal of Political Economy* 58 (December 1950): 494–512; Rendigs Fels, "American Business Cycles, 1865–79," *American Economic Review* 41 (June 1951): 325–49; Charles P. Manias Kindleberger, *Panics and Crashes: A History of Financial Crises*, 5th ed. (New York: John Wiley and Sons, 2005), 137; Peter Mixon, "The Crisis of 1873: Perspectives from Multiple Asset Classes," *Journal of Economic History* 68 (September 2008): 722–57.

14. "Mr. Bradlaugh and the Internationals," *New York Times*, September 29, 1873, 8.

15. "Board of Aldermen," *New York Times*, November 25, 1873, 2; letter of W. A. A. Carsey, George W. Maddox, and H. M. Walton, November 9, 1873, in *The Papers of Ulysses S. Grant*, ed. John Y. Simon, 32 vols. (Carbondale: Southern Illinois University Press, 2000), 24: 220. Maddox is spelled Madox in some press accounts.

16. Herbert G. Gutman, "The Tompkins Square Riot in New York City on January 13, 1874," *Labor History* 6 (Winter 1965): 60–62; Samuel Gompers, *Seventy Years of Life and Labor* (New York: E. P. Dutton, 1925), 32–34. Embrey Bernard Howson mentioned Carsey along with "a few important men" arguing the government is obliged to provide work for the unemployed in the 1870s ("Jacob Sechler Coxey: A Biography of a Monetary Reformer, 1854–1951," PhD diss., Ohio State University, 1973, 125.

17. "The Working Men's Assembly," *New York Times*, January 28, 1874, 1; "The Workingmen's Assembly," *New York Herald*, January 30, 1874, 5. The latter closed with an appeal to all classes to join with them.

18. "Chief Matsell's Alarm," *The Sun* [New York], February 2, 1874, 1; "The Police and the Law," *New-York Tribune*, February 3, 1874, 4; "Jefferson Market Police Court," *New York Herald*, February 3, 1874, 8. A policeman named Edmund Buchanan is listed as living at 168 Bleeker according to *Trow's New York City Directory* (New York: J. F. Trow, 1871), 152.

19. "Communists in New York," *Galveston Daily News*, February 12, 1874, 2.

20. For Carsey, see his comment as an IWA spokesman in the *Chicago Daily Tribune*, February 12, 1874.

21. "The Immigration Question," *Little Rock Daily Republican*, February 3, 1874, 7.

22. "The Internationalists and Governor McEnery," *Houston Daily Mercury*, January 16, 1874, 2. See too the untitled item in the *Daily Mercury*, February 17, 1874, 2. On J. W. Mack as secretary: Carsey did serve as secretary of an IWA meeting in New York toward the end of 1874 ("A Panacea for Panic," *New York World*, December 31, 1873, 8).

23. "Cheap Transportation Association," *Sacramento Daily Union*, February 12, 1874, 1; *Marysville Daily Appeal*, February 12, 1874, 2; "The Internationalists Divided," *Memphis Public Ledger*, February 25, 1874, 2. On mercantile antimonopolism, see David Moisseiff Scobey, "Empire City: Politics, Culture, and Urbanism in Gilded-Age New York," PhD diss., Yale University, 1989, 168–69.

24. "Grievances of Internationals," *New-York Tribune*, January 26, 1874, 8. Maddox submitted the "Declaration of Principles and Bill of Grievances of the Internationals of the United States of America," in which he called for a working-class political party.

25. "Immigration," *Little Rock Daily Republican*, February 7, 1874, x.

26. "The Difference the Ballot Makes," subhead under "New York," *Nashville Union and American*, February 12, 1874, 1.

27. John H. B. Howland, *Sketches of Prominent Citizens of 1876* (Indianapolis: Tiford & Carlon, Printers, 1877), 545–46. See also Lause, *The Civil War's Last Campaign: James B. Weaver, the National Greenback-Labor Party and the Politics of Race and Section* (Lanham, MD: University Press of America, 2000), and Gretchen Ritter, *Goldbugs and Greenbacks: The Antimonopoly Tradition and the Politics of Finance in America, 1865–1900* (Cambridge: Cambridge University Press, 1997).

28. See also "The Workingmen," *Chicago Daily Tribune*, March 2, 1874; Thomas S. Mach, "George Hunt Pendleton, The Ohio Idea and Political Continuity in Reconstruction America," *Ohio History* 108 (Summer 1999): 125–44.

29. *Diary and Letters of Rutherford Birchard Hayes, Nineteenth President of the United States*, ed. Charles R. Williams, 5 vols. (Columbus, OH: Ohio State Archaeological and Historical Society, 1914–26), 3: 344.

30. The American internationalists and socialists followed this development; see the coverage in in *The Toiler* (New York), "Industrial Political Party," July 25, 1874, 1, and "The Industrial Labor Party," August 8 and 22, both p. 1. The last issue also noted on p. 2 that the "Committee of Public Safety," from which the "party" claimed authority, actually no longer existed. See further Thomas E. V. Smith, *Political Parties and Their Places of Meeting in New York City* (New York: for the author, 1893).

31. "The Mayoralty" and "Mr. Dana and the Mayoralty," *New York Herald*, October 13, 1874, 5, 8. See also "Declined," *Alexandria Gazette*, October 13, 1874, 3; untitled among "Political Notes," *National Republican*, October 14, 1874, 2; "News Items," *Belmont Chronicle*, October 22, 1874, 1; The meeting misnames one of the officers as "William A. Carson"; "The Mayoralty," *New York Herald*, October 13, 1874, 5.

32. "Mr. Dana Declines," *New York Herald*, October 13, 1874, 5; Frank Michael O'Brien, *The Story of the "Sun": New York, 1833–1918* (New York: George H. Doran, 1916), 229. See also "Political Notes," *National Republican*, October 14, 1874, 2; "New York City," *Wheeling Intelligencer*, October 14, 1874, 1; "Political Notes," *Omaha Daily Bee*, October 15, 1874, 2.

33. "Meeting of the Industrial Political Party," *New York Herald*, October 22, 1874, 10. See also "The Labor Convention," *Chicago Daily Tribune*, July 29, 1884, 4. See further Robert Waters, *Career and Conversation of John Swinton, Journalist, Orator, Economist* (Chicago: C. H. Kerr, c. 1902), and Sender Garlin, *Three American Radicals: John Swinton, Crusading Editor Charles P. Steinmetz, Scientist and Socialist William Dean Howells and the Haymarket Era* (Boulder, CO: Westview, 1991).

34. "Mr. Swinton Accepts," *New York Herald*, October 28, 1874, 10.

35. "Political" notice, *New York Herald*, November 1, 1874, 18; "The Elections," *New York*

Herald, November 3, 1874, 3; "The Right Way," *Woodhull and Clafflin's Weekly*, November 7, 1874, 11. The new party also nominated Conrad Kuhn for register, and Carsey, Blair, Joseph Taylor, and J. Graham for aldermen at-large. Some radicals, old internationalists and others allied with the Committee of Public Safety, fell into line behind the nomination. William A. Casey got 117 votes for alderman at-large in November 1874 (William C. Gover, *The Tammany Hall Democracy of the City of New York, General Committee for 1875* [New York: Martin B. Brown, 1875], 137).

36. "Industrial Political Party," *New York Herald*, November 3, 1875, 3.

37. "International Workingmen's Association" and notices on the SDWP, *The Toiler*, May 23, August 22, 1874, and Bernstein, *First International*, 247–48, 250–51, 258–62, 262–63, 267, 269–70; *Platform and Constitution of the Social Democratic Workingmen's Party of North America* (New York, 1876), printed in *The Socialist*, April 15, 1876.

38. For labor, see "Demonstration of Working Men" and "An Anti-Tammany Demonstration," *New York Daily Times*, September 1, 1874, 8, and August 15, 1875, 12. See also "Tompkins Square, or the Philanthropist," a dialogue in *The Toiler*, May 23, 1874; *The Toiler* also included two pieces on the "Industrial Political Party" and one on political action in the numbers of July 18 and 25, August 8, and September 26, 1874, as well as one on Christian Mayer, *The Toiler*, July 18, 1874, 2.

39. See, for example, the announcement under "Special Notices," *Philadelphia Times*, July 26, 1875, 3.

40. "The Rag-Men," *Chicago Daily Tribune*, November 26, 1874, 2; "More Money," *Chicago Daily Inter-Ocean*, November 26, 1874, 1. And see coverage in the *New York Times*, November 18, 1874.

41. "Greenback Meeting," *St. Louis Globe Democrat*, January 30, 1878, 4.

42. "The Rag Men Come to the Surface," "The Greenback Party," "Greenback Men in Council at Cleveland, O.," "Greenback Convention," "The Greenback Party," *Chicago Daily Tribune*, March 11, 1875, 2, 5; March 12, 2, 5; March 13, 1; "More Greenbacks" and "Greenback Enthusiasts," *Chicago Daily Times*, March 12, 1875, 3; March 13, 9. Joseph G. Tregle Jr., "Thomas J. Durant, Utopian Socialism, and the Failure of Presidential Reconstruction in Louisiana," *Journal of Southern History* 45 (November 1979): 485–512.

43. "The Anti-monopoly Convention," *New York Daily Times*, March 4, 1875, 1. Day's group followed with "Cincinnati Conference of Mechanics and Working-men," described in "The Working-men's Convention," *Cincinnati Daily Enquirer*, September 8, 1875, 8.

44. *Appleton's Cyclopedia 1876*, 599–602. See also "The Currency Question," *New York Daily Times*, July 29, 1875, 2, "Greenback Democrats," February 20, 2, "The New York Inflationists," March 3, 2, "The Democratic Inflationists," March 15, 1, 2, "Democratic Greenback Convention," March 22, 8, and "A Greenback Convention," March 25, 8.

45. Herbert J. Clancy, *The Presidential Election of 1880* (Chicago: Loyola University Press, 1958), on Tilden: 52–53, 56–57, 58–62, 62–63, 70–77; on Bayard: 64–65, 66–68, 78–79, 132–33, 137–39, 142–43; William J. Linton, *In the House That Tweed Built: Dedicated to Every True Reformer [Republican or Democrat]* (New York: The American News

Company, 1871). For a few examples of midwestern and southern Democratic papers pressing for a reform agenda—or said that they did—see *Fort Wayne Weekly Sentinel*, October 6, 1880, 2; "Gen. Weaver's Speech," *Opelika* [Alabama] *Observer-Locomotive*, July 29, 1880, 2; *Opelika* [Alabama] *Times*, July 23, 1880, 3.

46. "A New Party," *New York Herald*, November 2, 1875, 3. See also "Fourteenth District Reformers," *New York Times*, October 22, 1875, 10. For the historic lay of the land in a metropolis that changed almost entirely in rather rapid succession, see Real Estate Record Association, *A History of Real Estate Building and Architecture in New York City during the Last Quarter of a Century* (New York: Record and Guide, 1898; repr., New York, Arno, 1967).

47. "The Labor World," *Chicago Workingmen's Advocate*, January 15, 1876, 2; "New York Working Men at Albany," *New York Times*, January 27, 1876, 8.

48. "Business Editorials" [from the *Springfield Republican*], *Woodhull and Clafflin's Weekly*, February 12, 1876, 3.

49. "The Greenback Convention," *Rutland Daily Globe*, March 16, 1876, 3; "Greenback Fanatics," *New York Herald*, March 16, 1876, 3; "The Democratic Inflationists," *New York Times*, March 16, 1876, 1.

50. *Peter Cooper's "New Departure": An Answer by Him to Certain Criticisms on His "Letter on the Currency,"* broadside (New York, 1875); see also his posthumously published *Ideas for a Science of Good Government* (New York: Trow's Printing and Bookbinding, 1883); J. C. Zachos, *The Political and Financial Opinions of Peter Cooper, with an Autobiography of His Early Life* (New York: Trow's Printing and Bookbinding, 1877); Charles E. Lester, *Life and Character of Peter Cooper* (New York: J. B. Alden, 1883); Thomas Hughes, *Life and Times of Peter Cooper* (London: Macmillan, 1886); William F. Beller, *Peter Cooper: A Tribute in Commemoration of the Hundredth Anniversary of His Birth* (New York: Alumni Association of the Cooper Union, 1891); Rossiter W. Raymond, *Peter Cooper* (Boston: Houghton, Mifflin, 1901); Edward Mack, *Peter Cooper: Citizen of New York* (New York: Duell, Sloan and Pearce, 1949).

51. "Independent Labor Party," *New York Evening Post*, May 6, 1876, 4.

52. "Looking at the Work Beforehand," *New-York Tribune*, July 18, 1878, 2.

53. "Independent Labor Party," *New York Herald*, May 6, 1876, 4; "The Labor Convention," *Chicago Daily Tribune*, July 29, 1884, 4.

54. *Official Proceedings of the National Democratic Convention, Held in St. Louis, Mo., June 27th, 28th and 29th, 1876* (St. Louis: Woodward, Tiernan and Hale, 1876), 63.

Chapter 2. Independents and Partisan Pantomimes

1. "Rah for Rags," *Chicago Daily Times*, May 18, 1876, 3, and "Base and Bottomless," May 19, 3; "The Greenback Party," *Chicago Daily Inter-Ocean*, May 17, 1876, 5, "The Greenbackers," May 18, 5, and "The Greenback Party," May 19, 5. For the most complete and favorable coverage, see "Independents" in Buchanan's paper, the *Indianapolis Sun*, May 20, 1876, 1–2, 5, and editorial on 3.

2. "The Independent National Convention," *Workingman's Advocate*, May 20, 1876, 1; Reginald C. McCrane, "Ohio and the Greenback Movement," *Mississippi Valley Historical Review* 11 (March 1925): 526–42; Reginald C. McCrane, *William Allen: A Study in Western Democracy* (Columbus: Ohio State Archaeological and Historical Society, 1925).

3. "The Independent Labor Party," *New York Evening Post*, August 12, 1876, 1; "James Gordon Bennett," *National Republican*, August 12, 1876, 1.

4. "The Greenback Party," *Galveston Daily News*, September 27, 1876, 1; "Peter Cooper's Party," *Garnett* [Kansas] *Journal*, October 7, 1876, 1; "The Greenback Party," *New York Herald*, September 27, 1876, 4; "Campaign of the Greenback Party," *New York Times*, October 25, 1876, 2.

5. Vernon Parrington, *Main Currents in American Thought*. 3 vols. (New York: Harcourt, Brace, 1927–30) 3: 282, quoted in Allan Nevins, *Abram S. Hewitt, with Some Account of Peter Cooper* (New York : Harper and Brothers, 1935), 289; *North Mount Vernon Plain Dealer*, June 4, 1884, 7. See also "Political," *Bloomington Telephone*, June 7, 1884, 2, and "Political," *Albion New Era*, June 12, 1884, 2.

6. Illinois, Indiana, Michigan, and Iowa delivered nearly 45,000; Kansas and Pennsylvania added almost 15,000; and over 11,000 came from Missouri, Ohio, Nebraska, and Minnesota (*American Almanac and Treasury of Facts, Statistical, Financial, and Political, for the Year 1880*, ed. Ainsworth R. Spofford (New York: American News, 1880), 281. Mention of Peter Cooper's name in 1880, though, still drew cheers in Boston ("The Third Party—General Weaver's Address in Faneuil Hall," *Boston Daily Globe*, August 28, 1880, 1).

7. In smaller communities, where local authorities remained closer to their working citizens than to the railroads, government met corporate arguments that the strike endangered property by deputizing armed strikers to take the yards. In larger cities, strike committees often did the same, though Pittsburgh and Chicago experienced virtual insurrections of the desperately unemployed. In St. Louis and Toledo, strikers from various trades formed citywide leadership bodies that seized control of those cities, in the former under leadership of the socialist Workingmen's Party of the United States (WPUS) and the latter under the local Greenbackers. (Aside from some minor vandalism, the armed workers provided their communities with the most crime-free days of the Gilded Age.) For national overviews, see Robert V. Bruce, *1877: Year of Violence* (Indianapolis: Bobbs-Merrill, 1959), and Philip S. Foner, *The Great Labor Uprising of 1877* (New York: Monad, 1977).

8. Richard Slotkin discusses a coincidence of Indian war and social war that created metaphors of a "Red menace" that continued to shape US views for many years (Slotkin, *The Fatal Environment: the Myth of the Frontier in the Age of Industrialization, 1800–1890* [Middleton, CT: Wesleyan University Press, 1985], 338–45, 478–500).

9. See the quotes under "Monopolist Arguments" or "The True Inwardness of Old-Party Organs" in the *Winamac Greenback Journal*, March 6, 1880, 2, and August 14 and 21, 1880 (both on 1). The *Chicago Tribune* argument was prophetic, as the 1886

10. Neil L. Shumsky, *The Evolution of Political Protest and the Workingmen's Party of Cali-*

fornia (Columbus: Ohio State University Press, 1991), and Ira B. Cross, *A History of the Labor Movement in California* (Berkeley: University of California Press, 1935).

11. "Greenbackers," *Chicago Daily Inter-Ocean*, June 9, 1880, 82; his public declarations for the Republicans appeared in the *Iowa State Register*, July 12 and 13, 1877, but Weaver announced he had left the GOP in a letter to John Gear, August 29, 1877, Haynes quoted in Frederick E. Haynes, *James Baird Weaver* (Iowa City: State Historical Society of Iowa, 1919); see also 91–93, 95; Weaver, *A Call to Action: an Interpretation of the Great Uprising, Its Source and Causes* (Des Moines: Iowa Printing, 1892), 269; see also 269–84. Thomas B. Colbert ably addressed whether he had been a "Disgruntled 'Chronic Office Seeker' or Man of Political Integrity: James Baird Weaver and the Republican Party in Iowa, 1857–1877," *Annals of Iowa* 49 (Winter–Spring, 1988): 187–207.

12. "Work before Reformers," *New York Daily Times*, July 15, 1877, 6; "A Row among the Nationalists," *New York Daily Times*, May 9, 1878, 5. See also "Trouble in City Politics," *New York Daily Times*, June 9, 1878, 12.

13. John R. Commons, David J. Saposs, Helen L. Sumner, E. B. Mittelman, Henry E. Hoagland, John B. Andrews, Selig Perlman, and Henry W. Farnam, *History of Labour in the United States*, 2 vols., 2nd ed. (New York: Macmillan, 1946), 2: 221–22, 232, 232n, 235–36, 236n, 237–39; Samuel Bernstein, *The First International in America* (New York: Augustus M. Kelly, 1962), 247–48, 250–51, 262–63, 267, 269–70; *National Labor Tribune*, January (proceedings) 8, 9, 15, March 11, April 22, 29, 1876; "Declaration of Unity," *The Socialist*, May 6, 1876, 1; "Unity Convention," and "Unity," *The Socialist*, July 25, August 19, 1876, 1.

14. "The Nationals" and "Nationals," *Chicago Daily Inter-Ocean*, February 22, 23, 1878, both on 2; "The National Party," *Cincinnati Daily Enquirer*, February 23, 1878, 1–2; "Lunacy's Legacy," *Chicago Daily Times*, February 23, 1878, 2; and "The Greenback-Industrial Workingmen in Session at Toledo," *Chicago Daily Tribune*, February 23, 1878, 4.

15. Richard M. Doolen, "'Brick Pomeroy and the Greenback Clubs," *Journal of the Illinois State Historical Society* 65 (Winter 1972): 434–50; Mary E. Tucker, *Life of Mark M. Pomeroy* (New York: G. W. Carleton, 1868); Ruth A. Tucker, "M. M. Pomeroy: Forgotten Man of the Nineteenth Century," PhD diss., Northern Illinois University, 1979; Frank L. Klement, "'Brick' Pomeroy and the Democratic Processes: A Study in Civil War Politics," *Wisconsin Academy of Science, Arts and Letters* 51 (1962): 159–69; Marcus Mills Pomeroy, *Journey of Life: Reminiscences and Recollections of 'Brick' Pomeroy* (New York: Advance Thought Company, 1890).

16. "The Nationals Organizing," *New York Times*, June 28, 1878, 5.

17. "Libelling a Clergyman," *New York Herald*, October 4, 1876, 5; and "A Greenbacker in Trouble," *Middletown Daily Press*, July 31, 1878, 3.

18. "Shupe's Statutory Barrier," *New York Herald*, August 4, 1878, 4; "An Able Financier," *Fort Wayne Daily Sentinel*, August 13, 1878, 4; untitled item in the *Chariton Patriot*, August 6, 1878, 3. On the rumored arrest, "Sick of Shupe," *Cuba Patriot*, September 6, 1878, 2.

19. "The Condenser," *Indianapolis Journal*, August 9, 1878, 5.

20. "A Boss Communist" [from *Washington Post*], *Memphis Public Ledger*, June 19, 1878, 2.

21. "Accused of Treachery," *The Sun* [New York], July 11, 1878, 1; "Bad Greenbackers" [from the *Keokuk Constitution*], *Jackson Sentinel*, August 1, 1878, 4; "New York National Convention" and "The Greenback-Labor Movement" [from *New York Herald*], *Indiana* [PA] *Progress*, August 1, 1878, 4.

22. "Looking at the Work Beforehand," *New-York Tribune*, July 18, 1878, 2; Robert Griffith, machinist, former Democrat, but Labor Reform for several years. George W. Madox, real estate. "Was Once a Radical Republican. Is Now a Socialist." He was a candidate for office on the Socialist ticket last year.

23. "New York," *Terre Haute Weekly Gazette*, July 25, 1878, 4; "The New York Nationals," *Indianapolis State Sentinel*, July 31, 1878, 21; "The New-York Nationals," *New-York Tribune*, July 18, 1878, 2; "Looking at the Work Beforehand."

24. "The Labor Question," *Alexandria Gazette*, August 3, 1878, 3. See also "New York," *Rock Island Argus*, August 3, 1878, Page 1, c4; "The Labor Investigation," *Washington* [DC] *Evening Star*, August 3, 1878, 1, c7; "The Labor Question," *Memphis Daily Appeal*, August 4, 1878, image 1, c5; "Tulaendische Nachrichten," *Westliche Blätter*, August 4, 1878, 6; "A Row among the Nationalists: Meeting of the New-York Committee on Organization," *New York Times*, May 9, 1878, 5; "Congressional Investigation of the Causes and Cure of the Hard Times," *Macomb Journal*, August 8, 1878, 2; "The Red Flag," *New York Herald*, August 11, 1878, 7; untitled item, *Canton* [OH] *Stark County Democrat*, August 15, 1878, 3. "The American Rowdy Party," *Spectator*, August 24, 1878, 1064–65, advocated a Homestead Act (which was passed years earlier and provided employment in public improvements—"on which only American citizens should be employed"). A. S. Hewitt chaired a meeting at which Carsey spoke, attended by Mrs. S. Myra Hall of the Congress of Humanity and Robert W. Hume of the Labor League. See also untitled item, *Independent*, August 8, 1878, 11; "Some Barriers between Labor and Capital," *Catholic World* 28 (November 1878): 241–42; Albert V. House Jr., "Proposals of Government Aid to Agricultural Settlement during the Depression of 1873–1879," *Agricultural History* 12 (January 1938): 58; Samuel Rezneck, "Distress, Relief, and Discontent in the United States during the Depression of 1873–78," *Journal of Political Economy* 58 (December 1950): 502–3.

25. "Shupe's Wing," "Greenbackers," and "Cosmopolitan Greenbackers," *New York Herald*, August 15, 1878, 4; "Greenback-Labor Party," *New York Herald*, September 8, 1878, 12; "Anti-Tammany" and "The Shupe-O'Reilly Greenback Primaries," *New York Herald*, October 5, 1878, 4.

26. "Quarrelsome Nationals," *New York Times*, August 17, 1878, 8, "The Fight of the Factions: Can a Harmonizing Committee Harmonize?" August 18, 12, "The Harmonizing Committee: Claims of the Contending Factions—Peter Cooper's Electioneering Expenses," August 20, 8, and "The Greenback-Labor Comedy," August 21, 8.

27. "The Greenbackers' Convention," *New York Times*, October 6, 1878, 1, "Local

Political Matters: The Contest against Tammany," October 10, 2, "W. A. A. Carsey's Convention," October 11, 2, and "Deserting the Greenbackers," October 29, 5.

28. New York Labor Union, W. A. A. Carsey, Chairman; B. M. Abell, Secretary; Frank Waters, M. Farrell, and committee, *City Record* [New York] 6 (October 9, 1878): 1457.

29. *City Record* 6 (December 3, 1878): 1749, 1750, *City Record* supplement (December 9, 1878); and *Tribune Almanac and Political Register for 1879* (New York: Tribune Association, 1879). 92.

30. For the congressional returns, see Congressional Quarterly, *Guide to U.S. Elections*, (Washington, DC: Congressional Quarterly, 1975, with subsequent editions in 1985 and 1994), corrected by *The Tribune Almanac for 1879* (New York: Tribune Association, 1878), and for 1880 (New York: Tribune Association, 1881), as well as "Representatives Elect to the Forty-Sixth Congress—March 4, 1879, to March 4, 1881," in *American Almanac and Treasury of Facts, Statistical, Financial, and Political, for the Year 1879*, ed. Ainsworth R. Spofford (New York: American News, 1879), 297–99. See also *Cincinnati Daily Enquirer*, November 5, 1878, 1; *Chicago Daily Inter-Ocean*, November 5, 1878, 2, and November 7, 1. On their role in Congress, see "Those Thirteen," *Courtland Friend of the Labourer*, April 10, 1879, 2.

31. "Work before Reformers," *New York Daily Times*, July 15, 1877, 6, "Trouble in City Politics," June 9, 1878, 12, "The Nationals Organizing," June 28, 5, "'Dick' Schell for Mayor," October 4, 8, "The Greenbackers' Convention," October 6, 1; "W. A. A. Carsey's Convention," *New York Times*, October 11 (2), 1878; "Cheap Transportation," *New York Daily Times*, September 10, 1873, 8, "Work before Reformers," September 11, 1, 4–5, and "Trouble in City Politics," July 15, 1877, 6, June 9, 1878, 12.

32. "A Greenback Fizzle," *New York Herald*, September 19, 1879, 4.

33. For Carsey, see "A Row among the Nationalists," *New York Daily Times*, May 9, 1878, 5. As with Carsey's meetings, these gatherings often had very few participants other than their "leader." "Work before Reformers," *New York Daily Times*, July 15, 1877, 6. See also "Trouble in City Politics," *New York Daily Times*, June 9, 1878, 12; "Kewaunee Smith" Democritus, "Political," *Indianapolis Journal*, August 20, 1878, 2. It covered other aspects of these local parties on October 2, 1874, 5, October 18, 7, August 12, 1875, 2, and October 9, 1877, 5.

34. "What Shupe Says," *Chicago Daily Tribune*, November 10, 1878, 13. See also Eugene Beebe to the editor, "The Nationals and the Mayoralty," *New York Herald*, September 8, 1878, 12.

35. "The Rag Baby Advocates: The New-York State Greenback Convention," *New York Times*, August 28, 1879, 1, and "Convention of Greenbackers at Utica," and August 29, 1.

36. Carsey to Wright, November 22, 1878, in Daniel J. Curran, "Hendrick B. Wright: A Study in Leadership," PhD diss., Fordham University, 1963, 354.

37. For Weaver's background and emergence as an insurgent leader, see Lause, *The Civil War's Last Campaign: James B. Weaver, the Greenback-Labor Party, and the Politics of Race and Section* (Lanham, MD: University Press of America, 2001).

38. "What Shupe Says," *Chicago Daily Tribune*, November 10, 1878, 13.

39. T. A. Bland, *Life of Benjamin F. Butler* (Boston: Lee and Shepard; New York: Charles T. Dillingham, 1879), 5–10, 13, 17, esp. 14–16. See also Butler's "Absolute Money," *Winamac Greenback Journal*, November 2, 1878, 1.

40. Bland, *Life of Benjamin F. Butler*, 19–21, 23, 30–31, 32–35, 163–73, 173–75, 187–88, 185–86, 186–87, and, on women's suffrage, 180–84; Clancy, *The Presidential Election of 1880* (Chicago: Loyola University Press, 1985), 48 and 48n; "Our Standard-Bearer," *Irish World*, May 15, 1880, 5. See also "Butler's Nomination," *New York Herald*, October 13, 1874, 5.

41. Foner, *History of the Labor Movement*, 563; Don D. Lescohier, "The Knights of St. Crispin, 1867–1874," *Bulletin of the University of Wisconsin: Economics and Political Science Series* 7 (July 1910): 56, 58–59, 59n. See also "The Greenbackers," *Boston Daily Globe*, September 23 (morning ed.), 1880, 1. For some of the many preliminary meetings, see "Danvers Greenbackers," "Gloucester Greenbackers," "Newburyport Greenbackers," and "Salem Greenbackers," *Boston Daily Globe*, August 29 (morning ed.), 1880, 8; "Greenback Caucus at Natick," *Boston Daily Globe*, September 12, 1880, 8.

42. "Our Standard-Bearer," *Irish World*, May 15, 1880, 5; Frank H. Brooks, "Ideology, Strategy, and Organization: Dyer Lum and the American Anarchist Movement," *Labor History* 34 (Winter 1993): 60–61, 62, 65. See also Brooks, "Anarchism, Revolution, and Labor in the Thought of Dyer D. Lum: 'Events Are the True Schoolmasters,'' PhD diss., Cornell University, 1988, which is honest about race but misunderstands Lum's break with the Greenbackers as an indication of his radicalism. Lum had enlisted in 1862 to serve as a sergeant in the 121st New York, eventually gaining a commission in the Fourteenth New York Cavalry.

43. "Gen. Horace Binney Sargent," *Chicago Weekly Express*, October 12, 1880, 8. The Chicago dailies—the *Times*, the *Tribune*, and the *Inter-Ocean*—published thorough accounts of the convention in the issues of June 9–12, 1880.

44. "Ben Butler and the Greenbackers," *The Sun* [New York], May 28, 1880, 2.

45. Alexander Saxton, *The Indispensable Enemy: Labor and the Anti-Chinese Movement in California* (Berkeley: University of California Press: 1971), 161–63.

46. Missouri's shift must have represented considerable maneuvering. Going into the convention, only Joshua A. Bodenhamer, the editor of the *Carthage People's Press*—published "in the interest of the industrial and business classes"—had been the only member of that state's delegation for Butler (*The History of Jasper County, Missouri . . .* [Des Moines, IA: Mills, 1883], 291, 323).

47. McGuire's letter in *Irish World*, July 31, 1880, 1; *Biographical and Historical Memoirs of Mississippi*, 2 vols. (Chicago: Goodspeed, 1891), 2: 1013–15; J. H. Stone, "General Absolom Madden West and the Civil War in Mississippi," *Journal of Mississippi History* 42 (May 1980): 135–44.

48. "Weaver on the War-Path," *New York Daily Times*, July 7, 1880, 1.

49. "Gen. Weaver's Acceptance," *New York Daily Times*, July 3, 1880, 5; "Gen. J. B. Weaver," *Winamac Greenback Journal*, July 10, 1880, 1; William B. Hesseltine, *Third-Party*

Movements in the United States (Princeton, NJ: Van Nostrand, 1962), 142–45; *The Platform of the National Greenback Labor Party and the Letter of Acceptance of General J. B. Weaver* (n.p.: National Greenback Party, 1880).

Chapter 3. Counterfeiting Class

1. Rowland Hill Harvey, *Samuel Gompers: Champion of the Toiling Masses* (Stanford, CA: Stanford University Press, 1935), 40–41; William Trant, *Trade Unions: Their Origins and Objects, Influence and Efficacy*, 18th ed. (Washington, DC: AFL, 1916), 39.

2. "Four Leading Greenbackers All for Hancock," *Point Pleasant Weekly Register*, September 22, 1880, 2. See also "A Fair Exchange" [from *National View*], *Chicago Weekly Express*, September 28, 1880, 5. For Cooper's presence on the platform, see "Gen. Weaver in New York," *New York Daily Times*, September 14, 1880, 5. Cooper supposedly gave some financial support to Weaver's campaign right up into its final week. See further Thomas Card, "Questions and Answers," *Chicago Weekly Express*, October 26, 1880, 2.

3. On the meeting, see "The Third Party—General Weaver's Address in Faneuil Hall," *Boston Daily Globe* (morning ed.), August 28, 1880, 1. See also "The Greenback Candidate," *Boston Evening Transcript*, August 27, 1880, 4. Weaver's remark paraphrased in "General Weaver in Faneuil Hall," August 28, 1880, 2. See also "Gen. Weaver in Boston," *New York Daily Times*, August 28, 1880, 4. On Boston, see "Weaver in Boston" [from *Irish World*] and "Gen. Weaver," *Winamac Journal*, September 25, October 27, 1880, both on 1. See further *Boston Daily Globe*, (morning ed.), August 29, 1880, 1.

4. The *Iowa State Tribune* comment on Butler is quoted in *Chicago Weekly Express*, October 12, 1880, 8.

5. "Gen. Weaver in New York," *New York Daily Times*, September 14, 1880, 5; notice in "Campaign Notes," *Irish World*, September 18, 1880, 5, and September 25, 8. For schedule, see "Political Notes," *Boston Daily Globe* (morning ed.), September 9, 1880, 1, with "General Weaver's Prediction" (morning ed.), September 12, 1880, 8. For the New York speech, see "Gen. Weaver," *Winamac Journal*, October 1, 1880, 1. See also "Gen. Butler in Conference with Gen. Hancock," *Bangor Daily Commercial*, September 20, 1880, 1; *Iowa State Tribune* comment on Butler is quoted in *Chicago Weekly Express*, October 12, 1880, 8.

6. "Weaver Too!" *Grand Rapids Daily Eagle*, October 26, 1880, 1; *Des Moines Independent*, October 27, 1880, 1.

7. "Dyer D. Lum's Sensation," *Chicago Weekly Express*, October 5, 1880, and "Dyer D. Lum's Proof," October 26, 1; *Des Moines Independent*, October 6, 1880, 1, October 13, 5; "Weaver's Sell Out," *Fort Wayne Weekly Sentinel*, October 6, 1880, 2, 4; "A Word to Greenbackers," *Boston Daily Globe* (morning ed.), October 3, 1880, 4. See also "Weaver's Web," *Grand Rapids Weekly Democrat*, October 6, 1880, 1. For charges in the *Washington Post* of a three-hour interview behind closed doors that left Weaver $329 richer, see "A Sale That Don't Work" [from *Philadelphia Times*], *Fort Wayne Weekly Sentinel*, October 6, 1880, 2. See also Martin in "A Traitor to the Greenbackers," *New York Daily Times*, Oc-

tober 3, 1880, 2, and "Warwick Martin on Lum" in "Lum's Charges and Their Prompt Refutation by Gen. Weaver, Warwick Martin and George O. Jones," *Chicago Weekly Express*, October 5, 1880, 5.

8. "Another Traitor," *Chicago Weekly Express*, November 9, 5, and the same title in *Irish World*, November 9, 5. Mulford's letter first appeared in *The Sun* [New York]. See also "Mr. Mulford's Greenback Clubs" and notice in a circular, *New York Daily Times*, March 27, 1880, 8, and August 17, 4. See further items noted under "Campaign Notes," *Irish World*, July 17, 1880, 5, September 4, 5, and Robert Blissert, "To the Men of New York," November 6, 1880, 5.

9. Weaver proved to be as "bright and encouraging" as any politician when he chatted with reporters. He once said that he "usually considered 10,000 but a small meeting." Repeatedly, he made "very sanguine" predictions of upset GLP victories in Alabama, West Virginia, Arkansas, Texas, Mississippi, Maine, and California, with possible wins in Missouri, and "a vote which will astonish both parties" in Michigan, Wisconsin, Illinois, Indiana, and Massachusetts ("General Weaver's Views," *Indianapolis Journal*, September 25, 1880, 3; "How Gen. Weaver Feels," *Winamac Journal*, October 16, 1880, 1; "The Greenback Candidate," *Boston Evening Transcript*, August 27, 1880, 4; "Words with Weaver," *Wheeling Daily Intelligencer*, August 2, 1880, 4; "General Weaver's Prediction," *Boston Daily Globe*, September 12 [morning ed.], 1880, 8; "Weaver's Triumphant March" [from *Philadelphia Times*], *Mobile Daily Register*, July 21, 1880, 2). When Weaver made claims about California in Chattanooga, Republican commentators back home in Iowa reported that he "rates Kearney too high" (*Davis County Republican*, September 9, 1880, 1; "A Slim Chance," *Mobile Daily Register*, July 23, 1880, 2).

10. US Congress, *Report of the Tariff Commission, Appointed under Act of Congress Approved May 15, 1882*, 2 vols. (Washington, DC: Government Printing Office, 1882), 1: 341–42.

11. "Political Bandits, These People," *New York Times*, October 22, 1893, 2.

12. "Knights Badly Organized, Surplus of Labor the Cause of All Trouble," *New York Times*, February 13, 1887, 3.

13. "Nearly 150 Miles by River for Ten Cents," *Memphis Daily Appeal*, September 20, 1882, 3; "Practical Anti-monopoly," *Ottawa Free Trader*, September 20, 1882, 2; untitled item, *Shelbyville Daily Evening Democrat*, September 27, 1883, 1. See also "Sons of Columbia" from an old temperance hymnal (Mrs. C. H. Waterman, "Come, Sons of Columbia," *Temperance Hymn Book and Minstrel: A Collection of Hymns, Songs and Odes for Temperance Meetings and Festivals*, ed. J. Marsh (New York: American Temperance Union, New York, 1842), 66.

14. "Wage-Workers' Demands," *The Sun* [New York], April 5, 1881, 1; Harvey, *Samuel Gompers*, 40–41. See also "Like the Knights of Labor: A New Secret Order in Course of Formation in Boston," *Washington Evening Star*, March 23, 1886, 3.

15. "Wage-Workers' Demands," *The Sun* [New York], April 5, 1881, 1, c3; Harvey, *Samuel Gompers*, 40–41. See also *Preamble to the Declaration of Principles of the Knights of Industry*; "Like the Knights of Labor."

16. "Wage-Workers' Demands,'" *The Sun* [New York], April 5, 1881, 1.

17. "The Industrial Party. Their National Convention Meets Today," *Washington Evening Star*, February 22, 1888, 1; "Confederated Industrial Unions," *Indianapolis Journal*, November 19, 1891, 2. See also G. F. Zedaker, Lewis L. Driver, and John W. Somers, "In Memoriam," *Fort Wayne Weekly Gazette*, April 28, 1892, 5.

18. "That Campaign of Argument—One of the 'Capital's' Samples," *Advocate and Topeka Tribune*, August 3, 1892, 5; untitled item, *Laramie Daily Boomerang*, March 12, 1892, 8.

19. Harvey, *Samuel Gompers*, 40–41; Trant, *Trade Unions*, 39; Hermann Schluter, *Brewing Industry and the Brewery Workers' Movement in America* (Cincinnati, OH: International Union of United Brewery Workmen of America, 1910), 210.

20. "Current Events," *Brooklyn Daily Eagle*, January 27, 1880, 2. The Amalgamated Labor Union held a mass meeting in the Cooper Union to endorse bills before the legislature for a bureau of labor statistics, the abolition of prison labor, an eight-hour law, the abolition of tobacco factories in tenement houses, and a mechanics' lien law. "Current Events," *Brooklyn Daily Eagle*, January 27, 1880, 2; and Participation with the Central Labor Union. Saturday afternoon "Short Hour League" meeting on the bowery. K of L central labor union and A.L.U. "Saturday Half Holiday," *The Sun* [New York], July 8, 1883, 5.

21. An Amalgamated Labor Union promised support to the Cohoe strikers ("The Cohoes Strikers," *Port Jervis* [NY] *Evening Gazette*, May 27, 1882, 2). See also "Determined Mechanics," *The Sun* [New York], May 27, 1882, 1; "Saturday Half Holiday," *The Sun* [New York], July 8, 1883, 5; "Maryland Miners' Strike," *The Sun* [New York], May 27, 1882, 1.

22. "City News," *Terre Haute Evening Mail*, June 11, 1881, 5; Mike McCormick, "Historical Perspective: American Federation of Labor Born in Terre Haute," *Terre Haute Tribune-Star*, November 13, 2016, https://www.tribstar.com/features/history/historical-perspective-american-federation-of-labor-born-in-terre-haute/article_7eec9842-b5e3-5043-82d0-1020f34de8d8.html.

23. See, too, the involvement of Carsey's old ally, Sanford Church, in the discussion of Rapid Transit ("The Rapid Transit Commission. The Press and Inventors Still Excluded from Its Rooms," *New York Daily Herald*, July 15, 1875, 5, which describes Carsey and William Wedemeyer waiting to present their plans to the commission). See further Church on Rapid Transit ("Workingmen's Lyceum," *New York Toiler*, September 26, 1874, 2, and also "State News," *Geneva Daily Gazette*, February 27, 1884, 2).

24. "'You Pays Your Money,' etc.," Town Talk, and "The Fourth," City News, *Terre Haute Evening Mail*, July 9, 1881, 1, 5.

25. Schluter, *Brewing Industry*, 210; Harvey, *Samuel Gompers*, 40–41; Trant, *Trade Unions*, 39.

26. Trant, *Trade Unions*, 39.

27. Untitled item, *Terre Haute Evening Mail*, August 6, 1881, 5; Mark Crawford, "'Large Oaks from Little Acorns Grow': Some Information Concerning the Early History of What Is Now Known as the American Federation of Labor," *American Federations* 27 (February 1920): 140, 142, 142–43 (full essay is on 140–49); McCormick, "Historical Perspective." Key figures among the unionists were John E. Coughlin, president of the National Tanners and Curriers Union and Richard Powers of the Lake Seamen's Union from Chicago; Peter J. McGuire, the carpenter and socialist from the St. Louis Trades and Labor Assembly; William C. Pollner of the Cleveland Trades Assembly; Thomas Thompson of the Iron Molders Union of Dayton, Ohio; George W. Osborne of the Iron Molders Union from Springfield, Ohio; Samuel L. Leffingwell of the Indianapolis Trades Assembly; and Lyman A. Brant of the International Typographical Union from Detroit.

28. Crawford, "Large Oaks," 143; untitled item, *Terre Haute Evening Mail*, August 6, 1881, 5, c1.

29. Harvey, *Samuel Gompers*, 40–41; Trant, *Trade Unions*, 39; Crawford, "Large Oaks," 145–49; *Report of the First Annual Session of the Federation of Organized Trades and Labor Unions of the United States and Canada, Held in Pittsburg* [sic], *Pennsylvania, December 15, 16, 17, and 18, 1881* (n.p.: by the Authority of the Federation, n.d.) in *Proceedings of the American Federation of Labor 1881 . . . 1888*, collected and reprinted (Bloomington, IL: for the AFL, 1906), 3–24.

30. David Hochfelder, *The Telegraph in America, 1832–1920* (Baltimore: Johns Hopkins University Press, 2012), 47. Carsey's credentials as a movement spokesman were given as his attendance at the Farmers Alliance convention in Ocala in 1890. In 1893, the "Supreme Council of the Knights of Industry in New York" also won an interview with the newly inaugurated President Grover Cleveland and his attorney general to discuss their petition "To Abolish the Bell Telephone Patent," likely made on behalf of its aspiring rivals (*Washington Evening Star*, March 15, 1893, 5).

31. "Court Calendar," *Akron Summit County Beacon*, October 15, 1873, 1; "Fragments," *Akron Summit County Beacon*, November 12, 1873, 3.

32. "Little They Don't Want," *New York Times*, January 21, 1893, 8.

33. "Still Think It's a Trick," *The Sun* [New York], August 23, 1890, 2; "Influence Bought and Paid For" [from *The Sun*], *Buffalo Weekly Express*, May 18, 1893, 5.

34. For the elaboration of Carsey's views given over the subsequent three paragraphs, see US Congress, *Report of the Tariff Commission, Appointed under Act of Congress Approved May 15, 1882*, 2 vols. (Washington, DC: Government Printing Office, 1882), 1: 341, 343; full testimony on 341–44.

35. US Congress, *Report of the Tariff Commission*, 1: 342.

36. Untitled item, *Indianapolis News*, September 4, 1882, 2; US Congress, *Report of the Tariff Commission*, 1: 343.

37. US Congress, *Report of the Tariff Commission*, 1: 344.

38. Untitled item, *New-York Tribune*, January 17, 1883, 4, c2; New York Association for the Protection of American Industry, *Proceedings of the Mass Meeting Held at Cooper Institute*, New York, February 1, 1883.

39. Herbert J. Bass, "David B. Hill and the Steal of the Senate, 1891," *New York History* 41 (July 1960): 299–311; Bass, *"I Am a Democrat": The Political Career of David Bennett Hill* (Syracuse, NY: Syracuse University Press, 1961). See also State of New York, *Public Papers of David B. Hill, Governor, 1887* (Albany, NY: Argus, 1888). On his ascendancy, Hill hired Cleveland's executive clerk to be his own private secretary, who had also served in that capacity as early as during the administration of Samuel Tilden ("State News," *Geneva Daily Gazette*, February 27, 1884, 2).

40. Bass, *"I Am a Democrat,"* 67, 68, 69, 120, 251.

41. United States. Congress. House. Committee on Commerce, Wayne MacVeagh, J. H. Reagan, *Arguments and Statements before the Committee on Commerce in Relation to Certain Bills Referred to That Committee Proposing Congressional Regulation of Interstate Commerce*, February 21, 1882 (Washington, DC: Government Printing Office, 1882), 151, 55, 97.

42. "Nearly 150 Miles by River for Ten Cents," *Memphis Daily Appeal*, September 20, 1882, 3; "Practical Anti-monopoly," *Ottawa Free Trader*, September 20, 1882, 2.

43. "Practical Anti-monopoly." Shupe listed Butler among his allies and Thomas Ewing as one of his lawyers in New York.

44. "Obituary," *The Sun* [New York], May 27, 1893, 3; John Francis Henry Sr. (February 25, 1834–May 25, 1893), burial, Hope Cemetery Waterbury, Washington County, Vermont. Henry also had business ties to Henry E. Bowen.

45. "Knights Badly Organized."

46. "The Conference of the Anti-monopolists of America," *Monmouth* [IL] *Evening Gazette*, July 6, 1883, 1.

47. "Father Columbia's Paper," *Boston Daily Globe*, December 19, 1883, 8.

Chapter 4. Monopolizing Antimonopolism

1. "The Antimonopolists," *Chicago Daily Inter-Ocean*, May 15, 1884, 3, dates the meeting on April 18, and the following date it on the 20th: "Butler to Be Nominated," *Baldwinsville* [NY] *Gazette and Farmers' Journal*, April 24, 1884, 4; "Electric Flashes," *Monmouth* [IL] *Evening Gazette*, April 1, 1884, 2. See also "Political Notes," *Washington Evening Star*, April 5, 1884, 5; untitled item, *Galveston Daily New*, April 24, 1884, 3.

2. "Electric Flashes," *Monmouth* [IL] *Evening Gazette*, April 1, 1884, 2. See also "Political Notes," *Washington Evening Star*, April 5, 1884, 5; untitled item, *Galveston Daily New*, April 24, 1884, x.

3. "Father Columbia's Paper," *Boston Daily Globe*, December 19, 1883, 8.

4. Frank M. O'Brien, *The Story of the Sun—New York, 1833–1918* (New York: George H. Doran, 1918), 420–21. See also Janet Steele, *The Sun Shines for All: Journalism and Ideology in the Life of Charles A. Dana* (Syracuse, NY: Syracuse University Press, 1993).

5. "The Workingmen in Politics," *New York World*, September 1, 1883, 2; A. J. Canary from Cuba, Missouri, "Lyer Dum," *New York The People*, July 24, 1892, 2.

6. The National Committee later said to have been appointed was named, after the fact, six months later. "The Labor Convention," *Chicago Daily Tribune*, July 29, 1884, 4;

"The Labor Convention," *Daily Republican*, January 11, 1884, 4; "Democracy Succumbs to Monopoly," *Watertown* [WI] *Republican*, January 16, 1884, 4. In general, see Harold B. Raymond, "Ben Butler's Last Hurrah: The Presidential Campaign of 1884," *Colby Library Quarterly* 10 (March 1973): 26–38.

7. "Workingmen to Organize," *New York Evening Telegram*, January 9, 1884, 3; "Antimonopolists to Meet," *New York World*, January 12, 1884, 2; and "Labor and Wages," *Monmouth* [IL] *Evening Gazette*, January 14, 1884, 1.

8. "The Antimonopolists," *Chicago Daily Inter-Ocean*, May 15, 1884, 3, dates the meeting on April 18, and the following date it on the 20th: "Butler to Be Nominated," *Baldwinsville* [NY] *Gazette and Farmers' Journal*, April 24, 1884, 4; "Electric Flashes," *Monmouth* [IL] *Evening Gazette*, April 1, 1884, 2. See also "Political Notes," *Washington Evening Star*, April 5, 1884, 5; untitled item, *Galveston Daily New*, April 24, 1884, x.

9. Nichols to Reagan, March 27, Reagan to Nichols, March 28, 1884, "Selections from the Reagan Papers: The Butler-Reagan Ticket of 1884," *Journal of Southern History* 21 (August 1955): 381–82, 382–83. Butler's letters to Major, May 8, to Lichtman, May 22, and to Shupe, May 29, reflect this developing strategy.

10. Weaver to Reagan, April 22, 1884, "Selections from the Reagan Papers: The Butler-Reagan Ticket of 1884," *Journal of Southern History* 21 (August 1955): 383–84.

11. Reagan to Andrew Young, May 24, 1884, and to Weaver, May 26, 1884, "Selections from the Reagan Papers," 385–86.

12. "Political," *Chicago Times*, May 15, 1884, 6; "Antimonopolists," *Chicago Daily Inter-Ocean*, May 14, 1884, 3. See also Harold B. Raymond, "Ben Butler's Last Hurrah: The Presidential Campaign of 1884," *Colby Library Quarterly* 10 (March 1973): 26–38, and Hans Trefousse, "Ben Butler and the New York Election of 1884," *New York History* 37 (April 1956): 185–96. On the campaign, see Mark W. Summers, *Rum, Romanism, and Rebellion: The Making of a President, 1884* (Chapel Hill: University of North Carolina Press, 2003).

13. "Anti-monopoly Seceders," *Chicago Times*, May 18, 1884, 3.

14. "The Greenbackers," *Chicago Times*, May 30, 1884, 1; "Greenbackers," *Cincinnati Enquirer*, May 29, 1884, 4; "Butler Boom," *New-York Daily Tribune*, May 31, 1884, 4.

15. "Butler Again," *Cincinnati Enquirer*, May 28, 1884, 1, and "'Tis Done. The Greenbackers Wait on Their Butler," May 30, 4; "The Greenbackers," *Indianapolis News*, May 28, 1884, 4; "The Greenbackers. National Convention," *Chicago Daily Inter-Ocean*, May 29, 1884, 2.

16. "The Greenbackers," *Chicago Times*, May 30, 1884, 1; "The Greenbackers," *Chicago Times*, May 30, 1884, 1; *Biographical and Historical Memoir of Pulaski, Jefferson, Lonoke, Faulkner, Grant, Saline, Perry, Garland and Hot Spring Counties, Arkansas* (Chicago: Goodspeed, 1890), 438–49.

17. "Butler Again."

18. For Butler's role in the convention discussed here and in the following two paragraphs, see *Official Proceedings of the National Democratic Convention*, Saint Louis, June 5, 6, and 7, 1888 (St. Louis: Woodward and Tiernan, 1888), 202–3, 203–4, 204–5, 206,

208, 209. See also "A Short but Instructive History," *The Sun* [New York], November 2, 1884, 4.

19. Untitled item, *Norton's Union Intelligencer* [Dallas], July 17, 1884, 1.

20. Item, *Chicago Tribune*, February 13, 1874, 4; "The Workingmen," *Chicago Inter-Ocean*, February 26, 1874, 4.

21. "The Labor Convention," *Chicago Daily Tribune*, 4.

22. "The Convention Is Claimed Both by Butler and Blaine Adherents"; "Independent Labor Party" under "Convention of the Independent Labor Party at Chicago—No One Knows Yet Who They Will Support for President," *Maysville* [KY] *Daily Evening Bulletin*, July 30, 1884, 1; "The Labor Convention," *Cincinnati Enquirer*, July 30, 1884, 4.

23. "A Postponement," *San Francisco Daily Alta California*, July 29, 1884, 5, c1. See also identified as United Labor Party; "On Their Dignity," *Dallas Daily Herald*, July 29, 1884, 1; "The Labor Party," *Washington Evening Star*, July 29, 1884, 1; "Political Notes. Dissensions in the United States Labor Party," *Philadelphia Inquirer*, July 30, 1884, 1; "Another National Convention," *Palatka* [FL] *Daily News*, July 30, 1884, 4, c4; "A Slight Misunderstanding," *Butte* [MT] *Semi-weekly Miner*, July 30, 1884, 2.

24. "Efforts to Deceive Workingmen," *Albany Times*, July 31, 1884, 2.

25. For these accounts, see "The Labor Convention," *Chicago Daily Tribune*, July 29, 1884, 4, and "Disappointed Delegates," July 31, 5.

26. "The Labor Convention," *Chicago Daily Tribune*, July 30, 1884, 6.

27. "Anti-monopolists. Gathering of the Clans at Chicago," *Buffalo Evening Telegraph*, July 29, 1884, 1; "The Tale Is Told," *Burlington* [IA] *Hawk-Eye*, July 30, 1884, 4; "National Labor Committee," *New Haven* [CT] *Morning Journal and Courier*, July 30, 1884, 3.

28. Untitled item, *Buffalo* [NY] *Evening Republic*, August 6, 1884, 1.

29. For this meeting, see "A Story of Steve Elkins," *New York World*, August 9, 1884, 3.

30. "Labor's Love for Blaine: Diligent Search Fails to Reveal It," *New York Times*, August 13, 1888, 1. Years later, a headline called some members of the group in Brooklyn "Fine 'Blaine Republicans': George D. Lennon and 'Judge' Rooney Worthy Allies," *New York Times*, November 5, 1893, 2.

31. "Butler Losing," *Chicago Daily Tribune*, August 1, 1884, 6.

32. "Ben Butler," *Chicago Daily Tribune*, October 7, 1884, 2; and "Ben Butler? No, Samuel Johnson Did Not Allude to Benjamin," *Terre Haute* [IN] *Daily Wabash Express*, October 2, 1884, 4.

33. Untitled item, *Idaho Avalanche* [Silver City], October 4, 1884, 2; untitled item, *Galveston Daily News*, October 13, 1884, 4.

34. "A Denial from Gen. Butler," *The Sun* [NY], October 27, 1884, 1.

35. Chandler to James B. Blaine, June 8, 1R84, in Richard West, *Lincoln's Scapegoat General* (Boston: Houghton Mifflin, 1965), 394, and see also 399–401, 404–5; David Muzzey, *James G. Blaine* (New York: Dodd, Mead, 1934), 92–93; Hans Trefousse, "Ben Butler," 185–86; Gail Hamilton, *James G. Blaine* (Norwich, CT: Henry Bill, 1895), 578.

36. "Butler's Campaign Plans," *New York Daily Times*, September 17, 1884, 1; "Gen.

Butler at Natick," *The Sun* [NY], November 4, 1884, 1. "Our cause is evidently booming all along the line"; Democrats complaining "about you selling out to Blaine" (A. B. Leonard, Logansport IN, to Butler, October 26, 1884, box 141, f. Oct. 21–31, Benjamin F. Butler Papers, Manuscript Reading Room, Library of Congress, Washington, DC).

37. "Passing of Colonel Noah Allen Plympton," *The Standard* [New York], 69, October 7, 1911, 329; "Erastus E. Potter for Congress," *The Sun* [NY], October 5,1884, 1, "Butler Strength in Jersey City," November 2, 5. See also Levi Badger Chase, *A Genealogy and Historical Notices of the Family of Plimpton or Plympton in America: And of Plumpton in England* (Hartford, CT: Plimpton, 1884).

38. "The Reception for Gen. Butler," *New York Daily Times*, August 21, 1884, 2, "The Butler Mass Meeting," August 26, 2, and "Butler Speaks His Piece," August 31, 1; "Butler in the Field," and "Monday's Parade," *John Swinton's Paper*, August 31, 1884, 1.

39. "The Result in Doubt," *The Sun* [NY], November 6, 1884, 1. For the full official count, see *American Almanac and Treasury of Facts, Statistical, Financial, and Political, for the Year 1888*, ed. Ainsworth R. Spofford (New York: American News, 1888), 198–272. See also Gretchen Ritter, *Goldbugs and Greenbacks: The Antimonopoly Tradition and Finance in America* (Cambridge: Cambridge University Press, 1997).

40. "The Labor Convention: Outlines of President George Blair's Address," *New York Times*, August 12, 1884, 5.

41. "A Hot Meeting in Prospect," *New York Times*, August 18, 1884, 8; "No Use for Butler. Workingmen Advising Co-operation with the Regular Parties," *New York Times*, August 23, 1884, 8; "The Political Headquarters," *New York Times*, August 27, 1884, 2. Signers included James A. Thompson, John Cavanagh, and G. D. Lennon.

42. "Workingmen Correcting General Butler," *Cairo* [IL] *Bulletin*, September 2, 1884, 4; "Back Talk to Butler," *Indiana State Sentinel*, September 3, 1884, 3. See also "Grover Cleveland," *Pontiac* [IL] *Bill Poster*, September 10, 1884, 1, supplement, 1. "Butler Rebuked," *Cheboygan* [WI] *Democrat*, September 4, 2.

43. "Candidates of the Labor Party," *New York Times*, September 30, 1884, 5.

44. "A Hot Meeting in Prospect," *New York Times*, August 18, 1884, 8, "Candidates of the Labor Party," September 30, 5. See also David Nemec, ed., *Major League Baseball Profiles, 1871–1900*. Vol. 2, *The Hall of Famers and Memorable Personalities Who Shaped the Game* (Lincoln: University of Nebraska Press, 2011), 2. Kid Carsey became famous for his slow curve and pitched twenty-two strikeouts in a single game (David Nemec, ed., *Major League Baseball Profiles, 1871–1900*. Vol. 2, *The Hall of Famers and Memorable Personalities Who Shaped the Game* (Lincoln: University of Nebraska Press, 2011), 131–32. See also Stephen V. Rice, "Kid Carsey," *Society for American Baseball Research*, accessed May 26, 2023, https://sabr.org/bioproj/person/kid-carsey/.

45. "On with the Butler Boom," *The Sun* [NY], October 10, 1884, 3, "Butler Clubs," October 14, 1, "Where to Get Butler Electoral Tickets," November 1, 1.

46. "Why Did John Kelly Call?" *The Sun* [NY], October 17, 1884, 1; "Campaign Notes," *Irish World*, December 4, 1880, 4.

Chapter 5. The Path through Populism

1. The secretary of the Civil Service Examining Board found Carsey qualified for appointment as an inspector of sewers and masonry on April 29, 1885 (*Minutes and Documents of the Board of Commissioners of the Department of Public Parks for the Year Ending April 30th, 1885* [New York: Martin B. Brown, 1885)] 648); John Whalen, *Report for Year Ending December 31, 1900* (New York: Martin B. Brown, 1901), 711.

2. "Favoring a Fifth-Avenue Railroad," *New York Times*, September 13, 1885, 7.

3. Daniel Bell, "Marxian Socialism in the United States," in *Socialism and American Life*, vol. 1, ed. Donald Drew Egbert and Stow Persons (Princeton, NJ: Princeton University Press, 1952), 367–68; Max Shachtman, "Footnote for Historians," *New International* 4 (December 1938): 377–79.

4. "Trades-Unions for Hill," *New York World*, October 24, 1885, 3.

5. "Their Law for the Mayor," *New York Times*, November 13, 1885, 8, December 24, 3.

6. "Talking to Tammany," *New York Times*, December 29, 1883, 2; "Anti-monopoly Men," January 12, 1886, 3; "Joining the County Democrats," February 19, 3. See also "Opposition to O'Donnell," *Boston Globe*, May 5, 1887, 2.

7. See Leon Fink's *Workingmen's Democracy: The Knights of Labor and American Politics* (Urbana: University of Illinois Press, 1983) for labor politics in smaller communities. On Chicago in this period particularly, see William Cronon, *Nature's Metropolis: Chicago and the Great West* (New York: W. W. Norton, 1991). For more recent work on the Haymarket riot, see Paul Avrich, *The Haymarket Tragedy* (Princeton, NJ: Princeton University Press, 1984); Bruce C. Nelson, *Beyond the Martyrs: A Social History of Chicago's Anarchists, 1870–1900* (New Brunswick, NJ: Rutgers University Press, 1988); James R. Green, *Death in the Haymarket: A Story of Chicago, the First Labor Movement and the Bombing That Divided Gilded Age America* (New York: Pantheon, 2006); Timothy Messer-Kruse, *The Trial of the Haymarket Anarchists: Terrorism and Justice in the Gilded Age* (New York: Palgrave Macmillan, 2011); Messer-Kruse, *The Haymarket Conspiracy: Transatlantic Anarchist Networks* (Urbana: University of Illinois Press, 2012). See also the excellent guides and anthologies by David Roediger and others.

8. On George's background, see my "Progress Impoverished: Origins of Henry George's Single Tax," *Historian* 52 (May 1990): 391–410.

9. *Irish World*, December 11, 1880, 8; Henry George Jr., *The Life of Henry George* (New York: for the author, 1900), was most recently published, with an introduction by Paul M. Gaston, as *Henry George* (New York: Chelsea House, 1981).

10. On the events of 1886, see Edward O'Donnell, *Henry George and the Crisis of Inequality: Progress and Poverty in the Gilded Age* (New York: Columbia University Press, 2017); Ronald Mendel, "Workers in Gilded Age New York and Brooklyn, 1886–1898," PhD diss., City University of New York, 1989.

11. "The Anti-monopoly League," *New York Times*, September 14, 1886, 5.

12. "Found His Place Filled," *New York Times*, November 5, 1886, 2; "Men and Women,"

The Standard [New York], January 29, 1887, 3. See also "Yank's Criticism," *Workmen's Advocate*, March 5, 1887, 1.

13. "For and against Mr. George," *New York Times*, October 23, 1886, 3, "Injuring Hewitt's Cause: Serious Mistakes Which His Managers Are Grieving," October 31, 9, "Found His Place Filled," November 5, 2.

14. "The Democrats Anxious," *New York Times*, October 27, 2, "Injuring Hewitt's Cause," October 31, 9.

15. "Knights Badly Organized, Surplus of Labor the Cause of All Trouble," *New York Times*, February 13, 1887, 3. See also, for Carsey, "List of Registered Voters for the Year 1886," *The* [New York] *City Record: Official Journal*, October 27, 1886, supplement.

16. "Found His Place Filled," *New York Times*, November 5, 1886, 2, "Knights Badly Organized," February 13, 1887, 3; "Men and Women," *The Standard*, January 29, 1887, 3.

17. "Knights Badly Organized," *New York Times*, February 13, 1887, 3.

18. Untitled item, *The Standard*, March 3, 1887, 4.

19. Bass, *"I Am a Democrat,"* 66, "Hot Words in the Labor Party," both in *New-York Tribune*, May 6, 1887, 5.

20. The SLP closed its national office in September 2008.

21. "Anti-monopolists, Not to Attend," *Cincinnati Enquirer*, February 22, 1887, 8. For Curtiss, Acting Commissioner, Board of Police at Buffalo, *Manual of the Common Council, Containing a Sketch of Buffalo* . . . (Buffalo, NY: Wenborne-Sumner, 1897), 213, 242.

22. "The Coming Party," *The Standard*, February 26, 1887, 4.

23. "The Coming Party."

24. Untitled item, *The Standard*, March 3, 1887, 4.

25. W. J. Atkinson, "Can Unite Only on Principle," *The Standard*, August 20, 1887, 4.

26. "Yank's Criticism," "Parties and Parties," *Workmen's Advocate*, March 5, 1887, 1, July 16, 2.

27. "Humbugs," *Workmen's Advocate*, July 21, 1888, 1, "The Union Labor Party Derided," *New York Times*, August 11, 1887, 8. Some Republicans organized their own "labor party" to endorse their ticket ("Harrison and Morton Indorsed," *Port Huron Times Herald*, July 18, 1888, 4; "Independent Labor Party for Harrison and Morton," *Mt. Pleasant* [MI] *Isabella County Enterprise*, July 20, 1888, 4). See also "Labor's Love for Blaine," *New York Times*, August 13, 1888, 1.

28. "Cranks and Politicians: The Union Labor Party Holds a Conference," *New York Times*, June 16, 1887, 1.

29. "Not Unlike a Famous Trio: The Anti-monopoly League Suggests the Tailors of Tooley-Street," *New York Times*, February 8, 1888, 5.

30. "Using Governmental Control," *Waterbury* [CT] *Evening Democrat*, February 14, 1888, 1; "Against Wanamaker's Scheme," *Los Angeles Herald*, February 22, 1890, 4; "Mr. Wanamaker's Bill Opposed," *Philadelphia Inquirer*, February 22, 1890, 3; "Opposed to Wanamaker's Scheme," *Sacramento Daily Union*, February 22, 1890, 1. See also David Hochfelder, *The Telegraph in America, 1832–1920* (Baltimore: Johns Hopkins University Press, 2012), 47.

31. "Subway Laborers Organize," *Evening World*, June 1, 1888 (3 o'clock ed.), 1. Gallahue warned that electric light and telephone wires were "dangerous and should be put underground as quickly as possible" ("Active Subway Laborers," *Evening World*, June 8, 1888 [5 o'clock extra], 3). On Carsey's job, see "The Legislature," *Watertown* [CT] *Re-union*, March 12, 1890, 4.

32. "Ten-Cent Steamboating," *Biddeford* [ME] *Daily Journal*, August 15, 1888, 1; "Father Columbia's Dime Trips," *New York Evening World*, September 17, 1888 (sporting ed.), 3; "Fancies in Cognomens," *Helena* [MT] *Independent*, May 6, 1890 (morning ed.), 2.

33. "Anti-monopoly League," *Galveston Daily News*, February 9, 1888, 3. William A. A. Carsey is listed as a builder on 146th Street in *Trow's New York City Directory... for the Year Ending May 1, 1888* (New York: Trow City Directory, 1888), 300.

34. "The Industrial Party," *Washington Evening Star*, February 22, 1888, 1.

35. "Redstone and Colvin," *Washington Evening Star*, February 23, 1888, 3; "Another Reform Party," *Washington Critic*, February 23, 1888, 1; Albert E. Redstone, "Land Monitor," August 18, 1862 (watercolor on paper 16 7/8 x 13 3/8, National Archives and Records Administration, Records of the Office of the Chief of Ordnance; "Four Tickets Already in the Field," *New York Times*, May 20, 1888, 10. See also Jay O'Connell, *Co-operative Dreams: A History of the Kaweah Colony* (Van Nuys, CA: Raven River, 1999), 24–25, 60–61, 71, 82, 171. John H. Redstone and "Al" Redstone were sons.

36. Laura Kerr, *The Girl Who Ran for President* (New York: Thomas Nelson, 1947); Jill Norgren, *Belva Lockwood: The Woman Who Would Be President* (New York: New York University Press, 2007). See also "Four Tickets Already in the Field," *New York Times*, May 20, 1888, 10.

37. "Labor and Politics," *Cincinnati Enquirer*, May 14, 1888, 8; "For Labor's Cause," *Cincinnati Enquirer*, May 15, 1888, 5; "Union Labor," *Cincinnati Commercial Gazette*, May 15, 1888, 4. See also "Men of Two Labor Parties," *Chicago Herald*, May 15, 1888, 3.

38. "Protection for Revenue Only," *New York Times*, September 19, 1888, 5.

39. Charles W. Calhoun, *Minority Victory: Gilded Age Politics and the Front Porch Campaign of 1888* (Lawrence: University Press of Kansas, 2008), 56–57, 58, 59–60, 164–65, 167–68; "Humbugs," *Workmen's Advocate*, July 21, 1888, 1.

40. Bass, *"I Am a Democrat,"* 99–102, 128, 133–35, 147–48.

41. William A. A. Carsey is listed as a builder at 80 W Ninety-First Street in *Trow's New York City Directory... for the Year Ending July 1, 1894* (New York: Trow City Directory, 1894), 216; John Whalen, City of New York Law Department, *Report for Year Ending December 31, 1900* (New York: Martin B. Brown, 1901). See also *Index to the Grover Cleveland Papers* (Washington, DC: Library of Congress, 1965), 63; William A. A. Carsey, $840, in the "U.S. Register of Civil, Military, and Naval Service, 1863–1959," in *Official Register of the United States, Containing a List of the Officers and Employees in the Civil, Military, and Naval Service Together with a List of Vessels Belonging to the United States*, 1: 670. Around the same time, William A. Carsey, also a New Yorker, petitioned the president on August 22, 1894 (*Index to the Grover Cleveland Papers* [Washington, DC: Library of Congress, 1965], 63).

42. "Discussing Rapid Transit," *New-York Tribune*, April 4, 1889, 2; *Trow's New York City Directory . . . for 1888–1889* (New York: Trow City Directory, 1888).

43. "Labor Agitators Busy," *New York Times*, September 20, 1889, 5.

44. "Labor Men Oppose Tammany," *New York Times*, October 25, 1889, 3.

45. "On the Last Million," *New-York Tribune*, November 20, 1889, 3.

46. "Backing Up 'The World,'" *Evening World*, March 10, 1890 (2 o'clock extra ed.), 1; "The Legislature," *Watertown* [CT] *Re-union*, March 12, 1890, 4.

47. "Assaulted a Reporter," *New York Times*, March 6, 1890, 1. The Trow's city directories indicate that the *World* reporter assaulted was surely Curtis W. Dunham ("Baseball," *Outing*, June 1888, 280).

48. "Brooklyn. Proceedings of the Brooklyn C.L.U.," *Workmen's Advocate*, March 15, 1890, 8.

49. Carsey's son was "Kid Carsey," who was just beginning to feel his oats as a professional baseball player ("Baseball," *Outing*, June 1888, 280).

50. "City and Suburban News," *New York Times*, April 1, 1890, 3; "Carsey Stood at the Bar," *Evening World*, April 4, 1890 [sporting extra], 5.

51. "Organized Labor," *Workmen's Advocate*, March 29, 1890, 1.

52. "City and Suburban News," *New York Times*, April 8, 1890, 3. Joseph Archer of Missouri advocated a congressional bill to loan money to farmers at 1 percent ("Bogus Labor Man Carsey," *Evening World*, April 10, 1890, 2).

53. William A. Carsey filed for pension on July 30, 1890, as an invalid and V. I. Kansas Adelle filed as a widow on June 15, 1914; William A. A. Carsey in "U.S. Register of Civil, Military, and Naval Service, 1863–1959." The record indicates his birthplace and date as New York, July 1, 1891 (Provo, UT: Ancestry.com, 2014), 1: 670.

54. "The Farmers' Alliance," *Chicago Weekly Express*, October 5, 1880, 2, October 19, 1880, 5. See also Lawrence Goodwyn, *Democratic Promise: The Populist Moment in America* (Ann Arbor: University of Michigan Press, 1976) Thomas E. Alter, *Toward a Cooperative Commonwealth: Transplanted Roots of Farmer-Labor Radicalism in Texas* (Urbana: University of Illinois Press, 2022); Kyle Wilkison, *Yeomen, Sharecroppers and Socialists: Plain Folk Protest in Texas, 1870–1914* (College Station: Texas A&M University Press, 2008); James R. Green, *Grass Roots Socialism: Radical Movements in the Southwest, 1895–1943* (Baton Rouge: Louisiana State University Press, 1978).

55. "Want to Start a Third Party," *Indianapolis Journal*, December 5, 1890, 1; "National Alliance Meeting," *Prairie Farmer*, December 13, 1890, 792; "A New Party Is Forming: Kansas Alliance Men Now at Ocala Behind," *New York Times*, December 5, 1890, 1, "W. H. Carsey," in Hochfelder, *Telegraph in America*, 47.

56. J. I. H., "Down with Traitors," *American Nonconformist and Kansas Industrial Liberator*, March 12, 1891, 2. On the meeting with President Benjamin Harrison, see "Washington Letter," *Washtenaw Saline Observer*, December 3, 1891, 4.

57. "Local Labor Matters," *New York Times*, May 15, 1891, 2; "The National Conference Opening of the Proceedings in Cincinnati," *New York Times*, May 20, 1891, 1.

58. Untitled item, *The People*, May 17, 1891, 4.

59. "Labor in Council," *Jackson Mississippi Leader*, March 3, 1892, 1; for Powderly's comments, see "Wild and Wooly," *Rock Island* [IL] *Argus*, February 25, 1892, 4; "St. Louis Conference," *Dublin* [TX] *Progress*, March 11, 1892, 3; "The St. Louis Conference," *The People*, February 28, 1892, 1,

60. "Oil for Troubled Labor," *New York Press*, July 13, 1892, 6.

61. "Morning Matters," *Wheeling* [WV] *Daily Intelligencer*, June 9, 1892, 1; "The Enemy of Labor," *St. Joseph Herald*, August 31, 1892, 4.

62. "Henry A. Hicks for Mayor," *New York Times*, October 11, 1892, 5.

63. "Chats with the Brethren," *Progressive Farmer*, May 16, 1893, 7; unsigned letter from New York printed in "That Campaign of Argument—One of the 'Capital's' Samples," *Advocate and Topeka Tribune*, August 3, 1892, 5.

64. "A Political Fraud," *The People*, June 12, 1892, 2; "Silver Men in a Big Row: 'Blood to the Bridles' Plan Almost Enacted," *New York Times*, July 26, 1893, 1; "History of a Silver Meeting," *New York Times*, April 12, 1895, 1; "A Snare for New-York Farmers," *New York Times*, August 13, 1893, 2. Lawrence Goodwyn had written of the silver lobby and Bryan as "shadow movements" in his groundbreaking study of Populism, *Democratic Promise: The Populist Moment in America* (New York: Oxford University Press, 1976). See also "History of a Silver Meeting," *New York Times*, April 12, 1895, 1.

65. "Knights of Reciprocity," *New York Times*, January 11, 1891, 17. "A Secret Political Society," *New York Times*, June 3, 1891, 1; "Like the Farmers' Alliance," *New York Times*, June 5, 1891, 2; "Knights of Reciprocity," *New York Times*, June 8, 1891, 1; "Lyons Laconics," *Wichita* [KS] *Daily Eagle*, June 30, 1891, 1; "Knights of Reciprocity," *New York Times*, June 10, 1892, 2.

66. Kim Moody, *Tramps and Trade Union Travelers: Internal Migration and Organized Labor in Gilded Age America, 1870–1900* (Chicago: Haymarket, 2019).

67. "Did Not Represent Labor," *New York Times*, July 27, 1893, 8; "Chats with the Brethren," *Progressive Farmer*, May 16, 1893, 7; "Municipal Lodging-Houses," *Evening World*, January 31, 1893, 5; "Political Bandits, These People," *New York Times*, October 22, 1893, 2. See also "Fine 'Blaine Republicans': George D. Lennon and 'Judge' Rooney Worthy Allies," *New York Times*, November 5, 1893, 2.

68. "Dyer D. Lum Dead," *Geneva* [NY] *Advertiser*, April 11, 1893, 2; and "The Late Dyer D. Lum, Anarchist," *Seattle Post-Intelligencer*, April 16, 1893, 1.

69. "Carsey Had Had a Fight," *New York Times*, May 27, 1893, 3. Carsey's pugilistic opponent was one of half a dozen members of Ellsworth's Zouaves named Shaw ("Farnham Post Undismayed: Attacks and Ridicule Will Not Change Its Position," *New York Times*, May 28, 1893, 16). See also John DeWitt Warner, "Half a Million Dollars a Day for Pensions," *The Forum* 15 (June 1893): 439–51, Allen R. Foot, "The Decisive Breach in the Grand Army," (June 1893): 452–58, Charles McKnight Leoser, "The Grand Army as a Pension Agency," (June 1893): 522–31, and John J. Finn, "Complete History of the Farnham Post Revolt," (July 1893), 532–40. Finn was commander of Noah L. Farnham Independent Veterans, No. 1, and was "one of the oldest members of Typographical Union No. 6."

Epilogue

1. "Editorials by the Boss," *Colby* [KS] *Free Press*, July 31, 1913, 4; "Boy Grabs Third-Sacker's Wig; She's a Man, Ructions," *Winnipeg* [MB] *Tribune*, August 2, 1913, 22.

2. Joseph Dorfman, *The Economic Mind in American Civilization, 1606–1935*, 5 vols. (New York: Viking, 1946–59), 3: 17. Others understandably misinterpreting Carsey as a genuine insurgent are Nathan Weiss, "The Political Theory and Practice of General Benjamin Franklin Butler," PhD diss., New York University, 1961, 150; Daniel J. Curran, "Hendrick B. Wright: A Study in Leadership," PhD diss., Fordham University, 1962, 354n; and Embrey B. Howson, "Jacob Sechler Coxey: A Biography of a Monetary Reformer, 1854–1951," PhD diss., Ohio State University, 1973, 125.

3. "Local Briefs," *Aspen* (CO) *Tribune*, February 6, 1901, 4; C. A. Henrie, 49, born in Illinois, was the assistant docket clerk of the Senate (*Senate Journal: Proceedings of the Senate of the State of Kansas. Thirteenth Biennial Session, Topeka, January 13 to March 13, 1903* [Topeka: State of Kansas, 1903], 2, 1099); Edith E. Davenport, coll. and arr., *David Benton and Nancy Pitts: Their Ancestors and Descendants, 1620–1920* (Rochester, NY: DuBois, 1921), 95; "Kansas Newspapers and Periodicals Now Received," "Kansas State Publications," and William R. Rightmire, "The Alliance Movement in Kansas—Origin of the People's Party," in *Transactions of the Kansas State Historical Society* 4 (1890): 98; 6 (1900): 449; 9 (1906): 3; *A List of Kansas Newspapers* (Topeka, KS: State Historical Society, 1913), 20, 138, 1632, 1635.

4. "Vanderbilt in the West," *New York Times*, October 9, 1882, 1, noted in David Hochfelder, *The Telegraph in America, 1832–1920* (Baltimore: Johns Hopkins University Press, 2012), 47.

5. Some biographies of Bryan are Robert W. Cherny, *A Righteous Cause: The Life of William Jennings Bryan* (Boston: Little, Brown, 1985); Paul W. Glad, *The Trumpet Soundeth: William Jennings Bryan and His Democracy, 1896–1912* (Lincoln: University of Nebraska Press, 1960); Louis William Koenig, *Bryan: A Political Biography of William Jennings Bryan* (New York: Putnam, 1971); Gerald Leinwand, *William Jennings Bryan: An Uncertain Trumpet* (New York: Rowman and Littlefield, 2006); M. R. Werner, *William Jennings Bryan* (New York: Harcourt, Brace, 1929).

6. *Official Proceedings of the Democratic National Convention Held in Chicago, Ill., July 7th, 8th, 9th, 10th and 11th, 1896* (Logansport, IN: Wilson, Humphreys, 1896).

7. *Proceedings of the Convention of the National Democratic Party, Held at Indianapolis, Indiana, September 2 and 3, 1896* (Indianapolis: Sentinel, 1896), 141. The New York delegates sent one Henry George.

8. Letter from New York printed in "That Campaign of Argument—One of the 'Capital's' Samples," *Advocate and Topeka* [KS] *Tribune*, August 3, 1892, 5.

9. For Carsey's positions on the Bureau for Collection of Arrears of Personal Taxes and his construction work in the city, see John Whalen, *Report for Year Ending December 31, 1900* (New York: Martin B. Brown, 1901), 711; 1; "The Building Department: List of Plans Filed for New Structures and Alterations," *New York Times*, March 30, 1902,

19; "North Castle" in *Katonah* [NY] *Times*, November 27, 1903, 1; "The Civil Service," *New York Times*, May 30, 1912, 19; "The Civil Service," *New York Times*, October 8, 1913, 16. See also "The Building Department: List of Plans Filed for New Structures and Alterations," *New York Times*, March 30, 1902, 19; "North Castle" in *Katonah* [NY] *Times*, November 27, 1903, 1; "The Civil Service," *New York Times*, May 30, 1912, 19; "The Civil Service," *New York Times*, October 8, 1913, 16.

10. "Dead Woman a Missing Wife," *New York Herald*, May 20, 1905, 5. By the 1910 census, the family lived in Brooklyn on Division Avenue in Ward 19. Carsey remained at work as an inspector in the city's Bridge Department and certainly remained loyal to the perspectives of Governor Hill and the New York machines.

11. "William A. Carsey," *Brooklyn Daily Eagle*, June 2, 1914, 2.

12. Adelle filed as a widow on June 15, 1914 ("General Index to Pension Files, 1861–1934" [Washington, DC: National Archives and Records Administration], T288, 546 rolls). The death of Adelle Ostrander Carsey on May 27, 1924, at age 72 is in Pittsfield deaths 1886–1941, posted at https://sites.rootsweb.com/~maberksh/towns/pittsfield/pitt_deaths/c-1.html.

13. T. C. Jeffries, "Nearly All Locals Have Similar Trouble," *Appeal to Reason*, April 17, 1909, 5.

14. Anand Giridharadas, *Winners Take All: The Elite Charade of Changing the World* (New York: Random House, 2018).

Index

MARK A. LAUSE is a professor in the department of history at the University of Cincinnati. His many books include *Free Spirits: Spiritualism, Republicanism, and Radicalism in the Civil War Era* and *Free Labor: The Civil War and the Making of an American Working Class.*

The University of Illinois Press
is a founding member of the
Association of University Presses.

University of Illinois Press
1325 South Oak Street
Champaign, IL 61820-6903
www.press.uillinois.edu